Views and Opinions

by

Ouida

Views and Opinions
by Ouida

ISBN: 978-93-64287-39-5

Published by

DOUBLE 9 BOOKS

2/13-B, Ansari Road
Daryaganj, New Delhi – 110002
info@double9books.com
www.double9books.com
Tel. 011-40042856

This book is under public domain

ABOUT THE AUTHOR

Ouida was the pen name of Marie Louise de la Ramée (1839–1908), a Victorian–era English novelist, short story writer, and critic. She was born in Bury St Edmunds, England, and spent much of her life in London and abroad in continental Europe. Ouida gained fame for her flamboyant and romantic writing style, which captivated readers and critics alike during the late 19th century. Her literary career began with the publication of her first novel, "Granville de Vigne," in 1859, but she achieved broader recognition with subsequent works such as "Under Two Flags" (1867) and "Moths" (1880). Ouida's novels often featured themes of passion, adventure, and social criticism, set against lavish and exotic backdrops. Beyond her fiction, Ouida was also known for her essays and articles, collected in volumes such as "Views and Opinions." In these writings, she expressed her views on various subjects including literature, society, politics, and the arts, reflecting her progressive and often controversial perspectives. Ouida's writing style was characterized by lush descriptions, melodrama, and a keen sense of satire. She was critical of Victorian society's moral constraints and advocated for greater personal freedom and artistic expression. Though her popularity waned in the early 20th century, Ouida remains a significant figure in Victorian literature, known for her bold and unconventional approach to storytelling and social commentary.

CONTENTS

THE SINS OF SOCIETY

'Ses divertissements sont infiniment moins raisonnables que
ses ennuis.'—Pascal.

A brilliant and daring thinker lately published some admirable papers called 'Under the Yoke of the Butterflies.' The only thing which I would have changed in those delightful satires would have been the title. There are no butterflies in this fast, furious and fussy age. They all died with the eighteenth century, or if a few still lingered on into this, they perished forever with the dandies. The butterfly is a creature of the most perfect taste, arrayed in the most harmonious colours: the butterfly is always graceful, leisurely, aerial, unerring in its selection of fragrance and freshness, lovely as the summer day through which it floats. The dominant classes of the present day have nothing in the least degree akin to the butterflies; would to Heaven that they had! Their pleasures would be more elegant, their example more artistic, their idleness more picturesque than these are now. They would rest peacefully on their roses instead of nailing them to a ballroom wall; they would hover happily above their lilies and carnations without throwing them about in dust and dirt at carnivals.

Butterflies never congregate in swarms; it is only locusts which do that. Butterflies linger with languorous movement, always softly rhythmical and undulating even when most rapid, through the sunny air above the blossoming boughs. The locust is jammed together in a serried host, and tears breathlessly forward without knowing in the least why or where he goes, except that he must move on and must devour. There is considerable analogy between the locust and society; none between society and the butterfly. But be the yoke called what it will, it lies heavily on the world, and there is no strength in the strongest sufficient to lift it up and cast it off, for its iron is Custom and its ropes are Foolishness and Bad Example, and what is termed Civilisation carries it as the steer carries the nose-ring and the neck-beam.

Some clever people have of late been writing a great deal about society, taking English society as their especial theme. But there are certain facts and features in all modern society which they do not touch: perhaps they are too polite, or too politic. In the first place they seem to except, even whilst attacking them, smart people as elegant people, and to confuse the two together: the two words are synonymous in their minds, but are far from being so in reality. Many leaders of the smart sets are wholly unrefined in taste, loud in manner, and followed merely because they please certain personages, spend or seem to spend profusely, and are seen at all the conspicuous gatherings of the season in London and wherever else society congregates. This is why the smart sets have so little refining influence on society. They may be common, even vulgar; it is not necessary even for them to speak grammatically; if they give real jewels with their cotillon toys and have a perfect artist at the head of their kitchens, they can become 'smart,' and receive royalty as much and as often as they please. The horrible word smart has been invented on purpose to express this: smartness has been borrowed from the vocabulary of the kitchenmaids to express something which is at the top of the fashion, without being necessarily either well born or well bred. Smart people may be both the latter, but it is not necessary that they should be either. They may be smart by mere force of chance, impudence, charm, or the faculty of making a royal bored one laugh.

It is, therefore, impossible for the smart people to have much influence for good on the culture and manners of the society they dominate. A *beau monde*, really exclusive, elegant and of high culture, not to be bought by any amount of mere riches or display, would have a great refining influence on manner and culture, and its morality, or lack of it, would not matter much. Indeed, society cannot be an accurate judge of morality; the naughty clever people know well how to keep their pleasant sins unseen; the candid, warm-hearted people always sin the sole sin which really injures anybody — they get found out. 'You may break all the ten commandments every day if you like,' said Whyte Melville, 'provided only you observe the eleventh, "Thou shalt not be found out."' There is a morality or immorality, that of the passions, with which society ought to have little or nothing to do; but there is another kind with which it should have a good deal to do, *i.e.*, the low standard of honour and principle which allows persons in high place to take up *richards* for sheer sake of their wealth, and go to houses which have nothing to recommend them except the fact that convenient rendezvous may be arranged at them, or gambling easily prosecuted in them. But it is not society as constituted at the present year of grace which will have either the courage or the character to do this. Theoretically, it may condemn what it calls immorality and gambling, but it will always arrange its house-party in accord with the affinities which it sedulously remembers and ostensibly ignores, and will allow bac' to follow coffee after dinner rather than illustrious persons should pack up and refuse to return.

At risk of arousing the censure of readers, I confess that I would leave to society a very large liberty in the matter of its morality or immorality, if it would only justify its existence by any originality, any grace, any true light and loveliness. In the face of its foes lying grimly waiting for it, with explosives in their pockets, society should justify its own existence by its own beauty, delicacy and excellence of choice and taste. It should, as Auberon Herbert has said, be a centre whence light should radiate upon the rest of the world. But one can only give what one has, and as it has no clear light or real joy within itself it cannot diffuse them, and in all probability never will. 'The Souls' do, we know, strive in their excellent intentions and their praiseworthy faith to produce them, but they are too few in numbers, and are already too tightly caught in the tyres of the great existing machinery to be able to do much towards this end. After all, a society does but represent the temper of the age in which it exists, and the faults of the society of our time are the faults of that time itself; they are its snobbishness, its greed, its haste, its slavish adoration of a royalty which is wholly out of time and keeping with it, and of a wealth of which it asks neither the origin nor the solidity, and which it is content only to borrow and bask in as pigs in mud.

It is not luxury which is enervating; it is over-eating, over-smoking, and the poisoned atmosphere of crowded rooms. Edmond de Goncourt likes best to write in a grey, bare room which contains nothing to suggest an idea or distract the imagination. But few artists or poets would desire such an *entourage*. Beauty is always inspiration. There is nothing in a soft seat, a fragrant atmosphere, a well-regulated temperature, a delicate dinner, to banish high thought; on the contrary, the more refined and lovely the place the happier and more productive ought to be the mind. Beautiful things can be created independently of place; but the creator of them suffers when he can enjoy beauty only in his dreams. I do not think that the rich enjoy beauty one whit more than the poor in this day. They are in too great a hurry to do so. There is no artistic enjoyment without repose. Their beautiful rooms are scarcely seen by them except when filled with a throng. Their beautiful gardens and parks are visited by them rarely and reluctantly. Their treasures of art give them no pleasure unless they believe them unique, unequalled. Their days, which might be beautiful, are crammed with incessant engagements, and choked with almost incessant eating.

In England the heavy breakfasts, the ponderous luncheons, the long, tedious dinners, not to speak of the afternoon teas and the liqueurs and spirits before bedtime, fill up more than half the waking hours; 'stoking,' as it is elegantly called, is the one joy which never palls on the human machine, until he pays for it with dyspepsia and gout. People who live habitually well should be capable of denying their appetites enough to pass from London to Paris, or Paris to London, without wanting to eat and drink. But in point of fact they never dream of such denial of the flesh, and they get out at the buffets of Boulogne and Amiens with alacrity, or order both breakfast and dinner, with wines at choice, in the club-train. A *train de luxe* is, by the way, the epitome and portrait of modern society; it provides everything for the appetite; it gives cushions, newspapers and iced drinks; it whirls the traveller rapidly from capital to capital; but the steam is in his nostrils, the cinder dust is in his eyes, and the roar of the rattling wheels is in his ears. I do not think that plain living and high thinking are a necessary alliance. Good food, delicate and rich, is like luxury; it should not be shunned, but enjoyed. It is one of the best products of what is called civilisation, and should be duly appreciated by all those who can command it. But feeding should not occupy the exaggerated amount of time which is given to it in society, nor cost the enormous amount of money which is at present spent on it.

Luxury in itself is a most excellent thing, and I would fain see it more general, as the luxury of the bath was in Imperial Rome open to one and all; with the water streaming over the shining silver and snowy marbles, and the beauty of porphyry and jade and agate gleaming under the silken awning, alike for plebeian and patrician. It is not for its luxury for a moment that I would rebuke the modern world: but for its ugly habits, its ugly clothes, its ugly hurry-skurry, whereby it so grossly disfigures, and through which it scarcely even perceives or enjoys the agreeable things around it.

Luxury is the product and result of all the more delicate inventions and combinations of human intelligence and handicraft. To refuse its graces and comforts would be as unwise as to use a rudely-sharpened flint instead of a good table-knife. A far more lamentable fact than the existence of luxury is that it is so little enjoyed and so rarely made general. We deliberately surrender the enjoyment of the luxury of good cooking because we most stupidly mix up eating with talking, and lose the subtle and fine flavours of our best dishes because we consider ourselves obliged to converse with somebody on our right or our left whilst we eat them. We neutralise the exquisite odours of our finest flowers by the scent of wines and smoking dishes. We spoil our masterpieces of art by putting them together pell-mell in our rooms, smothered under a discordant mingling of different objects and various styles. We allow nicotines to poison the breath of our men and women. We desire a crowd on our stairs and a crush in our rooms as evidence of our popularity and our distinction. We cannot support eight days of the country without a saturnalia of slaughter. We are so tormented by the desire to pack forty-eight hours into twenty-four, that we gobble our time up breathlessly without tasting its flavour, as a greedy schoolboy gobbles up stolen pears without peeling them. Of the true delights of conversation, leisure, thought, art and solitude, society *en masse* has hardly more idea than a flock of geese has of Greek. There is in the social atmosphere, in the social life of what is called 'the world,' a subtle and intoxicating influence which is like a mixture of champagne and opium, and has this in common with the narcotic, that it is very difficult and depressing to the taker thereof to leave it off and do without it. As La Bruyère said of the court life of his time, it does not make us happy but it makes us unable to find happiness elsewhere. After a full and feverish season we have all known the reaction which follows on the return to a quiet life. There is a magnetic attraction in the great giddy gyrations of fashionable and political life. To cede to this magnetism for a while may be highly beneficial; but to make of it the vital necessity of existence, as men and women of the world now do, is as fatal as the incessant use of any other stimulant or opiate.

The great malady of the age is the absolute inability to support solitude, or to endure silence.

Statesmanship is obscured in babbling speech; art and literature are represented by mere hurried impressions snatched from unwillingly-accorded moments of a detested isolation; life is lived in a throng, in a rush, in a gallop; the day was lost to Titus if it did not record a good action; the day is lost to the modern man and woman unless it be spent in a mob. The horror of being alone amounts in our time to a disease. To be left without anybody else to amuse it fills the modern mind with terror. 'La solitude n'effraie pas le penseur: il y a toujours quelqu'un dans la chambre,' a witty writer has said; but it is the wit as well as the fool in this day who flies from his own company; it is the artist as well as the dandy who seeks the boulevard and the crowd.

There is nothing more costly than this hatred of one's own company, than this lack of resources and occupations independent of other persons. What ruins ninety-nine households out of a hundred is the expense of continual visiting and inviting. Everybody detests entertaining, but as they all know that they must receive to be received, and they cannot bring themselves to support solitude, people ruin themselves in entertainment. There can scarcely be a more terrible sign of decadence than the indifference with which the *grands de la terre* are everywhere selling their collections and their libraries. Instead of altering the excessive display and expenditure which impoverish them, and denying themselves that incessant amusement which they have grown to consider a necessity, they choose to sell the books, the pictures and the manuscripts which are the chief glories of their homes; often they even sell also their ancestral woods.

This day, as I write, great estates which have been in the same English family for six hundred years are going to the hammer. This ghastly necessity may be in part brought about by agricultural depression, but it is far more probably due to the way of living of the times which must exhaust all fortunes based on land. If men and women were content to dwell on their estates, without great display or frequent entertainment, their incomes would suffice in many cases. It is not the old home which ruins them: it is the London house with its incessant expenditure, the house-parties with their replica of London, the women's toilettes, the men's shooting and racing and gaming, the Nile boat, the Cairene winter, the weeks at Monte Carlo, the Scotch moors, the incessant, breathless round of intermingled sport and pleasure danced on the thin ice of debt, and kept up frequently for mere appearances' sake, without any genuine enjoyment, only from a kind of false shame and a real inability to endure life out of a crowd.

There is a stimulant and a drug, as I have said, in the curious mixture of excitement and *ennui*, of animation and fatigue, produced by society, and without this mixture the man and woman of the world cannot exist; and to find the purchase-money of this drug is what impoverishes them, and makes them indifferent to their own degradation, and sends their beautiful old woods and old books and old pictures to the shameful uproar of the sale-rooms. If the passion for the slaughter of tame creatures which is almost an insanity, so absorbing and so dominant is it, could be done away with in England, and the old houses be really lived in by their owners all the year round with genuine affection and scholarly taste, as they were lived in by many families in Stuart and Georgian days, their influence over the counties and the villages would be incalculable and admirable, as Mr Auberon Herbert and Mr Frederick Greenwood have recently said; and the benefit accruing to the fortunes of the nobles and gentry would be not less.

It is not only in England that men have become bored by and neglectful of their great estates. All over Italy stand magnificent villas left to decay or tenanted by peasants, the lizard creeping in the crevices of forgotten frescoes, the wild vine climbing over the marbles of abandoned sculptures, the oranges and the medlars falling ungathered on the mosaics of the mighty and desolate courts. Why is this? In the earlier centuries men and women loved pleasure well, and had few scruples; yet they loved and honoured their country houses, and were happy in their fragrant alleys and their storied chambers, and spent magnificently on their adornment and enrichment with a noble pride. It is only now in the latest years of the nineteenth century that these superb places are left all over Europe to dust, decay, and slow but sure desolation, whilst the owners spend their time in play or speculation, call for bocks and brandies in the club-rooms of the world, and buy shares in mushroom building companies.

Marion Crawford observes dryly 'that it is useless to deny the enormous influence of brandy and games of chance on the men of the present day.' It is indeed so useless that no one who knows anything of our society would dream of attempting to deny it, and if we substitute morphia for brandy, we may say much the same of a large proportion of the women of the present day. Drinking and gambling, in some form or another, is the most general vice of the cultured world, which censures the island labourer for his beer and skittles, and condemns the continental workman for his absinthe and lotteries. It is a strange form of progress which makes educated people incapable of resisting the paltry pleasures of the green-table and the glass; a strange form of culture which ends at the spirit frame, the playing cards, and the cigar box. The poor Japanese coolie amongst the lilies and lilacs of his little garden is surely nearer both culture and progress than the drinker and the gambler of the modern clubs.

Reflect on the enormous cost of a boy's education when he belongs to the higher strata of social life, and reflect, also, that as soon as he becomes his own master he will, in ninety-nine cases out of a hundred, take advantage of his liberty only to do what Crawford's young Don Orsino does, i.e., drink brandy, gamble at bac', and try to gain admittance into the larger gaming of the Bourses. It will certainly be allowed by any dispassionate judge, that a better result might be arrived at with such exorbitant cost; that a nobler animal ought to be produced by such elaborate and wholly useless training.

Drinking and gambling (in varied forms it is true, but in essence always the same) are the staple delights of modern life, whether in the rude western shanty of the navvy, the miner and the digger, or in the luxurious card-rooms of the clubs and the country houses of the older world. We have even turned all the rest of creation into living dice for us, and the horse trots or gallops, the dog is fastened to the show-bench, the pigeon flies from the trap, even the rat fights the terrier that our fevered pulses may beat still quicker in the unholy agitation of a gamester's greed.

We are great gamblers, and the gambler is always a strangely twisted mixture of extravagance and meanness. Expenditure is not generosity; we are lavish but we are not liberal; we will waste two thousand pounds on an entertainment, but we cannot spare five pounds for a friend in distress. For the most part we live not only up to but far beyond our incomes, and the necessary result is miserliness in small things and to those dependent on us.

'Ses divertissements sont infiniments moins raisonnables que ses ennuis,' says Pascal of the society of his day, and the statement stands good of our own. Society has no pleasure which is graceful or elevating, except music; but music listened to in a crowd loses half its influence; and it is an insult to the most spiritual of all the arts to regard it, as it is regarded in society, as a mere interlude betwixt dinner and the card-table. There is little except music which is beautiful in the pageantries of this day. A ball is still a pretty sight if it takes place in a great house, and if not too many people have been invited. But except this, and this only in a great house, all entertainments are unsightly. No decoration of a dinner-table, no gold plate, and orchidæ, and electric light, and old china can make even tolerable, artistically speaking, the sight of men and women sitting bolt upright close together taking their soup around it. A full concert-room, lecture-room, church, are a hideous sight. A garden party in fair weather and fine grounds alone has a certain grace and charm; but garden parties, like all other modern spectacles, are spoilt by the attire of the men, the most frightful, grotesque and disgraceful male costume which the world has ever seen. When the archæologists of the future dig up one of our bronze statues in trousers they will have no need to go further for evidence of the ineptitude and idiotcy of the age. What our historians call the dark ages had costumes, alike for the villein and the seigneur, adapted to their needs, serviceable, picturesque and comely; this age alone, which vaunts its superiority, has a clothing for its men which is at once utterly unsightly, unhealthy, and so constructed that all the bodily beauty of an Apollo or an Achilles would be obscured, caricatured, and deformed by it. The full height of its absurdity is reached when the glazier comes in his black suit to mend your windows, and brings his working clothes in a bundle to be put on ere he works and put off ere he goes into the street. The political incapacity with which the natives of Ireland are charged by English statesmen never seemed to me so conclusively proven as by their persistence in wearing ragged tail-coats and battered tall hats in their stony fields and on their sodden bogs. A man who cannot clothe his own person reasonably is surely a man incapable of legislating for himself and for his kind. This rule, however, if acted on, would disfranchise Europe and the United States.

To a society which had any true perception of beauty, grace, or elegance, the masher would be impossible; the shoulder-handshake, the tall hat, the eternal cigarette, the stiff collar, the dead birds on the ball-dresses and bonnets, the perspiring struggles of the sexes on the tennis ground, and a thousand other similar things would not be for a moment endured. To a society which had any high standard of refinement such entertainments as are appropriately called 'crushes' would be insupportable; the presence and the speeches of women on public platforms would be intolerable; all the enormities of the racecourse would be abhorrent; its fine ladies would no more wear dead humming-birds upon their gowns than they would wear the entrails of dead cats; its fine gentlemen would no more gather together to murder hand-fed pheasants than they would shoot kittens or canaries; to a truly elegant society everything barbarous, grotesque and ungraceful would be impossible.

An incessant and *maladif* restlessness has become the chief characteristic of all cultured society nowadays: it is accounted a calamity beyond human endurance to be six months at a time in one place; to remain a year would be considered cause for suicide. The dissatisfaction and feverishness which are the diseases of the period are attributed to place most wrongly, for change of place does not cure them and only alleviates them temporarily and briefly. Here, again, the royal personages are the first offenders and the worst examples. They are never still. They are never content. They are incessantly discovering pretexts for conveying their royal persons here and there, to and fro, in ceaseless, useless, costly and foolish journeys.

Every event in their lives is a cause or an excuse for their indulgence in the *pérégrinomanie*; if they are well, they want change of scene; if they are ill, they want change of air; if they suffer a bereavement, nothing can console them except some agreeable foreign strand; and the deaths, births and marriages of their innumerable relations furnish them with continual and convenient reasons for incessant gyrations. In all these multiplied and endless shiftings of place and person the photographs fly about in showers, and the gold and silver offerings are tendered in return on bended knees.

It must be confessed that royalty confirms and keeps up many usages and obligations of society which are absurd and unpleasant, and which without royal support would die a natural death.

What can be more absurd, more childish, and more utter waste of money than the salutes with which it is the custom to celebrate the going and coming, the births and the deaths, of these royal people? The savage who expresses his joy by discharging his rusty musket is deemed a silly creature; but the civilised nation is less excusably silly which expresses its pleasure, its grief, and its homage by means of this hard, ugly, unpleasant noise which has no sense in it, and blows away in smoke vast sums of money which might easily be better spent. It is a barbarous practice, and it is difficult to comprehend a civilised world tamely submitting to its continuance.

The most vulgar form of salutation, the shake-hands, has been adopted and generalised by princes, until it is now usual in countries where it was unknown in the beginning of the century. Nothing can be more ludicrous and ungraceful, or more disagreeable, than the 'pump-handling' which is common in all ranks of society, and which great personages might easily have abolished altogether. They think it makes them popular, and so they resort to it on every suitable and unsuitable occasion. There can be no possible reason why people should go through this unpleasant action, and few sights are more absurd than to see two elderly gentlemen solemnly sawing each other's arms up and down as they meet before the doorsteps of their club. The slight smile and scarcely perceptible bend of the head which are all with which well-bred people recognise their acquaintances at a reception or a ball, is fully sufficient for all purposes of recognition at any period of the day, and can amply preface conversation. The pressure of hands should be left to lovers, or to friends in moments of impulses of emotion; on leave-taking before, or on welcome after, a long absence. There are many men still in Europe, not all old men either, who know how to greet a woman, and bend low over her hand and touch it lightly with their lips; and how graceful, how respectful, how suggestive of homage is that courtly salutation! It is the fault of women that it has become the exception, not the rule.

If we had Charles the First on the throne of England, and Louis Quatorze on the throne of France, whatever political difficulties might come of it, manners would certainly be considerably altered, corrected and refined. The influence of some great gentleman might do much to purge the coarseness and commonness of society out of it; but such a personage does not exist, and if he did exist, the Augean stable would probably be too much for his strength. He would retire, like Beckford, to some Fonthill and build a Chinese Wall between him and the world.

But alas! the vulgarity of the age is at its highest in high places. The position of sovereigns and their descendants is one which should at least allow them to be the first gentry of their countries in feeling as they are in precedence and etiquette; they might, were they capable of it, set an example of grace, of elegance, and of purity of taste. Strong as is the revolutionary leaven amongst the masses, the force of snobbism is stronger still, and all habits and examples which come from the palace are followed by the people with eager and obsequious servility. If, when princes and princesses were united in wedlock, they ordained 'No presents,' the abominable blackmail levied by betrothed people on their acquaintances would cease to be fashionable, and would soon become 'parcel and portion of the dreadful past.' If, when princes and princesses paid the debt of nature, the Court officials sent out the decree 'No flowers,' all other classes would take example, and the horrible, senseless barbarism of piling a mass of decaying wreaths and floral crosses upon a coffin and a grave would pass to the limbo of all other extinct barbaric and grotesque customs. But they are careful to do nothing of the kind. The bridal gifts are too welcome to them; and the funeral baked meats are too savoury; and all the royal people all over Europe unite in keeping up these tributes levied from a groaning world. Modern generations have made both marriage and death more absurd, more banal, and more vulgar than any other period ever contrived to do; and it is not modern princes who will endeavour to render either of them simple, natural and dignified, for the essence and object of all royal life in modern times is vulgarity, *i.e.,* publicity.

Of all spectacles which society flocks to see, it may certainly be said that the funeral and the wedding are the most intolerably coarse and clumsy. There is indeed a curious and comical likeness between these two. Both take place in a crowd; both are the cause for extortion and expenditure; both are attended unwillingly and saluted with false formulæ of compliment; both are 'seen out' and 'got through' with sighs of relief from the spectators; and both are celebrated with the sacrifice of many myriads of flowers crucified in artificial shapes in their honour.

Hymen and Pallida Mors alike grin behind the costly and senseless orchids and the sweet dying roses and lilies of the jubilant nurseryman. The princes and the tradespeople have in each case decreed that this shall be so; and society has not will or wisdom enough to resist the decree.

A poet died not long ago and left amongst his farewell injunctions the bidding to put no flowers on his bier. The wise press and public exclaimed, 'How strange that a poet should hate flowers!' Poor fools! He loved them so deeply, so intensely, that the tears would start to his eyes when he beheld the first daffodils of the year, or leaned his lips on the cool pallor of a cluster of tea roses. It was because he loved them so well that he forbade their crucified beauty being squandered, to fade and rot upon his coffin. Every true lover of flowers would feel the same. Nothing more disgusting and more offensive can be imagined than the cardboard and wires on which the tortured blossoms are fastened in various shapes to languish in the heated atmosphere of a *chambre ardente,* or in the sickly and oppressive air of a mortuary chamber. All the designs which serve to symbolise the loves of cook and potboy on St Valentine's Day are now pressed into the service of the princely or noble mourners; harps, crowns, crosses, hearts, lyres, and all the trash of the vulgarest sentiment are considered touching and exquisite when hung before a royal catafalque or heaped upon a triple coffin of wood, lead and velvet. In all these grotesque and vulgar shapes the innocent blossoms are nailed, gummed, or wired by workpeople, grinning and smoking as they work, and the whole mass is heaped together on bier, in crypt, or on monument, and left to rot and wither in sickening emblem of the greater corruption which it covers.

The fresh-gathered flowers laid by maidens' hands on the wet hair of Ophelia, or the white breast of Juliet, might have beauty both natural and symbolical. One spray of some best-loved blossom, placed by some best-loved hand on the silenced heart, may have the meaning and be the emblem of the deepest feeling. To put softly down upon a bed of moss and rose-leaves the dead white limbs of a little child may have fitness and beauty in the act. To go in the dusk of dawn into the wet, green ways of gardens, silent save for the call of waking birds, and gather some bud or leaf which was dear to our lost love, and bear it within to lie with him where we can never console or caress him in his eternal solitude: this may be an impulse tender and natural even in those first hours of bereavement. But to arise from our woe to order a florist to make a harp of lilies with strings of gold or silver wire; to stay our tears, to break the seals of boxes come by rail from Nice and Grasse and Cannes: this indeed is to fall into bathos beside which the rudest funeral customs of the savage look respectable and dignified.

When we realise what death is and what it means: that never will those lips touch ours again; that never will that voice again caress our ear; that never more will our inmost thoughts be mirrored in those eyes; that never more shall we say, 'Shall we do this to-day? shall we do that to-morrow?' that never more can we go together through the grass of spring, or together watch the sun drop down behind the hills; that never can we ask pardon if our love were fretful, human, weak; that never more can there be communion or comprehension; that all is silent, lonely, ended, an unchanging and unchangeable desolation:—when we realise this, I say, and think that there are persons who, left to this awful solitude, can give orders to floral tradesmen and take comfort in toys of cardboard and wire, we may be pardoned if we feel that the most bitter scorn of the cynic for human nature is flagellation too merciful for its triviality and folly.

Truly, in nine times out of ten it is but a conventional and unreal sorrow which thus expresses itself; truly, out of the millions of deaths which take place there are but few which create deep and abiding grief; still, the association of these elaborate artificial wreaths and garlands, these stiff and crucified blossoms, with the tomb would only be possible to the most vulgar and insensible of generations, even as decoration, even as mere common-place compliment, whilst to the true lover of flowers they must be ever a distressing outrage.

In Lopez de Vega's *Diego de Alcala* the humble servant of a poor hermit, lowliest of the low, begs pardon of the flowers which he gathers for the chapel, and begs them to forgive him for taking them away from their beloved meadows. This is a worthier attitude before those divine children of the dews and sun than the indifference of the lovers of the flower carnival or the funeral pageant.

If a daisy were but as scarce as a diamond, how would the multitudes rush to adore the little golden-eyed star in the grass!

One of the most exquisitely beautiful things I ever saw in my life was a thick tuft of harebell glittering all over with dew on a sunny morning where it grew on a mossy wall. It was not worth sixpence, yet it was a thing to kneel down before and adore and remember reverently for evermore.

Who will deliver us, asks George Sala, from the fashionable bridal, from the eternal ivory satin and the ghastly orange-blossom, and the two little shavers masquerading as pages?

The roughest and rudest marriage forms of savage nations are less offensive than those which are the received and admired custom of the civilised world. There cannot be a more Philistian jumble of greed, show, indecency and extravagance than are compressed into the marriage festivities of the cities of Europe and America. When the nuptials are solemnised in the country, something of country simplicity and freshness may enter into them, but almost all fashionable weddings are now taken to the cities, because a huge enough crowd cannot be gathered together even in the biggest of big country houses. Often the persons concerned go to an hotel, or borrow a friend's mansion for the celebration of the auspicious event.

Year after year the same trivial and tiresome usage, the same vulgar and extravagant customs, the same barbarous and uncouth ceremonies prevail, and are accepted as sacred and unalterable law. The most intimate, the most delicate, the most personal actions and emotions of life are set out in the full glare of light in the most unscreened and most unsparing publicity; and no one sees the odious and disgusting coarseness of it all. The more sensitive and refined temperaments submit meekly to the torture of its commands.

If marriage, so long as the institution lasts, could become in its celebration that which decency and good taste would suggest, a simple and sacred rite with neither publicity nor gaudy expenditure to profane it, there might come, with such a change, similar alteration in other ceremonies, and sentiment might have a chance to put in its modest plea for place unfrightened by the loud beating of the brazen drums of wealth. In all the annals of the social life of the world there has not been anything so atrocious in vulgarity as a fashionable wedding, whether viewed in its greedy pillaging of friends and acquaintances or in its theatrical pomp of costume, of procession and of banquet. It is the very apogee of bad taste, incongruity and indecency, from the coarse words of its rites to its sputtering champagne, its unvaried orations, and its idiotic expenditure. It is this publicity which is dear to the soul of our Gaius and Gaia; for were it not so there would be more special licences demanded, since these are not so costly that gentle-people could not easily afford to have their marriage ceremony as entirely private as they pleased. But they would not feel any pleasure at privacy; they despise it; they are always ready with gag and rouge for the foot-lights; if they had not an audience the bride and bridegroom would yawn in each other's faces. Every ceremony duly repeats and carefully imitates those which have preceded it. There is no originality, there is no modesty, there is no dignity or reserve. The plunder which is called 'presents' are laid out on exhibition, and the feverish anxiety of every bride-elect is to get more presents than any of her contemporaries. Even the in-door and out-door servants of each of the two households have this shameless blackmail levied on them; and gillies subscribe for a hunting-watch, and kitchen-maids contribute to the purchase of a silver-framed mirror. Scarcely even is a royal or aristocratic marriage announced than the laundries and the pantries are ransacked for sovereigns and half-sovereigns to purchase some costly article to be offered to their princely or noble employers. Imagine the slaves of Augustus presenting him with a gold whistle, or the comedians of Louis Quatorze offering him a silver cigar-box!

But all is fish which comes to the nets of the impecunious great folks of the *fin de siècle*, and the unhappy households must submit and buy a propitiatory gift out of their salaries. That households are notoriously dishonest in our day is but a necessary consequence. Who can blame a servant if, knowing the blackmail which will be levied on him, he recoups himself with commissions levied in turn upon tradesmen, or perquisites gleaned from the wine-cellars? It is said openly, though I cannot declare with what truth, that all the gifts in gold and silver and jewels which are offered to princes on their travels by loyal corporations or adoring colonists are sold immediately, whilst all the costly boxes and jewelled trifles which such princes are obliged by custom to leave behind them wherever they have been received are similarly disposed of by the greater number of their recipients. It is, perhaps, the reason why royal donors so frequently limit themselves to the cheap gift of a signed photograph. They know that photographs cannot be offered to them in return.

The diffusion of German influence, which has been general over Europe through the fatality which has seated Germans on all the thrones of Europe, has had more than any other thing to do with the vulgarisation of European society. The German eats in public, kisses in public, drags all his emotions out into the public garden or coffee-house, makes public his curious and nauseous mixture of sugar and salt, of jam and pickles, alike in his sentiments and in his cookery, and praises Providence and embraces his betrothed with equal unction under the trees of the public square.

And the influence of courts being immense, socially and personally, society throughout Europe has been Germanised; scholars love to point out the far-reaching and deeply penetrating influence of the Greek and Asiatic spirit upon Rome and Latium; historians in a time to come will study as curiously the effect of the German influence on the nineteenth and twentieth centuries, and that of royal houses upon nations in an epoch when royalty drew near its end.

It is to German and royal influence that English society owes the introduction of what are called silver and golden weddings, of which the tinsel sentiment and the greedy motive are alike most unlovely. Gaius and Gaia grown old, proclaim to all their world that they have lived together for a quarter or a half century in order that this fact, absolutely uninteresting to any one except themselves, may bring them a shower of compliments and of gifts. They may very probably have had nothing of union except its semblance; they may have led a long life of bickering, wrangling and dissension; Gaius may have wished her at the devil a thousand times, and Gaia may have opened his letters, paid his debts out of her dower, and quarrelled with his tastes ever since their nuptials: all this is of no matter whatever; the twenty-five or the fifty years have gone by, and are therefore celebrated as one long hymn of peace and harmony, the loving-cup is passed round, and blackmail is levied on all their acquaintances. 'Old as he is, he makes eyes at my maid because she is young and fresh-coloured!' says Gaia in her confidante's ear. 'The damned old hag still pulls me up if I only look at a pretty woman!' grumbles Gaius in his club confidences. But they smile and kiss and go before the audience at their golden wedding and speak the epilogue of the dreary comedy which society has imposed on them and which they have imposed on society. And the buffets of their dining-hall are the richer by so many golden flagons and caskets and salvers given by their admiring acquaintances, who are not their dupes but who pretend to be so in that unending make-believe which accompanies us from the nursery to the grave. The union may have been virtually a separation for five-sixths of its term; the ill temper of the man or the carping spirit of the woman, or any one of the other innumerable causes of dissension which make dislike so much easier and more general than affection, may have made of this 'married life' an everlasting apple of discord blistering the lips which have been fastened to it. Nevertheless, because they have not been publicly separated, the wedded couple, secretly straining at their chains, are bound after a certain term of years to receive the felicitations and the gifts of those around them.

The grotesqueness of these celebrations does not seem to strike any one. This century has but little humour. In a witty age these elderly wedded pairs would be seen to be so comical, that laughter would blow out their long-lit hymeneal torch, and forbid the middle-aged or aged lovers to undraw the curtains of their nuptial couches. Love may wither in the flesh, yet keep his heart alive maybe—yes, truly—but if Love be wise, he will say nothing about his heart when his lips are faded.

Old men and women, with grandchildren by the hundred, and offspring of fifty years old, should have perception enough of the ridiculous not to speak of a union which has so many living witnesses to its fruitfulness. The tenderness which may still unite two aged people who have climbed the hill of life together, and are together descending its slope in the grey of the coming night, may be one of the holiest, as it is certainly the rarest, of human sentiments, but it is not one which can bear being dragged out into the glare of publicity. What is respectable, and even sacred, murmured between 'John Anderson my jo, John,' and his old wife as they sit in the evening on the moss-grown wall of the churchyard, where they will soon be laid side by side together for evermore, is ridiculous and indecent when made the theme of after-dinner speeches and newspaper paragraphs. No true feeling should ever be trumpeted abroad; and the older men and women grow, the more bounden on them becomes the reserve which can alone preserve their dignity. But dignity is the quality in which the present period is most conspicuously deficient. Those who possess it in public life are unpopular with the public; those who possess it in private life are thought pretentious, or old-fashioned and stiff-necked.

The French expression for being fashionable, *dans le train*, exactly expresses what fashion now is. It is to be remarkable in a crowd indeed, but still always in a crowd, rushing rapidly with that crowd, and no longer attempting to lead, much less to stem it. Life lived at a gallop may be, whilst we are in the first flight, great fun, but it is wholly impossible that it should be very dignified. The cotillon cannot be the minuet. The cotillon is sometimes a very pretty thing, and sometimes a very diverting one, but it is always a romp. I would keep the cotillon, but I would not force every one to join in it. Society does force every one to do so, metaphorically speaking; you must either live out of the world altogether or you must take the world's amusements as you find them, and they are nowadays terribly monotonous, and not seldom very unintelligent, and a severe drain upon both wealth and health. Youth, riches and beauty may have 'a good time,' because they contain in themselves many elements of pleasure; but this 'good time' is at its best not elegant and always feverish; it invents nothing, it satisfies no ideal, it is full of slavish imitation and repetition, and it is bored by tedious and stupid ceremonies which everyone execrates, but no one has the courage to abolish or refuse to attend.

One is apt to believe that anarchy will sooner or later break up our social life into chaos because it becomes so appalling to think that all these silly and ugly forms of display and pompous frivolity will go on for ever; that humanity will be for ever snobbishly prostrate before princes, babyishly pleased with stars and crosses, grinningly joyful to be packed together on a grand staircase, and idiotically impotent to choose or to act with independence. There appears no possibility whatever of society redressing, purifying, elevating itself; the unsavoury crowd at the White House reception and the Elysées ball is only still more hopelessly ridiculous and odious than the better-dressed and better-mannered throng at St James's or the Hofburg. The office-holder in a republic has as many toadies and parasites as an archduke or a *kronprinz*. The man who lives in a shanty built of empty meat and biscuit tins on the plains of Nevada or New South Wales is by many degrees a more degraded form of humanity than his brother who has stayed amongst English wheat or Tuscan olives or French vines or German pine-trees: many degrees more degraded, because infinitely coarser and more brutal, and more hopelessly soaked in a sordid and hideous manner of life. All the vices, meannesses and ignominies of the Old World reproduce themselves in the so-called New World, and become more vulgar, more ignoble, more despicable than in their original hemisphere. Under the Southern Cross of the Australian skies, cant, snobbism, corruption, venality, fraud, the worship of wealth *per se*, are more rampant, more naked, and more vulgarly bedizened than beneath the stars of Ursa Major. It is not from the mixture of Methodism, drunkenness, revolver-shooting, wire-pulling, and the frantic expenditure of *richards* who were navvies or miners a week ago, that any superior light and leading, any alteration for the better in social life can be ever looked for. All that America and Australia will ever do will be to servilely reproduce the follies and hopelessly vulgarise the habits of the older civilisation of Europe.

What is decreasing, fading, disappearing more and more every year is something more precious than any mere enjoyment or embellishment. It is what we call high breeding; it is what we mean when we say that *bon sang ne peut mentir*. All the unpurchasable, unteachable, indescribable qualities and instincts which we imply when we say he or she has 'race' in him, are growing more and more rare through the continual alliance of old families with new wealth. We understand the necessity of keeping the blood of our racing and coursing animals pure, but we let their human owners sully their stock with indifference so long as they can 'marry money,' no matter how that money has been made. The effect is very visible; as visible as the deterioration in the manners of the House of Commons since neither culture nor courtesy are any longer exacted there, and as the injury done to the House of Lords by allowing it to become a retreat for retired and prosperous tradesmen.

It is reported that Ravachol, who was not especially sound at the core himself, stated it as his opinion that society is so rotten that nothing can be done with it except to destroy it. Most sober thinkers, who have not Ravachol's relish for the pastimes of crime, must yet be tempted to agree with him. Who that knows anything at all of the inner working of administrative life can respect any extant form of government? Who that has studied the practical working of elective modes of choice can fail to see that there is no true choice in their issues at all, only endless wire-pulling? Who can deny that all the legislation in the world must for ever be powerless to limit the *sub rosa* influence of the unscrupulous man? Who can deny that in the struggle for success, honesty and independence and candour are dead-weights, suppleness and falsehood, and the sly tact which bends the knee and oils the tongue, are the surest qualities in any competitor? Who can frame any social system in which the enormous, intangible and most unjust preponderance of interest and influence can be neutralised, or the still more unjust preponderance of mere numbers be counteracted?

Some thinkers predict that the coming ruler, the working man, will change this rottenness to health; but it may safely be predicted that he will do nothing of the kind. He will be at the least as selfish, as bribable, and as vain, as the gentry who have preceded him; he will be certainly coarser and clumsier in his tastes, habits, and pleasures, and the narrowness of his intelligence will not restrain the extravagance of his expenditure of moneys not his own, with which he will be able to endow himself by legislation. If Socialism would, in reality, break up the deadly monotony of modern society, who would not welcome it? But it would do nothing of the kind. It would only substitute a deadlier, a still triter monotony; whilst it would deprive us of the amount of picturesqueness, stimulant, diversity and expectation which are now derived from the inequalities and potentialities of fortune. The sole things which now save us from absolute inanity are the various possibilities of the unexpected and the unforeseen with which the diversity of position and the see-saw of wealth now supply us. The whole tendency of Socialism, from its first tentatives in the present trades unions, is to iron down humanity into one dreary level, tedious and featureless as the desert. It is not to its doctrines that we can look for any increase of wit, of grace and of charm. Its triumph would be the reign of universal ugliness, sameness and commonness. Mr Keir Hardie in baggy yellow trousers, smoking a black pipe close to the tea-table of the Speaker's daughters, on the terrace of the House of Commons, is an exact sample of the 'graces and gladness' which the democratic' apotheosis would bestow on us.

It is not the cap and jacket of the Labour member, or the roar of the two-legged wild beasts escorting him, which will open out an era of more elegant pleasure, of more refined amusement, or give us a world more gracious, picturesque and fair. Mob rule is rising everywhere in a muddy ocean which will outspread into a muddy plain wherein all loveliness and eminence will be alike submerged. But it is not yet wholly upon us. There is still time for society, if it care to do so, to justify its own existence ere its despoilers be upon it; and it can only be so justified if it become something which money cannot purchase, and envy, though it may destroy, cannot deride.

CONSCRIPTION

In a recent interview with Lord Wolseley, the visitor states that he obtained from that officer the following vehement declaration in favour of enforced and universal military service:—

'You develop his physical power, you make a man of him in body and in strength, as the schools he had been at previously had made a man of him mentally. You teach him habits of cleanliness, tidiness, punctuality, reverence for superiors, and obedience to those above him, and you do this in a way that no species of machinery that I have ever been acquainted with could possibly fulfil. In fact, you give him all the qualities calculated to make him a thoroughly useful and loyal citizen when he leaves the colours and returns home to civil life. And of this I am quite certain, that the nation which has the courage and the patriotism to insist on all its sons undergoing this species of education and training for at least two or three generations, will consist of men and women far better calculated to be the fathers and mothers of healthy and vigorous children than the nation which allows its young people to grow up without any physical training although they may cram their heads with all sorts of scientific knowledge in their national schools. In other words, the race in two or three generations will be stronger, more vigorous, and therefore braver, and more calculated to make the nation to which they belong great and powerful.'

It is obvious that such a rhapsody could only be uttered by one who has never studied the actual effects of conscription on a population, but speaks merely of what he has been led to believe is its effect from what he has watched on the drill-grounds of countries little otherwise known to him. It is a sweeping assertion, still less grounded on fact than its corresponding declaration, that school makes a man of its pupil mentally, which is by no means always or inevitably the case. I could not, of course, propose to contravene any purely military statement of a military celebrity, but this composite and wholesale and most amazing declaration I do dispute, and I think that I know more of the effects of compulsory service than does its speaker. Lord Wolseley has never certainly dwelt, even for a short time, in those countries which are cursed by conscription. He sees that the battalions of conscripted armies seem to him to march well and manœuvre finely, and he concludes, with natural military prejudice, that the results, moral and mental, of conscription on a nation are admirable, and are unattainable in any other manner.

To begin with, he considers evidently as beyond all dispute that the soldier is the highest type of humanity, which may be doubted, and that obedience is the highest human virtue, which may be also doubted. All the finest freedoms of mankind have been obtained, not by obedient, but by utterly disobedient, persons; persons who, if they had failed, would have been thrown into prison or sent to scaffolds. Obedience in the child is the first and the highest virtue, because the whole well-being of the child, material and moral, depends on it. But the man, to be a man, must be courageous enough to disobey if disobedience be needed by honour, justice, or wisdom. There are moments, even in war and even in a soldier's life, when the magnificent daring which disobeys is a more precious quality than the primmer and more decorous one of unquestioning deference to commands received. In older times the modes of warfare or the manner of civil life left much freer scope to idiosyncrasy and choice, much wider space for the play of spirit and originality. Modern warfare, like modern education, tends yearly to draw tighter the bonds with which it buckles down all natural growth of character and possibility of adventure. Mechanical reproduction is the chief note of military effort as of civil. The soldier, like the civilian, every year tends more and more to become only one infinitesimal atom of a rivet in the enormous and overwhelming engine of the State.

To a young man of genius, or even of merely great talent, it is certain that the enforced term of military service would be sorely and indelibly injurious. Genius does not easily obey, and all the harsh, unlovely, stupid routine of camp and barrack would be so odious to it that a youth of brilliant gifts and promise might easily be compromised and condemned, continually and fatally, in his passage through the ranks. Even were such a youth obedient to his duties, the sheer waste of time, the dispiriting influences of a long period of tedious, irksome, and detested occupations, would have the most depressing and dwarfing effect upon his talent. History teems with instances, which it would be tiresome to enumerate, in which revolt and refusal have produced for the world all that we most prize of liberty, of conscience, and of conduct. Revolt and refusal are disobedience, and they have frequently been quite as noble and fruitful as the more passive virtue of obedience, which not seldom has taken the form of timorous submission to, and execution of, conscious wrong. Would Lord Wolseley have admired or condemned a *mousquetaire* of the Louvre who should have refused to fire on the Huguenots from the windows?

But were obedience the first of virtues, conscription does not teach it: it enforces it, which is a very different thing. You do not put a quality into a man because you taught him and forced from him by fear the simulacrum of it. Because the conscript has for a term of years, to his bitter hatred and despite, been compelled to obey at the point of the bayonet, he does not thereby become a more willingly obedient man; he will, on the contrary, as soon as he is set free, revenge himself by insubordination to his parents, his employers, his superiors, in all the ways which may be open to him. The obedience exacted from the soldier is taken by force: he obeys because he knows that those stronger than himself will punish him badly if he do not. This is not an ennobling sentiment, nor is it one which can lend any beauty or nobility to a character. You are not a better or a kinder master because you been a slave, nilly-willy, for three of the best years of your life. Obedience which is rendered out of true veneration may be a tonic to the nature which is bent by it; but the obedience which is merely rendered, as all conscripts' obedience is, because if it be not given the irons and the cell will follow, does no one any moral good, teaches no virtue which can be productive hereafter. There is no servant, groom, artisan, farm-labourer, or hireling of any kind so lazy, so impudent, so insubordinate, and so useless as the young man who has recently come out from his term of compulsory service. It is natural that it should be so. As we cannot create morality by Act of Parliament, so we cannot create character by the knapsack and the cross-belts. Family education, even school education, can in a measure mould character, because it is the long, free, malleable, tender years of childhood and boyhood upon which it works; but after twenty-one, the character does not vitally alter much, though it will assimilate vice and vanity with fatal quickness. When Lord Wolseley utters the preposterous declaration that the education given by conscription teaches a lad 'all the qualities calculated to make him a thoroughly useful and loyal citizen,' has he the least idea of what is the actual moral state of the barrack-yards and barrack-rooms of the armies of the continent? Has he ever reflected on the inevitable results of the pell-mell confusion with which the clean-living young sons of gentle-people and commercial people are flung together with the lowest ruffians from the cellars of the cities and the caves of the mountains? Will he even credit how constantly the healthy, hard-working, obedient lad from the farmside or the counting-house, who left his people, happy in his duties and clean in body and mind, comes back to them, when his time is over, cankered body and soul, eaten up by disease, scornful of simple ways, too useless to work, too depraved to wed, too puffed up with foul desires and braggart conceits to earn the bread which he considers his father and brothers bound to labour to provide for him?

When the youth has had purity and strength of character and of mind enough to resist the contagion in which he has been steeped, he will in nine instances out of ten be a spoilt agriculturist, artisan, student, labourer. He has been torn from his chosen pursuit at the moment when he had begun to fairly master it, and he is spoilt for it, he is out of joint with it, he forgets its cunning. If he were engaged in any of those arts which require the utmost delicacy of touch, the ends of his fingers have become coarse, rough, blunted, and have lost all their sensitiveness; the porcelain-painters, the jewellers' artificers, the makers of the inimitable *articles de Paris*, suffer immeasurably from the injury done to their finger-tips by barrack work; whilst on the other hand the horny palms of the lads who push the plough and use the spade have grown so softened by what is to them the lighter work of the barracks, that they writhe with pain when they go out on their farms and the skin soon is stripped off the raw flesh.

To a military commander it is natural that the diffusion of the military temper should appear the beau ideal of improvement. Every class has its own intrinsic vanity, and sees in itself the salt and savour of society. But in truth there is a distinct menace to the world, in the present generalisation of the military temper, which is and must always be accompanied by narrowness and domination. What the young man acquires from his years of enforced service is much more often the hectoring and bullying temper characteristic of the soldier to the civilian, than it is the obedience, humility and loyalty which Lord Wolseley believes that he brings away with him. It is certainly most unjust that the soldier should be regarded, as in England, inferior to the civilian, and hustled out of theatres and concert-rooms; but it is still worse for the community when the soldier can fire on citizens, slash at greybeards, and run through children with impunity, as he can do in Germany, at his will and pleasure.

The very rules and qualities which are inevitable for the well-being of the soldier are injurious to the character of the civilian: mill-like routine, and unquestioning acceptance of orders, are not the makers of virile or high-minded men in civil life, however necessary they may be in battalions. Linesmen and gunners are admirable and useful persons, but they are not the supreme salt of the earth that we should endeavour to make all humanity in their likeness. The military education creates a certain sort of man, an excellent sort of man in his way, and for his purpose; but not the man who is the best product of the human race.

The story of Tell may be a myth or a fact, but whichever it be, the refusal to bow to the cap on the pole represents a heroism and a temper finer than any which militarism can teach, and which are, indeed, altogether opposed to it Even were the regiment the school which Lord Wolseley is pleased to believe it, why should he suppose that there are no others as good or better? The old apprenticeships, which have been done away with, were strict in discipline and insistent on obedience, and they are now considered too severe in consequence. Yet they were schools which kept a youth constantly within the practice of his art or trade. Conscription takes him away from it. It unsettles a young man at the precise moment in his life when it is most necessary that he should be confirmed in his tastes for and practice of his chosen occupation. It sends him from his village to some city, perchance hundreds of miles away, and keeps shifting him from place to place, imbuing him with the sickly fever of unrest, which is the malady of the age, and rendering his old, quiet, home-rooted life impossible to him. There can be nothing worse for him than the barrack life; at times very harsh and onerous and cruel, but with long, lazy pauses in it of absolute idleness, when the lad, lying in the sun on the stone benches, dozes and boozes his hours away, and the vicious rogue can poison at will the ear of the simple fool.

Lord Wolseley considers it an admirable machinery for creating citizens; it is not so, because the individual it creates is a mere machine, with no will of his own, with all virility and spirit beaten and cursed out of him, with no ideal set before him but to wait on the will of his corporal or captain. A soldier is at no time a good 'all round' man; the military temper and standard are, and must be, always narrow. In its most odious and offensive forms, as in Germany, it amounts to a brutal and most dangerous tyranny, overbearing in its intolerable vanity, and holding civilian life of no more account than dust.

Lord Wolseley seems to imagine that where conscription exists every man serves. In no country does every man serve. Even in Germany a very large proportion escape through physique or through circumstances, through voluntary mutilation or emigration. It is fortunate that it is so, for I can conceive nothing so appalling to the world as would be the forcing of the military temper down the throats of its entire multitudes. Militarism is the negation of individuality, of originality, and of true liberty. Its sombre shadow is spread over Europe; its garotting collar of steel is on the throat of the people. 'Forty-eight has produced nothing better than the universal rule of the tax-gatherer and the gendarme. The French Republic has the same corruption, the same tyrannies, and the same coercion by bayonets for which the two Empires were reviled. Germany is a hell of despotism, prosecution and espionage. Russia, a purely military nation, is given up to torture, corruption, filth, and drunkenness. Italy has recovered political freedom only to fall prostrate at the feet of her old foe, who has 'the double beak to more devour.' This is all that militarism and its offspring, conscription, has done for the three nations who most loudly protested their free principles. In the latter, at least, the whole people sweat, groan, perish under the burdens laid upon them for the maintenance of the vast battalions of young men imprisoned in barrack-yards in enforced idleness and semi-starvation, whilst the fruitful lands of the Veneto, of Apulia, of the Emilia, of Sardinia, and of Calabria lie untilled under the blue skies, the soil crying for its sons, the spade and the scythe rusting whilst the accursed sabre and musket shine.

When the gain of what is termed a whole nation under arms is estimated, the exaggeration of the pompous phrase hides the nakedness of the fact that large numbers of young men are lost to their country by the means to which they resort to escape military service. In Italy and Germany these may be counted by legions: in France fugitives from the military law are less numerous, because in France men are more wedded to the native soil, and take to service more gaily and more naturally, but in Italy and Germany thousands flock to emigrant ships, thus choosing lifelong self-expatriation; and every year, as the military and fiscal burdens grow heavier, will lads go away by preference to lands where, however hard be the work, the dreaded voice of the drill-sergeant cannot reach them, and they can 'call their soul their own.' Patriotism is a fine quality, no doubt, but it does not accord with the chill and supercilious apathy which characterises the general teaching and temper of this age, and a young man may be pardoned if he deem that his country is less a mother worthy of love than a cruel and unworthy stepmother, when she demands three of the fairest years of his life to be spent in a barrack-yard, and wrings his ears till the blood drops from them, or beats him about the head with the butt of a musket, because he does not hold his chin high enough, or shift his feet quickly enough.

For a hundred years humanity in this generation has been shouting, screaming, fighting, weeping, chaunting, bleeding in search and struggle for various forms of what has been called liberty. The only result hitherto deducible from this is the present fact that the nations of Europe are all watching each other like a number of sullen and suspicious dogs. We are told that this is peace. It is such excellent and perfect peace that it is merely their mutual uncertainty of each other's strength which keeps them from flying at each other's throats. It is not peace which Europe enjoys; it is an armed truce, with all the exhausting strain on the body politic and on the exchequer which must accompany such a state of things. Conscription enables this state of tension to exist, and the impatience which conscription excites in the people renders them perpetually thirsty and feverish for war.

They fancy that war would end it; would give them some good in return for all their sufferings. 'We cannot go on like this,' is the universal feeling on the Continent; it is the feeling created by conscription. Conscription is the pole-axe with which the patient labourer or citizen is brained, and it is cut from the wood of his own roof-tree. It is possible, probable, that conscription will be enforced in England also, with the many other forms of servitude which democracy assures us is liberty; but it is certain that when it is so, the country will be no longer the England which we have known in history.

GARDENS

In the charming essay called 'Caxtoniana' there is a passage on gardens which is supremely true, and which reminds us that whoever has a garden has one chamber roofed by heaven in which the poet and philosopher can feel at home. This passage was written beside a bay-window opening on the stately and beautiful gardens of the great author's home: to few is it given to possess such; but of any garden a certain little kingdom may be made, be it only green enough and well removed from city noise. Even within cities, little gardens, such as may be seen in the Faubourg St Martin and the Marais, where the population is poorest and densest, may be charmingly pretty, and a great solace to those who care for and look on them; and it is these little nooks and corners of gardens which give so much of its joyous and glad aspect to the whole of Paris. The great beauty of Rome (now since the Italian occupation irrevocably destroyed) was in the gardens; the shadowy, noble, antique gardens, with the embalmed breath of the past on their air, and the eternal youth of their flowers running wild over funeral sepulchre and fortress wall. It is their gardens which make the ancient cities and towns of Belgium so full of repose, of friendliness, of the calm of Nature and the romance of history. Public gardens, like public parks, may be beautiful, useful, health-giving, pleasure-giving; but still they must ever be public gardens: it is the private gardens, the green places dedicated to thought and to affection, which alone are lovable, and which alone make a home possible, even amidst the network of crowded streets.

It would be difficult for a Thoreau or a Wordsworth, for Alfred Austin or for Alphonse Karr, to find much pleasure in a public garden even historic as that of the Luxembourg, wondrous as those of the East, or beautiful as that of the Borghese in Rome or the English garden of Munich. Wherever intrusion is possible, and any movement other than that of birds is heard, we have no garden in the fullest, sweetest sense of the word. The lover of his garden is inevitably and essentially exclusive. He must be so, or the magic charm of his domain is gone. It may be a tiny plot fenced round by a privet or box hedge, or it may be stately pleasaunces walled in by clipped yew and gay terraces; but it must be his alone; his to wander in, to cherish, to dream through, undisturbed. A public garden is a valuable pleasure-ground for a city; but is no more a garden 'roofed by heaven,' in Bulwer-Lytton's sense of the word, than life in a hotel and at a *table d'hôte* is a home.

Gardens tend sadly to become more and more artificial with the ever-increasing artificiality of an age which, whilst demanding nature from its art and literature, becomes itself, with every breath it draws, farther and farther removed from nature. The great gardens of great houses in England, esteemed the finest gardens in the world, are spoiled for those who love them by the innumerable gardeners, by the endless and overdone sweeping and cleaning and clipping and pruning. A garden, like a woman may be too neat, too stiff, too *tiré à quatre éping les*. The remorseless brooms and barrows in autumn trundle away all the lovely carpet of golden and crimson leaves, and deprive the nightingales, when they come in spring, of their favourite and most necessary retreat. Sweep the paths, if you will, though even they need not be swept as smooth as a billiard-table; but to sweep and clear away the leaves from under the shrubberies, and from about the roots of trees, is a fatal error, most destructive to the trees themselves.

'Corisande's garden,' in 'Lothair,' is the ideal garden; and it is pathetic to think that, as an ideal, it was given to the world by one esteemed of all men the coldest and most world-hardened. But Disraeli had a warm and enduring devotion to flowers in his nature, and their loveliness and innocence and 'breath of heaven' never failed to touch the soul which slumbered behind that glittering, artificial, and merciless intelligence. He rightly abhorred the elaborately-patterned beds, the dazzling assorted colours, the formal mosaic of hues, in which the modern gardener delights. All the sweet-smelling, and what are now called old-fashioned, flowers are hustled out of the way by the bedding-out system and the present craze for geometrical arrangement. Numbers of delicious flowers which were dear to the heart of Herrick, fragrant, homely, kindly, hardy things, have been banished almost out of all knowledge, that the pelargonium, the dahlia, the calceolaria, the coleus, and various other scentless but fashionable flowers may fill group and border. It is a mistake. Even the petunia and the dwarf datura, though so sweet at sunset, cannot give such fragrance as will yield the humble favourites of yore—the musk-plants, the clove-pinks, the lavender, the lemon-thyme, the moss-rose, the mignonette, and many another sweet and simple plant which is rarely now seen out of cottage gardens.

Educated taste will spend large sums of money on odontozlossom, catleyia and orchid, whilst it will not glance perhaps once in a lifetime at the ruby spots on the cowslip bells and the lovely lilac or laburnum flowers blowing in a wild west wind. It will be a sorry day for the flowers and the nation when the cottage gardens of England disappear and leave the frightful villa garden and the painfully mathematical allotment field alone in their stead. An English cottage, such as Creswick and Constable, as old Crome and David Cox saw and knew them, and as they may still be seen, with roses clambering to the eaves, and bees humming in the southern-wood and sweetbriar, and red and white carnations growing beside the balsam and the dragon's-mouth, is a delicious rural study still linked, in memory, with foaming syllabub and ruddy cherries, and honey-comb yellow as amber, and with the plaintive bleating of new-born lambs sounding beyond the garden coppice. Who that knows England has not some such picture—nay, a hundred such pictures—in his recollection?

And it is in these gardens that Shakespeare's, Milton's, Ben Jonson's 'posies' may still be gathered; every flower and floweret of them still known by such names as Ophelia and Perdita gave them. Even in winter they are not wholly dreary or colourless; for there are their holly-bushes, their hellebore, their rosethorn, their hepatica, and their snowdrops to enliven them. In these times, when all the 'realism' of the lives of the poor is considered to lie in squalor, famine, crime, drunkenness, and envy, it is pleasant to know that such cottage gardens as these are still extant, though no longer frequent, in the land of Shakespeare and Ben Jonson; and that often, behind the door where the climbing white rose mounts to meet the thatch, there are still good humour, thrift, cheerfulness and cleanliness to be found in company with that manly content in existing circumstances which is the only form of durable happiness or solid virtue.

Children should never be allowed to pluck flowers, even in the fields and hedges, merely to throw them aside; they should be early taught reverence for this floral beauty which is around them, and never be permitted wantonly to break down boughs and branches, or fill their laps with buttercups and daisies only to leave them withered in the sun, discarded and forgotten. To teach the small child to care for flowers, to place them tenderly in water when gathered, and cherish them carefully in his nursery, is not only to give him a valuable moral lesson, but to lead him also to a taste and feeling which will give him, when he grows to manhood, many glad and innocent hours, and render him thoughtful and sympathetic when he deals with those sensitive plants,—the souls of women.

A love for flowers indicates the quickness for imagination and the delicacy of sentiment of those in whom it is strong. It will also be almost always accompanied by a feeling for all other kinds of natural beauty and woodland life. It would be difficult to love the rose without loving the nightingale, or cherish the hawthorn without caring for the thrushes that build in it. The fatal tendency of modern life is to replace natural by artificial beauty, where beauty is not driven out of the way altogether. Every child who is led to feel the loveliness of the water-lily lying on the green pond-water, or of the wild hyacinth growing in the home-wood grasses, will, as he grows up, lend his influence and his example to the preservation of all rural and sylvan loveliness.

In the great world, and in the rich world, flowers are wasted with painful prodigality. The thousands and tens of thousands of flowers which die to decorate a single ball or reception are a sad sight to those who love them. 'The rooms look well to-night,' is the utmost that is ever said after all this waste of blossom and fragrance. It is waste, because scarcely a glance is bestowed on them, and the myriad of roses which cover the walls do not effectively make more impression on the eye than the original silk or satin wall-hanging which they momentarily replace. Growing plants may be used in thousands for decoration without waste, but the inordinate display of cut flowers is a pitiable destruction of which scarcely one guest in fifty is sensible. In bowls and baskets and jars, cut flowers can live out their natural space; but nailed on walls, or impaled on wires, they are soon faded and yellow, and the ballroom in the morning is as melancholy a parable of the brevity of pleasure as any moralist could desire.

Church decoration is not a whit better; flowers are wantonly sacrificed to it, and in the winter the birds are starved through it for need of the evergreen berries torn down in woods and gardens to adorn the altars of men. The numbers of dead birds found in frost and snow on moor and field have increased enormously with the increase in church decoration. A sheaf of grain hung up for the seed-eating birds in winter, with some trays of meal-worms put on the ground for the insectivorous birds, would be a more useful form of piety than the cartload of branches and the garlands of berries given to church and cathedral.

The young should be led to cherish their flowers as wisely as, and more tenderly than, they cherish their gold and silver pieces in their money-boxes. The exquisite beauty of even the humblest blossom can only be appreciated by the eyes which gaze on it with attention and affection. If the wild thyme, or the shepherd's-purse, or the cuckoo's-eye, or any one of the tiny blossoms of the sward and the hedge-row were but as rare as sapphires are, the whole world would quarrel for them; but Nature has sown these little treasures broadcast with lavish hand, and scarcely any one is grateful. A single flower, if taken care of in winter, will gladden the eyes of an invalid or cripple for days; with care and thought for it a bunch of cut flowers, if cut at sunrise with the dew upon them, will live the week out in water in any cool weather; but these lovely, joy-giving things are wasted with the most reckless indifference.

Botany may be well in its way; but incomparably better is the practical knowledge of how to make flowers grow, and infinitely better still is the tenderness which turns aside not to tread on the wild flower in the path, not to needlessly disturb the finch's nest in the blossoming broom. Of all emotions which give the nature capable of it the purest and longest-lived pleasure, the sense of the beauty of natural things is the one which costs least pain in its indulgence, and most refines and elevates the character. The garden, the meadow, the wood, the orchard, are the schools in which this appreciative faculty is cultured most easily and enjoyably. Dostoïevsky may find food for it on the desolate steppe, and Burns in the dreary ploughed furrow; but to do this, genius must exist in the man who feels: it is to the ordinary sensibilities, the medium mind, the character which is malleable, but in no way unusual, that this training of the eye and of the heart is necessary: and for this training there is no school so happy and so useful as a garden.

All children, or nearly all, take instinctive delight in gardens: it is very easy to make this delight not merely an instinctive, but an intelligent one; very easy to make the arrival of the first crocus, the observation of the wren's nest in the ivy hedge, of the perennial wonders of frost and of sunshine, of the death and the resurrection of Nature, of the deepest interest to a young mind athirst for marvels. Then what greater joy and triumph does the world hold than these of the child gardener with his first bouquet of roses, his first basket of water-cress, his first handful of sweet peas! His garden, if he be taught to care for it in the right way, will be an unceasing happiness to him; he will not grudge the birds a share of his cherries, for he will value too well the songs they sing to him; he will breathe in the fresh home balm of the dewy sweet herbs, the wet flower borders, and he will draw in health and vigour with every breath; and if he reads his fairy stories and his lays of chivalry under the blossoming limes, poetry and history will keep for him in all after time something of his first garden's grace, something of the charm of a summer playtime.

If we did not know it as a fact, we should infer from the whole tenor of the verse of Tennyson that green old gardens, deep in their shade and placid in their beauty, had been about him all his life from infancy. The garden is a little pleasaunce of the soul, by whose wicket the world can be shut out from us. In the garden something of the Golden Age still lingers; in the warm alleys where the bees hum above the lilies and the stocks, in the blue shadows where the azure butterflies look dark, in the amber haze where the lime leaves and the acacia flowers wave joyously as the west wind passes.

The true lover of a garden counts time and seasons by his flowers. His calendar is the shepherd's calendar. He will remember all the events of his years by the trees or plants which were in blossom when they happened. 'The acacias were in flower when we first met,' or 'the hawthorns were in blossom when we last parted,' he will say to himself, if not to others; and no lovers are happier, or more spiritually in love than those whose sweetest words have been spoken in a garden, and who have fancy and feeling enough to associate their mute companions in memory with their remembered joys. No love can altogether die which comes back upon remembrance with every golden tuft of daffodil or every garland of growing honeysuckle. It is the garden scene in 'Faust,' it is the garden scene in 'Romeo and Juliet,' which embody passion in its fullest and its fairest hours.

O BEATI INSIPIENTES!

'Blessed are the poor in spirit,' says the Evangelist: he should have added, Blessed are the fools, the commonplace, the obscure, the mediocre; blessed those who have done nothing remarkable, thought nothing noteworthy, created nothing beautiful, and given nothing fair and fine to their generation! Unmolested may they dwell; unharassed may they live their lives at their own pleasure, unwatched may they take their daily walks abroad, ungrudged may they find happiness, unmolested may they indulge their grief. Their nursery days may rest forgotten; they will not be ransacked for reminiscences of childish petulance or babyish frowardness. Their school years may rest in the past, undisturbed by the grubbing of chroniclers and commentators, amongst the playground dust, and between the pages of the gradus. Their faults and follies will lie quiet in the grave, and no contemporary schoolfellow will recall their thefts of apples or their slips in parsings; or will write to the newspapers how they used a crib or smashed a tradesman's windows. Unworried, unenvied, unmisrepresented, they will pass through life inglorious, but at peace; and amongst the ashes of their buried years no curious hands will poke and rake in feverish zeal to find traces in their infancy of their bad passions, and drag out the broken pieces of the rattles or the ninepins they destroyed.

How ignorant is genius of what it does when it leaps up to the light of its sunrise! how little it recks of the hornet swarm which will circle round its head, of the viper brood which will coil round its ankles, of the horde of stinging, prying, buzzing, poisoning insects which will thicken the air as it passes, and hide in the heart of the roses it gathers!

It is not only the fierce light which beats upon a throne which genius has to bear, but the lurid glare of the sulphur fires of envy, making livid what is white, making hideous what is fair, making distorted and deformed what is straight and smooth and comely.

The world holds a concave mirror to the face of genius, and judges the face by the reflection.

The calm consciousness of power in the great writer, in the great artist, will always appear vanity to the majority, because the majority is incapable of seeing how entirely different to vanity it is, and how, if arrogant in the world, it is always humble in the closet; if it be conscious of its own superiority to its contemporaries, it will be none the less conscious of its inferiority to its own ideals. The intimate union of pride and of humility, which is characteristic of all genius, and pre-eminently sincere in it, can never be understood by the world at large.

Flaubert, as we know, corrected, effaced, reconstructed, erased and altered every line of his text a hundred times, in careless dissatisfaction with himself; but when an editor of a review asked him to make some corrections in the proof of St Julian Hospitador, he haughtily replied to the meddler: '*Des corrections? —j'en donne quelquefois, mais je n'en fais jamais!*' Inexorable self-scourger in his study or his studio, the man of genius is high-mettled and arrogant as an hidalgo before interference. How should the fool understand this?—the fool who deems himself perfect when strutting before his mirror, but is downcast before the first mocking glance or ridiculing word which he encounters in the public street!

Humanity loves to scoff, and say that genius is human. No doubt it is; but its humanity is always of a different kind to that of ordinary men. The nightingale is classified by naturalists amongst the tribe of the Sparrows, in the class of the Finches; but this fact does not make the nightingale only a sparrow, or only a finch. The nightingale sees life and nature very differently to the sparrow, though his physical organisation may, in some respects, resemble his kinsman's. It is one thing to sit on the housetops and drink rinsings from the gutter, and another to sit on a myrtle bough and drink dew from the heart of a rose. How shall those to whom the rinsings are sweet be able to judge those for whom the rose is chalice-bearer?

In a recent monograph upon his friend Meissonier, Alexandre Dumas has quoted some petulant and childish sayings of the great painter which would have been better left in oblivion. Dumas prefaces them by the phrase 'J'ai entendu Meissonier dire, mais peut-être, il est vrai, ne le disait-il qu'à moi:' in these last words, '*ne le disait-il qu'à moi,*' lies the whole gist of the matter, in these few words are contained the confession of the consciousness which should have preserved Meissonier's impetuous and unconsidered self-revelations from being, after his death, made public by his friend. It is just these things which are said only to us, which are said perhaps foolishly, perhaps hastily, perhaps stupidly, but in any way said in entire good faith, and in the conviction of the good faith of the confidant, which should never be repeated, above all when the ground is closed over the speakers of them. It will be said that there is nothing in this recollection of Meissonier which is in any way to his discredit. There is not. Yet it is none the less a violation of confidence; and in a sense it dwarfs the stature of him. One of the chief characteristics of genius is an extreme youthfulness of feeling and of impulse, often also of expression; the great artist is always in one side of his nature a child. But this fact, which is so lovable and engaging in him in his lifetime, makes him continually, in his careless and confidential utterances, say what is natural, and may even be beautiful in its spontaneity and suitability to the moment of its expression, but which loses its colour, its light, its charm, as a dried and pressed flower loses them when it is reproduced after death in the rigidity of type.

Taine set a fine example in his will when he enjoined on his heirs to burn all the documents in which he had written down all he had heard from his contemporaries. The rose should be always hung before the door wherever two or three are gathered together in familiar intercourse, and the inquisitive, censorious, malignant world is listening cunningly at the keyhole. The world will not go away for the rose; but those within should enforce respect for its symbol, and should stuff up the keyhole.

I once knew and liked for several years a diplomatist who was very popular in society. He was often with me, and one day he unfortunately told me that it was his habit to write down every night, no matter how late it might be when he went home, the record of everything witty, or interesting, or singular, that he had heard during the day, and the names of all the persons whom he had met and with whom he had conversed. 'I have done this,' he added, 'ever since I was an unpaid *attaché*, and these volumes, which are many, as you may imagine, will not be published until the time designated to my executors in my will.' Ever after this confession from him I saw him with much less pleasure; these bulky volumes, though unseen, cast their grim shadow over the present and the future; I never again laughed and talked with him without the recollection that he was treasuring up the nonsense I spoke or repeated to write it down in black and white before he allowed himself to sleep. The thought was a ghost at every intellectual banquet at which he and I met. I wanted to call out to our companions,

'There's a chiel amang you takin' notes.'

As he was a man who had his *petite entrée* into the arcana of politics, and was personally acquainted with the most distinguished people of Europe, he must have burned a good deal of post-midnight oil over his nightly chronicle, and I wonder he could keep awake to make it.

He died some years since, and of those voluminous records there is nothing said in the press as yet. No doubt, however, they will see the light some day; and some heir or heirs will make a round sum of money out of them. There is a kind of treason in this habit of committing to paper for ultimate publication what is said by those around us. If the matter be emended and emasculated when printed, it loses all interest; if published verbatim, the publication constitutes a betrayal. Social intercourse is surely based on the tacit assumption that what is said in it is said under cover of the white flag of mutual trust. I do not think that we have any right whatever to make any kind of private conversation public. The motive for doing so can never be a very high one. There is, no doubt, a great temptation in the wish to tell what we know about a friend whose character we see was unknown or misunderstood by the world in general, even probably by his intimate associates; but I doubt if we have the right to do so. If he revealed his natural inner self more completely to us than to others, it was no doubt because we inspired him with a more complete confidence or sympathy than did others. Shall that confidence or that sympathy be abused or betrayed by any man or woman of common honour?

It is a fact which is to be regretted that the faculty of inspiring confidence is, unfortunately, often allied to an utter faithlessness in keeping it. Those who most attract it are often those who most betray it. The sympathy which draws out our secrets is frequently united to considerable treachery in using them. Even those who are in many ways faithful and sincere betray after death those who trusted them in life, by revelations of their correspondence, either intentional or careless.

'Cachez votre vie: étalez votre esprit,' is a wise counsel; but it is this which the world will not permit if it can by any torment prevent it. He who has once allowed his wit to shine, and dazzle the eyes of his contemporaries, is expected to live his life for ever afterwards with open doors.

People who are famous are invariably accused of being self-conscious, reserved, monosyllabic, lacking in candour, in expansiveness, in inclination to converse. What more natural than that they should be so, since they know that their most intimate companion may not be able to resist the temptation of recording and retailing everything they say? If they speak as they feel, they are accused of 'giving themselves away,' as the English slang phrases it; if they be as reserved and as silent as it is possible to be without offence to society, they are accused of *morgue*, of vanity, of arrogance. In either case, whatever they do say, whether it be much or be little, will be certainly exaggerated, misrepresented, and disliked. Meissonier may, in a weak moment, wish he were Fortuny; Tennyson may, in an irritable hour, prefer money to fame; and each may say so to a trusted companion. But it is hard that the evanescent, unwise desire should be soberly published many years after in each case by a hearer who was deemed a friend.

We are none of us, perhaps, as loyal as we ought to be in speech. We are too thoughtless in what we repeat; and many, for sake of an epigram or a *jeu de mot*, sacrifice the higher duties of respect for confidence and silence on it. But speech may have the excuse of unpremeditation, haste, the contagion of conversation going on around. The indiscretions of written and of printed words share none of these excuses. Even if written in hurry or in carelessness, there is leisure enough when a proof sheet is received, between its reception and its publication, for all such revelations to be effaced. Have we a right to make public private conversations? I do not consider that we have. Intercourse, at all events the pleasure of intercourse, reposes on the tacit condition that its privacy is intangible. Intimate correspondence does the same. In letters we give hostages to our friends. It should be understood that such hostages are not to be led, like captives, into the public market-place and sold.

In the many memories of intimacy with Alfred Tennyson which have been published since his death, few would, I think, have pleased a man so reluctant to be observed and commented on as was he. The fulsome adulation would scarcely have sufficed to reconcile him to the cruel dissection.

Famous people, like obscure ones, do not weigh every syllable they speak; and the former pay heavily for imprudent utterance, whilst the latter sin scot-free because nobody cares a straw what they say or do not say. Tennyson, in an imprudent moment, said once to Henry Irving that Shelley had no sense of humour. It is quite true that Shelley had not: his life would have been brighter and happier if he had been able to laugh oftener; and it is exceedingly unfair to Tennyson to twist this statement of an actual fact into a depreciation of Shelley to his own self-praise. Even if he implied that he were the greater poet of the two, should a friend deride this, should a trusted companion record it?

Mr Knowles relates how Tennyson, speaking of his habit of composing verses which he never wrote down as he sat over the winter's fire, added, 'How many hundreds of fine lines went up the chimney and vanished!' The world cries out, 'What! did he call his own verses fine?' Why should he not? He must have known that he enriched the English language with scores of fine lines, as I suppose he must have known that he made many with false quantities, which halt painfully. But are these careless, natural phrases, utterances which should be produced in print? Nothing can divest such *post-mortem* revelations of a suspicion of treachery. They suggest the note-book of the diplomatist, in which at nightfall were recorded all the witty sayings and careless confidences heard during the daytime.

Mr Knowles, who admired Tennyson extremely, and lived for many years in his close intimacy, puts into print the saying of Tennyson that he wished he could have had the money which his books had brought without the nuisance of the fame which accompanied it. This was not an heroic speech, though it might be a natural one. It was probably a wrathful ebullition excited by the irritation of public comment and the prying impertinence of public curiosity. But it is the kind of speech which is never intended for reproduction in print. We all have these moments of ungrateful impatience with our lot. The king wishes himself in the hovel, the hind wishes himself on the throne. Whoso gathers the laurel longs for the cowslip, he who has the field flowers sighs for the myrtle and the bays. But it is not the place of a bosom friend to stereotype for all time the reproach of Fortune's favourites to the magnificent caprices of Fortune. Certainly Tennyson, having been compelled to choose, would have chosen the poverty and fame of Homer or of Cervantes rather than a life of inglorious ease and obscure eating of good dinners. The imperishable record in print, of a passing mood of irritability in which he said otherwise, is therefore a cruel injustice done to him.

It is impossible for the ordinary mind, which is usually dense of perception and greedy of observation, to attempt to measure or conceive in any degree the unsupportable torment to a sensitive temper and an exalted intelligence of the mosquito swarm of inquisitive interrogators and commentators; of the exaggeration, the misrepresentation, the offensive calumnies, and the still more offensive admiration, which are the daily penalty of all greatness. The adoring American, perched staring in the pear tree outside the dining-room window, may well have embittered to Tennyson the meats and wines of his dinner-table within. If he had got up from his table and shot the spy, such a pardonable impulse should certainly have been considered justifiable homicide. That because a man has done something higher, better, more beautiful than his fellows, he is therefore to be subjected without resistance to their curiosity and comment, is a premiss so intolerable that it should not be permitted to be advanced in any decent society. The interviewer is the vilest spawn of the most ill-bred age which the world has yet seen. If he be received, when he intrudes, with the toe of the boot, he has but his fitting reception.

There has been lately published the following personal description of a great writer whom I will not especially designate. It runs as follows: 'The first impression one gets is of a small man with large feet, walking as if for a wager, arms swinging hither and thither, and fingers briskly playing imaginary tunes in the air as he goes. Then, as the eccentric shape comes nearer, one is aware of a stubby beard and peeping eyes expressive of mingled distrust and aversion; a hideous hat is clapped down on the broad brow, which hat, when lifted, displays a bald expanse of skull bearing no sort of resemblance whatever to the counterfeit (*sic*) presentiments of Apollo; and yet, incongruous though it seems, this little vacuous, impatient, querulous being is no other than—' And then there is named one of the greatest masters of language whom the world has ever owned.

Yet who, having read this infamous portrait of physical defects, whether it be truth or libel, can ever again entirely divest his memory of it, can ever wholly prevent its arising in odious ridicule between him and his rapturous sense of the perfect music of a great style? Shakespeare cursed those who would not let his bones alone; the living genius may with equal justice curse those who will not let alone his living form and features. There are only two classes of persons who may be certain of seeing every physical fault or deformity or affliction in face or form brutally written down in print: they are the man of genius in the reports of his contemporaries, and the escaped criminal on the handbills and search-warrants of the police. Renan and Arton receive exactly the same measure.

The vulgar, the Herr Omnes of Luther, cannot comprehend the hatred, the loathing of observation and comment, which are of the very essence of the poetic temperament. Yet it is strange to think that being mobbed can be agreeable to anyone. The sense of being pursued by incessant curiosity, as often as not a merely malignant curiosity, must poison the hours of life to the proud and sensitive nature. Such curiosity existed, no doubt, in the days of Ovid, in the days of Alkibiades; but modern inquisitiveness is far worse, being armed with all the modern powers to torture. The intolerable Kodak, the intolerable interviewer, the artifices of the press, the typewriter, the telegraph, the telephone, the greedy, indelicate, omnivorous mind of the modern public—all contribute to make of celebrity a Gehenna.

Creation is the paradise of the artist or poet; sympathy, if it be also true, is balm to him; for the opinion of others he will never greatly care if his lips have been truly touched with the coal from the altar, yet the sense of his influence over them will be welcome to him; but the espionage of the multitude will be always to him irritating as mosquito bites, pestilent as a swarm of termites, darkening like a locust flight the face of the sun.

It is hard to think that one who has an illustrious name cannot idly gossip with an intimate friend without every careless word being stereotyped. One is grateful to Mr Knowles for telling us that Tennyson declared he would shake his fists in the face of Almighty God if He, etc., etc. One rejoices to know of this outburst of honest indignation at the unpitied sufferings of the helpless and the harmless, this grand flinging of the phylacteries in the face of a hypocritical and egotistic world. At the same time it is surely impossible to admit that such a spontaneous and impassioned expression of emotion ought, by any hearer of it, to have been, in cold blood, put on record and produced in print?

Poor dead singer of Ida and Œnone! The ruthless inquisitors who poisoned his life still pursue him even beyond the cold waters of the Styx! There is something infinitely pathetic in the knowledge of how, all his life long, Tennyson endeavoured to avoid the intrusion of the crowd, and of how utterly useless all his wishes and endeavours were, and how those whom he trusted and confided in, bring out the dead children of his spoken thoughts naked in the sight of the multitude whom he shunned.

The confidential utterances of great men and women should no more be desecrated by being told to the public than tears and kisses should be profaned by the publicity of a railway station.

The general reader can no more understand why Tennyson suffered so intensely at seeing a chestnut tree felled in full flower than they can understand the course in the heavens of Argol or Altair. To spread out before them these delicate, intricate, bleeding fibres of the soul is to slay Pegasus and Philomel to make a workhouse meal.

Mr Knowles alleges that it is necessary for him and other intimate friends of Tennyson to say all they thought of him, and repeat all he said, because a similar record of Shakespeare's conversations would be so precious a treasure to the world. This, also, is a questionable premiss. Shakespeare, happy in so much, was happiest of all in the obscurity in which his personality is sheltered; and the world is to be congratulated that it knows too little of the man to squabble and dwarf and disfigure him to the detriment of his works, as it does Byron and Shelley. What the man is matters so little. Psychology is but another name for curiosity, envy, or *dénigremené*. Whether the orchid grow on a rotten tree, or the lily on a dunghill, affects not the beauty of the orchid or the fragrance of the lily. What Horace was, or was not, at the Augustan Court cannot touch the exquisite grace of his style, the lovely lines of his pictures in words. The more we look at any writer the less we are likely to do justice to his creations, because his personality will exercise upon us either a great attraction or a great repulsion. It would be better for all works if, like Cologne Cathedral, they were without known progenitors.

Could Dante Rossetti ever have dreamed that Mr Leyland would preserve the poor, pathetic little note asking for the gift of more wine in his last illness, which Mr Val. Prinsep saw fit to publish in the *Art Journal* of September 1892? If we may not trust our most intimate friends with our necessities, in whom can we confide? The whole of this aforesaid correspondence of Rossetti was never intended for, nor is it fitted for, publication. The general world has a right to see any artist's completed work, and judge it as they may choose to do, but they have no right to be made acquainted with the hesitations, the self-torment, the fluctuations, the depression, the exultation, which preceded its birth. These are the ecstasies and the agonies which precede all gestation and parturition, and are not for public exhibition. Mr Leyland, loving Rossetti well, should have burned all these letters before, or immediately after, the artist's death. Mr Leyland was a man who knew his generation, and must have known the use which would be made of them. If a friend grant me a favour, and afterwards blab of that favour to our common acquaintances, I should prefer that such a favour had never been accorded. I think that most people will agree with this feeling. Yet reticence concerning favours done is not common in our times. Such reticence ought to be held the simplest obligation of honour; but the majority of persons do not so regard it. There is hardly a letter of any length ever written in which there are not some sentences liable to misconstruction, or open to various readings. It is grossly unfair to place any letter before those who are not in the possession of its key; that key which can alone lie in an intimate knowledge of its writer's circumstances and temperament. If Rossetti were not rich enough to buy the wine he wanted in his weakness, the shame is not his, but that of the world which left him poor. To think that he was too poor even to ever see Italy is an intolerable disgrace to his contemporaries. He would have been wiser to have left his patrons and to have lived in Italy on a black crust and a plate of bean soup.

If the man of genius amass wealth, he is accused of avarice or of mercenary sale of his own talent. If he remain poor, or be in trouble, no language can sufficiently condemn his extravagance, his improvidence, his immorality. If he live with any kind of splendour, it is display and profligacy; if he endeavour to avoid remark, it is meanness, hauteur or poverty.

Men and women of genius when they have money are too generous with it, and when they have it not are too careless about the lack of it. Shakespeare, we are told, had the prudence to put his money together and to buy houses and lands, with shrewd eye to the main chance; but this is, after all, mere supposition on the part of posterity. We know so little of the circumstances of his life that, for aught we can tell, he may have had some sharp-eyed, true-hearted friend or factor, who thus transmuted the poet's loose coins into solid fields and freeholds, as George Eliot had behind her George Lewis. I cannot believe that Titania's laureate ever quarrelled over deeds of copyhold and questions of fees and betterments with the burgesses and notaries of Stratford-upon-Avon. More likely, far, that he was lying in the sun, dreaming, deep cradled in cowslips and ladysmocks, as his winged verses flew up with the bees into the budding lime boughs overhead, whilst some trusty friend or brother did battle in his name with the chafferers and the scriveners in the little town. And when all was settled, and the deeds of transfer only wanted signature and seal, that trusty go-between would shout across the meadows to waken Will from his day-dream, and Will would lazily arise and come across the grass, with the pollen of the bees and the fragrant yellow dust of the cowslips on his clothes, and, with his sweet, serene smile, would scrawl his name to parchments which he scarcely even read. That is, I would take my oath, how the stores of Shakespeare increased, and how New Place became his. Pembroke's friend and Rosalind's creator never cared much for lucre, I am sure; for land he might care, because he loved England: he loved her fields, her woods, her streams, and he saw them as her sons can never see them now, uninjured and undimmed, the Lenten lilies growing tall beneath the untrimmed hedges of hazel and hawthorn, the water meadows spreading broad and fair, without a curl of smoke in sight, save that which rose from the cottage hearths. Elizabethan England was meadow where it was not coppice, park where it was not forest, heathery moorland where it was not reedy mere. It was natural that Shakespeare should care to call his own some portion of that beautiful leafy kingdom of his birth.

Even so Scott loved his Scottish soil, and Tennyson cared to own Farringford and Hazelmere. Even so George Sand's last dying words were of the trees of Nohant. Passion and pleasure and fame and love were in those last moments naught to her, but the green, fresh, dewy leafage of dead summers was still dear.

The psychologist Lombroso, in a recent essay, which must fill the *bourgeois* breast with exultation, finding that it is not possible for him to deny the mental fecundity of genius, denies its physical fertility, and endeavours to prove his assertion, after the customary method of scientists, by avoiding and omitting every fact which would in any manner tell against his theory. Evidence when manipulated by the scientist is like the colt when it issues, docked and clipped, from its training stable. Laying down the proposition that precocity is atavistic, founded on the declaration of the biologist, Dr Delaunay, that it is a sign of inferiority, he cites the marvellous precocity of Raffaelle, Pascal, Mozart, Victor Hugo, Mirabeau, Dante, Handel, Calderon, Tasso, and many others, who prove, on the contrary, that precocity is the sign of splendour, strength and durability of genius. He remarks that precocity is a mark of insignificance, and that the small and low organism develops with much greater rapidity than the higher order! Were we not used to the pompous self-contradictions of Science, we should be surprised to see a characteristic of so many great minds pronounced to be a defect and a deformity; it is certainly only a scientist who would dream of classing Raffaelle, Dante, Mozart, Hugo, amongst the lesser organisms.

The whole argument is built on the same quagmire of illogical assertion and false deduction. He first lays down as an axiom that men of genius are physically sterile, and supports it by the strange and curiously incorrect assertion that Shakespeare and Milton had no posterity! He proceeds to quote the saying of La Bruyère: 'Ces hommes n'ont ni ancêtres ni postérités; ils forment eux-seuls toute une descendance.' Now, as regards ancestry, it is clear that La Bruyère spoke figuratively: he did not and could not mean that men of genius have no progenitors: he meant that who their progenitors were did not matter to the world which cared only for themselves; in a similar way he spoke of their descendants, not as actually non-existent, but as counting for nothing beside the superior creation of their works.

Amongst the sterile *célibataires* Lombroso oddly enough includes Voltaire and Alfieri, whose loves and liaisons were famous and numerous. He entirely ignores Victor Hugo, whose philoprogenitiveness was so excessive as to be absurd; the extreme affection for their offspring of Tennyson and Renan, of George Sand and of Juliette Adam, of Millias and of Meissonier, of Mario and of Grisi, and of countless others whose names are famous and whose affections were or are most ardent. The offspring publicly recognised by man or woman is by no means necessarily the sole offspring of either. Allegra is not mentioned beside Ada in Burke's Peerage. Natural children frequently are not allowed to know even their own parentage; a woman may have children whom she does not openly acknowledge; a man may have children of whose birth even he knows nothing. It is not every celebrated woman who has the maternal courage of George Sand, nor every celebrated man who has the paternal tenderness of Shelley.

Lombroso confuses in a most unscientific manner the passion of love and the bond of marriage. Because Michael Angelo says that art is wife enough for him, Lombroso supposes that no passion, good or evil, ever moved him. The fact that a man or woman has not married does not prove that they have had no amours: the probability is that their ardour and caprice in love have withheld them from the captivity of a legal union, which is usually the tomb of love. Everything which disturbs the odd conclusion to which it has pleased him to come is put aside and left out by a writer whose treatise pretends to be based on an inexorable accuracy. He carefully omits all reference to the men of old who would, almost without exception, disprove his theory. The three greatest of these are surely Mahomet, Alexander and Julius Cæsar: all this triad were famous for sensual indulgence almost without limit. So far as the fact may be considered to honour genius, its alliance with the joys of voluptuous passions is fully established, and no ingenuity in paradox of a perverse hater of it can contravene the fact. As for the poets, from Catullus to Burns, they rise in their graves and laugh in the face of the biologist. Sterile? They? As well call sterile the red clover which yields its fecundating pollen to the bee in the glad sunlight of a summer day.

The great singer called Mario was a man of genius in every way, apart from the art in which he was unsurpassed: yet, he was a singularly handsome man, and possessed of magical seduction for women. Of the Spanish poet Zorilla, for whose recent death all Spanish women wept, the same may be said. Longfellow was very handsome, and his life was lovely, noble, and harmonious, from his youth to his grave. The physical beauty of Washington is well known, yet his genius cannot be contested. Vandyke had extreme physical beauty; Raffaelle also; the painters have nearly always been conspicuous for personal beauty, from Leonardo to Millais and Leighton. Gladstone has very fine features and a magnificent constitution; his physical strength is wonderful, yet his intellect has always been at full stretch, like a racing greyhound. The personal beauty and fine stature of Tennyson were accompanied by the most keen intellectual ardour, extant until the very latest day of his life. The beauty of Milton and of Goethe has become traditional in their respective countries. Wellington and Marlborough were singularly handsome men. Napoleon was a man of short stature, but his face had a classic beauty which resisted even death, as may be seen in the mask taken from his dead features at St Helena. Take Lamartine; place his verse where you will, it is impossible to deny his genius, the genius of intense poetic sympathy and insight, of eloquence, of magical music of utterance, of comprehension of all creatures which live and suffer; he himself was his finest poem, and as to his wonderful physical beauty there can be no dispute. Of three typical men of genius of modern times take Shakespeare, Goethe and Henri Quatre; all were of much beauty of person, and masculine vigour was not lacking in any; in the two latter it was even excessive. The hero of Arques and Ivry was the lover of more fair women than peopled the harem of Sardanapalus. Yet he had supreme genius; the genius of command, of wit, of intuition, of magnetic charm over the minds and wills and hearts of men; a charm which has been stronger than death, and has kept the fascination of his memory green throughout the length and breadth of France. Many more similar examples might be quoted. These, however, suffice to prove the inexactitude of the envious calumnies cast upon genius by Lombroso, who actually asserts that genius is never separated from physical degeneracy, and that the splendour of the brain is always paid for by atrophy of other organs! Were this true, the wretched, deformed, stunted creatures, the arrest of whose physical development is artificially obtained by the most cruel torture, and constitutes a trade in the Cevennes and the Pyrenees, would all of them become Napoleons, Goethes, Byrons, Mussets, Racines and Bismarcks. The manufacture of cripples would be the manufacture of heroes and poets! The favourite theory of scientists that genius is *caused* by physical imperfection is manifestly untrue, and grossly calumnious. It means, if it means anything, that the physically imperfect creature is the intellectually perfect; that the scrofulous and hunchbacked dwarf is the light-giver of the world, the Apollo Citharædus of the arts. What facts bear out such a theory?

Equally calumnious and false is the conclusion by Lombroso, that the man of genius (like the madman) is born, lives and dies, *cold, solitary, invisible.* A more abominable libel was never penned by mediocrity on greatness. The sweet, bright humour of Scott, buoyant even beneath woe and bodily pain; the gay, delightful kindliness of Molière, the cheerful, serene philosophies of Montaigne, the superb resistance to calamity of Cervantes, the playful, indulgent, affectionate temper of Thackeray, the noble tranquillity in adversity of Milton, the happy whimsical humour of Horace, the calm and fruitful leisure of Suetonius, the adoration of Nature of all the poets, from Theocritus to Lecomte de Lisle—all these and a thousand others arise to memory in refutation of this ignoble libel. Who held that the saddest things on earth were—

> 'Un cage sans oiseaux, une ruche sans abeilles,
>
> Une maison sans enfans?'

Victor Hugo: the master of one of the most fertile, puissant and imaginative minds ever known on earth. That genius seeks solitude is natural: it is only the fool who is afraid of his own company; the meditations and intellectual memories of genius must always be more delightful to it than the babble of society.

The commerce and conversation of the majority of persons is wearisome, trivial, dull; it is not wonderful that one who can commune in full harmony of thought with Nature, and with the wisdom of old, turns from the common babble of the common herd, and seeks the shelter of the library, or the silence of the forest and the moor. But such an one will always give more human sympathy than he can ever receive. None can see into his soul; but the souls of others are laid bare to him. To others he is a mystery which they fear; but others are to him as children whom he pities. If their folly and deadness of heart arouse his scorn, he yet weeps for them, because they know not what they do. They cannot hear, as he hears, the sigh in the leaves of the fallen tree, the woe in the cry of the widowed bird, the voices of the buried nations calling from the unseen tombs: no, in that sense he is alone, as the seer is alone and the prophet; but this loneliness comes not from the coldness of his own heart, but from the poverty of the hearts of other men. Who dares to say that those who alone can put into speech the emotions of a humanity, in itself dumb and helpless, are incapable of feeling those emotions which without them would find neither utterance nor interpreter.

Lombroso speaks exultingly of the cruelty to women of Musset, Byron, Carlyle and others; he has evidently no conception of the intense irritation roused in sensitive natures by uncongenial and enforced companionship. Jane Carlyle was a woman of fine wit and character, but she had no tact and little patience, and her sharp retorts must have been as thorns in the flesh of her bilious and melancholy Saul, as his uncouthness and ill-breeding must have been cruel trials to her. But this was no fault of either of them: it was the fault of that sad mistake, so common in the world, of an ill-assorted marriage, in which the prisoners suffered only the more because they were, in their different ways, of fine character, with a sense of duty so acute in each that it was a torture to both alike. What Lombroso calls the brutality of Carlyle was probably little else than the morbid gloom caused by a diseased liver, this disease in turn caused by the constraint and asphyxiation of a town life in a small house to a man born of hardy, outdoor, rustic stock, and farmed to breathe the strong, keen air of solitary Scottish moors and hills, to be braced by storm and sunshine, to battle with snow and wind and rain. The terrible folly which drives men of talent into cities, and leave them only the vitiated air of close and crowded streets, of feverish gatherings, and of unhealthy club-houses, is the origin of that alliance, so often seen in the present age, between the gifted mind and the suffering body, or the restless nerves, of a *névrosé*, of a hypochondriac, or of a bilious diabetic.

Lombroso, in the malignant spitefulness with which the scientists throw mud and stones at all genius, calls Byron a *Rachitique*, on account of his deformed foot; but when we remember Byron's splendid swimming powers, his endurance in the saddle, his passion for the mountains and the sea, his heroic calmness on his lonely deathbed, we must, if we are sincere, admit that this *Rachitique*, even apart from all his superb genius, was a man of no common courage and no common force, and that, whatever might be at birth the physical weakness accompanying his great physical beauty, he had known how to make himself the equal of the strongest even in outdoor sports. When we think of that great beauty before which women went down as corn before the flash of the reaping-hook, of the incomparable romance of that life, passing from the crowds of St James's to the pine solitudes of Ravenna, from the adulation of Courts to the silence of Alp and ocean, from the darksome glens and braes of Scotland to the azure light on the Hellespont and the Adrian Sea—when we think of its marvellous compass brought within the short span of thirty-six years, of its god-like powers, of its surpassing gifts, of its splendour of song, of wit, of melody, of passion, and of inspiration, of its tragic close, which broke off the laurel bough in its green prime, as Apollo would have it broken—when we think of this life, I say, it is easy to understand why its effulgence has been the mark for every petty malignity and jealous mediocrity ever since the light of the sun died down at Missolonghi.

Byron's must ever remain the most ideal, the most splendid, the most varied life which ever incarnated in itself the genius of man and the gifts of the gods: what joy, then, to the petty and the envious to point to his club foot, and to assure us he was *Rachitique*! The puling versifiers who spend their lifetime in elaborating artificial sonnets based on early Italian methods, straining, refining, paring, altering, transforming, trying to replace by effort all which is lacking to them in inspiration, may well be unable to comprehend aught of that fiery fury of scorn and invective, of that Niagara-like rush of thought and word and imagery, which made verse as natural an utterance to Byron as the torrent of its song is natural to the nightingale in the months of spring. To the grand verse of Byron there may be rivals, there may be superiors; but to the poetry of his life there is no equal in any other life. What greater, more unpardonable sin can he have in the sight of mediocrity?

I lately saw a tourist of small stature, mean appearance, and awkward gesture, criticising unfavourably the attitude of the beautiful Mercury in the Vatican Rotonda. I was irresistibly reminded of certain versifiers and newspaper essayists of the present moment criticising Byron!

Lombroso asserts that 'the man of genius has only contempt for other men of genius; he is offended by all praise not given to himself; the dominant feeling of a man of genius, or even of erudition, is hatred and scorn for all other men who possess, or approach the possession of genius or talent.' A greater libel was never penned. It is natural that those who are masters of their art should be less easy to please, less ignorant of its demands and beauties, than the crowd can be. The great writer, the great artist, the great composer, can scarcely fail to feel some disdain for the facility with which the public is satisfied, the fatuity with which it accepts the commonplace, the second-rate, the imitation, the mere catch-penny, as true and original creation. But this scorn for the mediocre, which is inseparable from all originality and is its right and privilege, does not for a moment preclude the ardent sympathy, the joyous recognition with which genius will salute the presence of kindred genius. What of the friendship of Coleridge and Wordsworth, of Byron and Shelley, of Flaubert and George Sand, of Shakespeare and Ben Jonson? Scarce a year ago two illustrious men conversed with sympathy and friendship under the green leaves by the waters of Annecy. Philippe Berthelet narrates how 'sous les vieux noyers de Talloires ils discutèrent pour la première fois de leur vie, Renan défendant son cher Lamartine, et Taine son poëte préféré Musset; je garde un pieux souvenir des nobles paroles de ces deux grands hommes qu'il m'a été donné d'entendre ce soir de Septembre sur le bord du lac limpide, au pied de la Tournette couronnée de neiges.'

The public likes inferior production; as a rule prefers it, because it understands it more easily; and this preference may irritate the supreme artist into a burst of wrath. Berlioz gave the *Damnation de Faust* to empty benches, and his Titanic disdain of his contemporaries for their preference of weaker men has been justified by the verdict of the present generation. But this sentiment of scorn is as far removed from the petty malignity of envy and injustice as the fury of the tempest amongst the Alps or Andes is unlike the sputtering of a candle guttering in a tin sconce. To the poet to see the poetaster crowned; to the great man to see his miserable imitator accepted as his equal; to the planet on high to know that the street lamp below is thought his rival, must ever be offensive. But this offence is just, and has grandeur in it; it is no more meanness and jealousy than the planet is the gaspipe or the Alpine storm the candle.

To the great artist it is a great affront to see the imitator of himself, the thief, the dauber, the mimic, the mediocre, accepted as an artist by the world. He is entitled to resent the affront and to scourge the offender. The intolerance of genius for mediocrity is called unkindness: it is no more unkind than the sentence of the judge on the criminal. In our time the material facilities given to production have multiplied mediocrity as heat multiplies carrion flies; it should have no quarter shown to it; it is a ravaging pest.

Cheap printing makes writers of thousands who would be more fittingly employed in stitching shoes or digging ditches; and the assistance of photography makes painters or draughtsmen of thousands who would be more harmlessly occupied whitewashing sheds or carding wool. Genius is as rare as ever it was in all the arts; but the impudent pretensions of nullity to replace and represent it increase with every year, because it finds readier acceptance from the ever-increasing ignorance of a universally educated public. The men of genius who do exist do not say this loudly enough or often enough: they are afraid to look unkind and to create enemies. It is not excellence which is malignant, envious, slanderous, mean: it is inferiority; inferiority dressed in the cheap garment of ill-fitting success.

There is a draughtsman who is very eminent in our time, and whose drawings have brought him in alike celebrity and wealth. He is esteemed one of the first artists in black-and-white of the century. Yet he never draws a line of any figure without resorting to his immense collection of photographs of all kinds and conditions of persons, in all attitudes and in all costumes, whence he selects whatever he may want to reproduce. This habit may perhaps not impair his skill as a draughtsman; but it certainly makes him a mere imitator, a mere copyist, and robs his works of all spontaneity, originality and sincerity. To draw from a photograph is mere copying, mere cheating; it is not art at all. Yet this popular draughtsman has not the least shame or hesitation in avowing his methods; nor do his public or his critics appear to see anything to censure or regret in them. If the true artist, who is sincere and original in all his creations, who draws from life, and would no more employ a camera than he would pick a pocket, feels, and expresses the contempt which he feels, for the draughtsman who is dependent on photographs, he is not moved either by hostility or jealousy, but by a wholesome and most just disdain. It is a disdain with which the general public can have little sympathy, because they cannot estimate the quality of the offence which excites it.

To the creator, whether of prose, of poem, of melody, picture, or statue, who is sincere in all he creates, to whom conscious imitation would have all the baseness of a forgery, and to whom sincerity and originality are the essence of creative talent, the fraud of imitation disgusts and offends as it cannot do the mere outsider. Such disgust, such offence, are no more envy or jealousy than the sublime fury of the storming-party is the secret stabbing of the hired bravo.

Oh, the obscure! the vile obscure! what shafts dipped in gall will they not let fly from the dusky parlour in which they sit and look with envious scowl out on the distant splendour of great lives!

The sweetest singer who ever sang on the classic Tyrrhene shore— Shelley, who soared with the skylark and suffered with the demi-god— Shelley leaves unhappily behind him a piteous little letter telling his friend Williams, in Dublin, of his poverty, and asking for the loan of five-and-twenty pounds; and this poor little letter is basely preserved and is sold by auction in London in the month of March of last year for the sum of eleven sovereigns! *O beati insipientes!* who cares whether you borrow five-and-twenty pounds, or five-and-twenty pence, or five-and-twenty thousand? Who cares to keep your humble request, your timid confession? Who cares whether you got what you craved, or were left to die of hunger? You, the mediocre, the commonplace, the incapable, are left in peace; but the sorry, carking, humiliating need of the beautiful boy-singer, whose name is blessed for all time, is dragged into the auction-mart and bid for rabidly by the curious! What joy for you, you well-fed, broad-bellied, full-pursed hordes of the commonplace, to think that this sensitive plant shivered and sickened under the vulgar hand of dun and bailiff, and withered in the sandy waste of want! He could write down the music of the lark, and hear the laughter of the fairies, and paint the changing glories of the sea, and suffer with the fallen Titan as with the trodden flower—but he was once in sore need of five-and-twenty pounds! *O beati insipientes!* Here lie your triumphs and your revenge. Clasp your fat palms above your ample paunch, and grin as you embrace your banker's pass-book. Take heed to keep that little letter of the poet of the 'Prometheus' safe under glass for all time, to comfort the jealous pains of the millions of nonentities whom you will continue to procreate until the end of time! Such are the consolations of inferiority.

Genius offends by its unlikeness to the general; it scorns their delights, their views, their creeds, their aspirations; it is at once much simpler and much more profound than they; it suffices to itself in a manner which, to the multitude, seems arrogance; the impersonal is always much more absorbing to it than the personal; there are qualities in it at once childlike and godlike, which offend the crowd at once by their ignorance and by their wisdom. In a word, it is apart from them; and they know that, they feel that, and they cannot forgive its unlikeness.

O Beati Insipientes! Unwatched, you eat and drink and work and play; unchronicled are your errors and your follies; would you weep, you may weep in peace; would you take a country walk, no spy, notebook in hand, will lurk in the hedges; when you pour out your trivial nonsense in the ear of a friend, he will not treasure it up to turn it into printer's copy as soon as you shall be cold in your coffin.

O Beati Insipientes! You know not what safety, what peace, what comfort are gained for you by your mantle of obscurity. You know not, and you would not believe though angels and archangels descended to tell it you, that the splendour of the sunlight of fame is darkened for ever to those whose path lies through it by the shadow which follows, mimicking, prying, listening, grinning, girding, slobbering, eagerly watching for a false step, cruelly counting the thorns trodden amidst the flowers—that shadow which dogs without mercy the whole of a life, and thrusts its prying fingers through the cere-clothes of death, that shadow of merciless and malign curiosity which follows genius as the assassin followed the fair youth Crichton through the streets of Mantua: the crime of Crichton being to excel!

CITIES OF ITALY

Whatever may be the opinion of Europe as to the political advantages accruing to it from the independence of Italy, it must be mournfully confessed that the losses to art and to history through it are greater than any which could have been caused by centuries of neglect or long years of hostile occupation and devastating war. It is scarcely to be measured, indeed, what those losses are; so immense are they in their extent, so incessant in their exercise, so terrible in their irreparable infamy. No doubt it could never be foreseen, never be imagined, by those who brought about and permitted the consolidation of Italy into one kingdom, that the people, nominally free, would become the abject slaves of a municipal despotism and of a barbarous civic greed. None of the enthusiasts for Italian independence possessed that power of foresight which would have told them that its issue would be the daily destruction, by hordes of foreign workmen, of its treasures of art and its landmarks of history. Yet there is no exaggeration in saying that this, and nothing less than this, is its chief issue.

Hermann Grimm published a powerful appeal to the scholars and artists of Europe against the Italian destruction of Rome. Having for thirty years written on Italian cities and their art and history, with scholarship and devotion, he had gained the right to raise his voice in indignant protest and scorn against the mercenary and vulgar shamelessness with which the Roman municipality is so dealing with the splendid heritage which it has received, that soon scarcely one stone will be left upon another of the sacred city. He said, and with truth, that the portion of the Italian nation which has the eyes to perceive and the soul to abhor all that is being done is so small a minority, and one so spiritless, hopeless and discouraged, that it is for all practical purposes non-existent. He appealed to what he termed that larger Rome which exists in the hearts of all who have ever known Rome with a scholar's knowledge, or an artist's love. The appeal may be powerless but at least it may be heard; and though it will scarcely be able to pierce through the thick hide of smug vanity and rapacity in which Italian municipalities are enveloped, it will put on record the courage and the scorn of one man for what is the greatest artistic iniquity of our time. It is idle and untrue for Italians to say that the rest of Europe has no right to interfere with what they do with the legacy they enjoy. In the first place, without the aid and acquiescence of Europe, the Italian kingdom as a unity could never have existed at all; without the permission of Europe the entry into Rome could never have been made at all. Europe has the title to observe and to condemn the manner in which the superb gift, which she permitted to be given to those very various peoples who are called Italians, is being squandered away and destroyed. The United Kingdom of Italy may, as a political fact, disappear to-morrow in any European war or any great Socialistic uprising; but historic Italy, classic Italy, artistic Italy, is a treasure which belongs to the whole world of culture, in which, indeed, the foreigner, if he be reverent of her soil, is far more truly her son than those born of her blood who violate her and desecrate her altars. Italy cannot be narrowed to the petty bounds of a kingdom created yesterday; she has been the mistress of all art, the muse and the priestess of all peoples.

What are the Italians doing with her? It is sickening to note and to record. Nothing can ever give back to the world what, day by day, municipal councillors having houses to sell, syndicates and companies merely looking for spoliation and speculation, contractors who seize on the land as a trooper seizes on a girl in a sacked town, are all taking from the fairest and the most ancient cities and towns on earth. The sound of the hatchet in the woods and gardens of Italy is incessantly echoed by the sound of the pickaxe and hammer in the cities and towns. The crash of falling trees is answered by the crash of falling marbles. All over the land, destruction, of the vilest and most vulgar kind, is at work; destruction before which the more excusable and more virile destruction of war looks almost noble. For the present destruction has no other motive, object, or mainspring than the lowest greed. It is absolutely incomprehensible how, after having been the leaders and the light of the far centuries, the Italians have, by common consent and with pitiable self-congratulation, sunk to the position of the most benighted barbarism in art. In everything which is now constructed the worst and most offensive taste is manifest, whilst that which has existed for centuries is attacked and pulled down without remorse. I wholly fail to account, on any philosophic or psychological grounds, for the utter deadness of soul which has come on the Italians as a nation. Born with loveliness of all kinds, natural and architectural, around them, the æsthetic sense should be as instinctive in them as their movements of limbs or lungs. Instead of this, it is entirely gone out of them. They have no feeling for colour, no sense of symmetry, and little or no sense of reverence for the greatness and the gloriousness of the past.

The only people in whom any of the native feeling for natural and artistic beauty still exists are those country people who dwell far removed from the contagion of the towns, and the marine populations of the Veneto.

But even in these it is slighter than any student of the past would expect. The sense of colour is *nil* in most Italians; they might as well be colour-blind for any heed they take of harmony of tones. They delight in *chinoiseries*, in photographs, in crétonnes, in all the rubbish bought in modern Exhibitions. In the superb and immense halls of a palace of the Renaissance one will see priceless tapestries on the walls, antique marbles on the consoles, frescoes of Veronese, of Giulio Romano, or of Sodoma on the ceilings; and at the same time see arm-chairs and couches, some yellow, some blue, some green, some scarlet; a table-cover of crimson; and the mosaic floor covered with a worthless *moquette* carpet of all hues, and of a set and staring pattern. I call to mind a similar palace on the Tiber, whose very name is as a trumpet-call to all the glories of the past; there the antique statues have been coloured, 'because white marble is so cold and sad;' an admirable copy in bronze of the Mercury of Gian' di Bologna has had his wings, his petasus, and his caduceus gilded; and the marble floors have been taken up to have French parquet flooring laid down in their stead, and varnished so highly that the woods glisten like looking-glasses; yet the owner of and dweller in this place is a great noble, who, after his own fashion, cherishes art. I have seen a Greek Venus, found in the soil at Baiæ, wreathed round with innumerable yards of rose-coloured gauze by its owner, an Italian princess. The excuse given is, '*Senza un'po di tinta sta cosi fredda!*'

It is the same feeling which makes the Italian peasant say of the field-flowers which you have arranged in your rooms, 'How well you have made those vulgar weeds look! Any one would take them now for *fiori secchi!*' (artificial flowers). Whence comes it, this absolute blindness of the eyes, this deadening absence of all consciousness of beauty? It is the same thing in their villages and their fairs. Go to a fair on a feast-day in any part of France; go to a kermesse in Belgium or Luxembourg; go to a merry-making in Germany or Austria, and you will see a picturesque and graceful sight; you will see a great deal of what the eyes of Teniers, of Ostade, of Callot, of Mieris saw in their day. There will be harmonised colours, unconscious grace of grouping, arrangements of common goods and simple things so made that beauty is got out of them. But in a village festival in Italy there is nothing, except in the water pageants of Venice, which is not ugly; it is all dusty, uninteresting, untempting; what colours there are, are arranged with the same disregard of fitness as is shown in the yellow, red and green arm-chairs of the palace chambers; and the whole effect is one of squalor and of vulgarity. The carnivals, which used to be fine and brilliant spectacles, are now, almost all, save that of Milan, mere tawdry, trivial, unlovely follies. Who can account for this?

Are we to infer that all the transmitted influences of race count for nothing? Would those who, rightly or wrongly, are tempted to explain all the problems of life by the doctrines of heredity tell me why the living representatives of the most artistic races on earth are almost absolutely deprived of all artistic instincts? Some have suggested that it is the outcome of the artificial habits and false taste of the eighteenth century; but this can scarcely be correct, because this artificiality existed all over Europe, not in Italy alone, and besides, never touched the country people in any way or in any of their habits.

The excuse made for the utter disregard and destruction of beauty in Italy is that the utility of all things is now preferred to beauty. But this is no adequate explanation. It may explain why a dirty steamboat is allowed to grind against the water-steps of the Ca'd'Oro, or why the fair shores of Poselippo and the blue bays of Spezzia and Taranto are made hideous by steam and bricks. But it will not explain why the peasant thinks a wax or cambric flower more lovely than a field anemone or daffodil, or why the nobleman paints his Athene and gilds the wings of his Hermes. This can only be traced to the utter decay of all feeling for beauty, natural or artistic, in the Italian mind, and, though we see, we cannot adequately explain, we can only deplore, it. There is no doubt a tendency all the world over to loss of the true sense of beauty; despite the æsthetic pretences of nations, the real feeling for natural and artistic perfection is very weak in most of them. If it were strong and pure, the utilitarian (*i.e.*, the money-getting spirit) would not prevail as it does in architecture, and forest solitudes would not be destroyed as they are; and men would see what hypocrites they be who make millions out of some hideous desecration of nature by factories, iron foundries, or petroleum wells, and think they can purchase condonation, and a reputation for fine taste, by buying pictures for their galleries or inlaying their halls with rare woods or stones. The whole world which calls itself civilised is guilty more or less of the most absolute barbarism; but modern Italy is guiltiest of all, even as he who has inherited a fair home and cultured intelligence is guiltier than he who has never known anything but a vitiated atmosphere and a squalid house. It is the immensity of her heritage which makes her abuse of all her opportunities so glaring and so utterly beyond pardon.

Nothing can ever give back to mankind what every day the Italian municipalities and people are destroying, as indifferently as though they were pulling down dead leaves or kicking aside anthills in the sand. There is not even the pretext for these acts that they are done to better the state of the people; to execute them the cheapest foreign labour is called in, ousting the men of the soil off it: house-rent is trebled and quadrupled, house-room narrowed, and in many instances denied, to the native population: and contracts are given away right and left to any foreign companies or syndicates who choose to bid for them. The frightful blocks of new houses, the hideous new streets, the filthy tramways, the naked new squares, are all made by foreign speculators who purchase the right of spoliation from the municipalities as the private owners of the soil. A few men are made temporarily richer: the country is permanently beggared.

'Rome' wrote Hermann Grimm, 'represents for humanity a spiritual value which cannot be easily estimated, but which is none the less precious because ideal.' Yet the vulgar and petty administration of an ephemeral moment is allowed to treat the capital of the world as though it were some settlement of shanties in the backwoods of America, fit only to disappear beneath the mallet and scaffolding of carpenters and masons. He said with justice that to call it vandalism is an injustice to the Vandals, for they, at least, were too ignorant to know the worth of what they destroyed, and acted in mere fierce instinct of conquest, with no ulterior greed; but they who are now destroying arch on arch, tower on tower, temple and church and palace, piling the sacred stones one on another like rubble, and effacing landmarks which had been respected through a thousand years, have the excuse neither of ignorance nor of war. They know not what to do, and we may add that they care not what they do, so long as their gain is made, their pockets filled.

Of all the grotesque barbarisms committed in Rome, the destruction of the cloister of Ara Cœli and of the tower of San Paolo upon the Capitol, to make room for an equestrian statue of Victor Emmanuel, has been one of the most offensive and ill-judged. All the world knows the beauty of the Capitol, the immemorial memories connected with it, and the great statue which for so many centuries has felt the Roman sunshine strike on its golden bronze. The placing of a modern statue in juxtaposition with the mighty Aurelian is an act so irredeemably vulgar, so pitiably incongruous, that it is a matter of infinite regret, even for the repute of the House of Savoy, that the present king did not peremptorily forbid such use of his father's manes. In the Superga, or on the mountain-side of the Piedmontese Alps he loved so well, a statue of Victor Emmanuel would be in keeping with his traditions, but it is a cruelty to him to dwarf him by such surroundings and such memories as are there on the Capitol of Rome. His fame is not of the kind which can bear, uninjured, such comparisons; and were it even ten times greater than it is, there could be no excuse for using the Capitol for such a purpose when there is the whole width of the Campagna for it, and when, in perfect accord with the abilities of modern sculptors, there are all the staring and naked modern piazzas waiting for their works. Will it be credited that it was actually proposed to place a statue of him between the columns of St Mark? In these matters the king could and should, with perfect propriety, intervene, and forbid a pretended homage for his father's memory being made a pretext and cover for the coarse and common vandalism of the epoch. In Florence, the beautiful wooded entrance of the Cascine was destroyed to make the bald, uninteresting square called the Piazza degli Zuavi, and a large, stony, open place, shadeless and unlovely, was reserved for a monument to Victor Emmanuel; for this the oval brick basement of the pedestal was raised many years ago, and there stands, unfinished and hideous, an eyesore to the city, an insult to the royal House.

There is scarcely a little town, there is no provincial capital on the whole peninsula, which has not some new, staring, stucco street named Corso Vittorio Emmanuele, or some historic and ancient square made absurd and pitiable by being re-baptised Piazza dell' Independenza. The effect is at once ludicrous and deplorable.

If it were necessary thus to deify the events of the last thirty years, and magnify them out of their true proportions, it would have been easy to build some wholly new city in some vacant spot, which might have borne any name or names deemed fitting, and thus have left in peace the great cities of the past, and not have made the present recall the fable of the frog and the bull.

Around Rome, as well as within it, the most luxuriant vegetation, a few years ago, alternated with the most sacred ruins: tombs and temples and triumphal arches were framed in the most abundant foliage; the banksia rose, the orange, the myrtle, the jessamine climbed and blossomed amidst the ruins of the palace of the Cæsars. In all these grand gardens, in these flowering fields, in these grass meadows, stretching between their marble colonnades, there was, as the German scholar says, an infinite calm, a loveliness and stillness in which the poet and the scholar could draw near to the mighty dead who had once been there as living men. There was nothing like it left on earth. Now it is destroyed for ever. Now,—in the stead of that tender silence of the tombs, that exquisite freshness of the spring, awakening in a thousand moss-grown dells and myrtle thickets which had seen Ovid and St Paul, Augustine and Raffael--now, in the stead of this there are the stench of engines, the dust of shattered bricks, the scream of steam whistles, the mounds of rubbish, the poles of scaffolding, long lines of houses raised in frantic haste on malarious soil, enormous barracks, representative of the martial law required to hold in check a liberated people: all is dirt, noise, confusion, hideousness, crowding, clamour, avarice.

The leaders of an invading and victorious army would have been ashamed to cause the havoc and the blasphemy which the Roman municipality have carried out with shameless callousness; the indignant voice of Europe would have bidden a Suwarrow, a Napoleon, a Constable de Bourbon stay his hand, had he dared to level with the dust the august monuments of which neither the majesty nor the memories have power to daunt the impious hand of the nineteenth century Edilizia. Common faith, even, has not been kept with the Roman people in the ruin of their city; the completed plan, put before the public in 1880, of the works which were intended, did not prepare the public for one-tenth of the devastation which has been wrought. In the words of Grimm, those who put forth the plan of '80 proposed tranquil, moderate and decent measures, and never contemplated the insensate haste, the brutal fury, the unsparing greed shown by those who, professing to accept its propositions, have utterly disregarded and far outstripped them. In the plan of '80 it was, for instance, expressly stated and provided that certain gardens, amongst them the Ludovisi, should be purchased by the city, but kept intact in their verdure and extent. This promise has been broken.

What traveller has not known the Ludovisi Gardens? What scholar, dreamer, painter, has not found his heaven there? Those immemorial pines, making twilight beneath them in the sunniest noon, those lofty walls of bays and of arbutus, those dim, green, shadowy aisles leading to velvet swards and violet-studded banks, the family of peacocks spreading their purples, their emeralds, their gold, out in the glory of the radiant light, the nightingales singing night and day in the fragrant solitudes, Sappho's angel in Corrinna's gardens—who has not known these? who has not loved these? And they are gone, gone forever; gone through the greed of men, and in their stead will stand the vile rows of cheap and staring houses: in their place will reign the devil of centralisation.

Centralisation is the heart-disease of nations. The blood, driven by it from the body and the limbs, becomes turgid and congested, overfills the vessels of the heart, and chokes them up; there is no more health, and later there is death. It has been the curse of France. It will be the curse of Italy. The violated nymphs and the slaughtered nightingales of the ruined gardens will be avenged. But what solace is that to us? We have lost them forever. No power on earth can give them back to us.

There is a violation of that sentiment which the Latins called Piety, so glaring, and so monstrous, in the destruction of Rome by the Italians, that it dwarfs all similar ruin being wrought elsewhere. All over Italy things are daily being done which might wring tears from the statues' eyes of stone. [A]

After the outrage to Rome, the injury done to Venice is the most irreparable, the most inexcusable.

The wanton destruction of the island of Saint Elena is, after the destruction of the Ludovisi and other historic gardens in Rome, the most disgraceful act of the sacrilege of modern Italy. It is barbarism without one shadow of excuse or plea of obligation. This loveliest isle had been spared by all hostile fleets and armies. It lies at the very mouth of the lagoon opening out from the Grand Canal. It arrests the eyes of all who go to and fro the Lido. It was, a little while ago, a little paradise of solitude, fragrance and beauty. Its thickets of wild rose, of jessamine, and of myrtle, were filled with song-birds. Its old church, the oldest in the Veneto, stood, grey and venerable, amidst the shade of green acacias and flowering oleanders. The little world of blossom and of melody, hung between the sea and sky, had a holiness, a pathos, a perfection of woodland loveliness not to be told in words; there no sound was heard except the bells of the matins and vespers, the lapping of the waves, the whir of the white gulls' wings, and the echo of some gondolier's boating song. To sit in its quiet cloisters, with the fragrance of its wild gardens all around, and see the sun set beyond Venice, and the deep rose of evening spread over the arch of the skies and the silver plain of the waters, was to live a little while in the same world that Giorgione and Veronese knew. It seems like a vision of a nightmare to find these cloisters levelled and these gardens and trees destroyed; the whole island made a grimy, smoking mound of clay and ruins. Yet thus it is. The government has chosen to make it a site for a factory and foundry; and, not content with this defilement, is throwing up, upon it and beside it, acres of the stinking sand and clay dredged up from the canals, intending in due time to cover this new soil with other factories and foundries, full in the face of the Ducal Palace, a few furlongs from the Piazza of St Mark. Viler devastation was never more iniquitously or more unpardonably wrought.

Meantime the very commonest care is refused to such interesting and priceless houses as the House of the Camel, which is let out to a number of poor and dirty tenants, with its eponymus alto-relievo made the target for the stones of the children; while in the same quarter of the Madonna dell' Orta, close at hand, a manufacturer is allowed to send the mouths of his steam-tubes hissing through the iron arabesques and between the carved foliage of a most noble Gothic doorway belonging to a deserted church.

I am aware that it is useless to protest against these things. The soul in the country is withered up by small greeds. All these irreparable injuries are done that municipal councillors may pocket some gain, and any stranger who has the money necessary can purchase from the Conscript Fathers of the hour the right to defile, to annex, to violate, to destroy the fairest and most sacred places in Italy. The goddess is given over to the ravishing of any boor who brings a money-bag.

The scholar, the poet, the archæologist are all abhorred in modern Italy; their protests are impatiently derided, their reverence is contemptuously ridiculed, their love of art, of nature, or of history, is regarded as a folly, ill-timed and inconvenient, lunatic and hysterical. But the new-comer who proposes a machine, a chimney, a monster hotel, a bubble company, or a tramway station, is welcomed with open arms; it is considered that he means 'progress,' *i.e.*, that he means a subsidy for some one, a general scramble for gold pieces.

Emile de Lavaleye has demonstrated, in his recent *Lettres d' Italie*, that these works in Venice, so fatal to the city, cannot ever result in any financial profit; that, with coal forty francs a ton, it is impossible they should ever bring any; that all industry of the kind is artificial and pernicious in Italy, and ends in impoverishing the many to enrich a few.

It is a wanton love of destruction which can alone lead a people who possess neither iron nor coal to make foundries and factories in Venice, the most lovely and luminous city of the sea. These works cannot be ever profitable at Venice, by reason of the immense cost of the transport there of the metals and combustibles necessary for their development. Yet in every direction their foul smoke is rising, and dimming that translucent air so dear to every painter from Carpaccio to Aïvarnovski. From the Zattere alone no less than fourteen factory chimneys are visible.

The Fondamenté Nuové was in the days of the Doges the *riva*, consecrated to the villas and pleasure-gardens of the Venetian nobles; their palaces were only for winter habitation or ceremonious use, but the beautiful garden-houses facing Murano were their retreat for mirth, ease and recreation of all kinds, with nothing between them and the silvery lagoon except the clouds of foliage and of blossom which then covered these little isles. Nothing would have been easier than to make this shore now what it was then, and it would even have been undoubtedly profitable to have done so. Will it be credited that, instead, it has been selected as the especial site of gas-works and iron-works and all abominations of stench and smoke, whilst, instead of the laughing loveliness of flowering lawns leaning to touch the sea, there is a long and dreary brick embankment, on which you can walk if you choose, and recall, if you can, the 'tender grace of a day that is dead'?

'*La lumière de Venise*' has been the theme of all poets and the enchantment of all travellers for centuries; that opal-hued, translucent, ethereal light has been the wonder of every wanderer who has found himself in the enchantment of its silvery radiance. *'On nage dans la lumière,'* is the just expression of Taine, to describe the exquisite effulgence of the light in Venice. Yet this wonder, this delight, this gift of Nature from sea and sky, the modern masters of the fate of Venice deliberately sacrifice, that a few greedy commercial adventurers may set up their chimneys on the shores consecrated to St Mark.

The Venetian populace have still in themselves a sense of colour and a passion for verdure; in every little *calle* and at every *traghetto* an acacia grows and a vine climbs; on the sails of the fishing and fruit boats there are painted figures, and in the garb of those who steer them there is still picturesque choice of form and hue. But in the Venetian municipality, as in every other Italian municipality, all taste is dead, all shame is dead with it; and the only existence, the only passion, left in their stead, are those of gain and of destruction. On the Giudecca hideous factories, which belch out the blackest of smoke close to the dome of the Church of the Redentore, have been allowed to pollute the atmosphere and disgrace the view; and in every shed or outhouse where anyone has a fancy to stick up the iron tube of an engine, similar smoke passes forth, making day frightful and clouding the lagoon for miles.

Reverence, and that sense of fitness which always goes with reverence, are wholly lacking in the modern Italian mind. There is a kind of babyish self-admiration in its stead, which is the most sterile of all moral ground, and with which it is impossible to argue, because it is deaf and blind, inwrapped in its own vanity. In a few years' time, if the Italian kingdom last, it will insist on its history being re-written, and the debts that it owed to the French Emperor in '59 and to the German Emperor in '70 being struck out of its balance-sheet altogether. Nothing was more untrue, more bombastical, or more misleading than the favourite phrase, *Italia fara da se*; but it is one of those untruths which have been caressed and repeated until they are accepted as facts; and the injury done by this conceit to the present generation is very great.

Nature has done all for Italy; it is a soil which is indeed blessed of the gods; from its pure and radiant air to its wildflowers, which spring as though Aphrodite were still here 'to sow them with her odorous foot,' it is by Nature perfectly dowered and thrice blessed. In its roseate dawns, its crystal, clear moonlight, its golden afternoons, it has still the lovely light of an unworn world. Art joined hands with Nature, and gave her best and her richest treasures to Italy. It is, to any scholar, artist, poet, or reverent pilgrim to her shrines, a thing of intolerable odium, of unutterable sorrow, that the very people born of her soil should be thus ignorant of her exquisite beauty, thus mercenary, venal and unshamed in their prostitution of it.

Even amongst those who follow art as their calling, there is no sense of colour or of fitness. When the old houses of the Via degli Archibusieri were pulled down in Florence, to lay bare the colonnade beneath them, a committee of artists deliberated for three months as to the best method of dealing with this colonnade. The result of their deliberations was to cover the old stone with stucco and paint the stones brown, with white borders! The effect is enhanced by upright lamp-posts, coloured brown, stuck in the middle of the way. The excuse given for the demolition of the houses was that the removal of them would widen a thoroughfare: as the lamp-posts are much more obstructive to drivers than the houses were, the correctness of the reasons given can be easily gauged. This is an example of all the rest. 'Are we to go in rags for sake of being picturesque?' said a syndic now ruling one of the chief cities of Italy, to a person who complained to him of the destruction of art and beauty now common throughout the peninsula. The reply is characteristic of that illogical stupidity and that absolute colour-blindness which are common to the modern Italian, or, let us say, the municipal Italian mind. They are insensible themselves to the horror of their work, just as they are unconscious why yellow, blue and green chairs on a red carpet offend a delicate taste. To whitewash frescoed walls; to make old monasteries look brand new; to scrub and peel and skin sculptured marbles; to daub over beautiful arches and columns and cloisters with tempera paintings, mechanically reproduced in one set pattern over and over again, over miles of stucco; to outrage the past and vulgarise the present; to respect nothing; to set the glaring seal of a despotic and bourgeois administration over all which ages have made lovely and reverent—all this they think an admirable and hygienic work, while they let human excrement be strewn broadcast over the fields and emptied in the street at midday under broiling heat, and set the guards of their rivers to drive out with blows of the scabbard the poor children who would fain splash and bathe in them under canicular suns. The excuse of hygiene is only the parrot cry which covers the passion for iconoclasm and destruction. To make their own *interessi* while the moment lasts is the only desire at the heart of all these civic councillors and engineers, architects and contractors, house-owners and speculators. To petty personal purposes and selfish personal profits everything is sacrificed by the innumerable prefects, syndics, and town councillors, by whom Italy is regarded as the Turkish pashas regarded the Egyptian fellah.

Florence, again, might, with great ease, have been made one of the most beautiful cities of Europe: if there had been only moderate care and decent taste displayed in its administration, its natural and architectural charms were so great that it would have been a facile task to keep them unharmed. If its suburbs, indeed, of ugliness and squalor, could show good roads and shady avenues; if its river banks, instead of brick walls, showed grass and trees; if its filthy cab-stands were kept out of sight, and its city trees allowed to grow at the will of Nature, Florence would be lovely and twice as healthy as it is. But there is no attempt to preserve what is beautiful, or to make what is of necessity modern accord in any manner with the old; whilst on trees there is waged a war which can only oblige one to conclude that those who are entrusted with the care of them have no eye except to the filling of their own wood-cellars. It is a very common thing to see an avenue of plane or lime trees with their heads cut off, whilst all the trees, whether in the public gardens or on the boulevards, are chopped and hacked out of all likeness to themselves, and of course dry up and perish long before their time.

Nothing can be more criminal that what is actually now being proposed in the Florence town council, i.e., to raise a loan of eight millions, at four per cent., to destroy the entire old centre of the city.[B] I repeat, nothing more criminal, more wasteful, or more senseless could be done. Florence is very poor; a few years ago she was on the brink of bankruptcy; taxation is enormous throughout Tuscany; the poorest are taxed for the very bed they lie on; the amount which she has to pay to the government from the *dazio consume* (that is, the octroi duty at the gates, on all food and produce of every kind entering the town) is extravagant and intolerable. So cruelly are the simplest productions of the soil mulcted by taxation that every class suffers, whether producer or consumer. The annual interest payable on the new loan will add immensely to the burdens which the city bears; and for what purpose is such a loan to be contracted? For the purpose of pulling down the oldest and most historic parts of Florence, to create a naked wilderness which will be changed into one of those squares, dusty and hideous, with metal lamp-posts round it and stunted shrubs in the centre of it, which represent to the municipal Italian the *ne plus ultra* of loveliness and civilisation. The excuse given of hygienic reasons is a lie. All the uncleanly classes which dwelt in the Ghetto have been bundled off wholesale to the S. Frediano quarters, where they will continue to dwell with unchanged habits, a few score of yards removed from where they were before. The dirt of Italian cities is not due to the age or shape of the streets, it is due to the filthy personal habits of the people, which are the same in a wide and roomy farm-house in the pine woods as in a garret of a town. They love dirt; water never touches their bodies all the year round, and never touches even their faces or hands in winter; they like their vegetables raw, their wine sour; their pipes are eternally in their mouths, and their clothes reek with every stench under heaven. It is the habits of the people, not the formation of the streets, which constitute the standing peril of pestilence in Italy. They would make a new house as filthy as an old one in a week. For what, then, is this enormous, useless, and unpardonable addition to the civil debt of Florence incurred? Only to put money in the pockets of a few speculators, and a few owners of the soil, at the cost of destroying all that is most interesting, valuable, and historical in the city.

Will it be credited by any readers of these words that it is actually in contemplation to turn the old piazza behind the Palazzo Strozzi into a range of glass-galleries like those of Milan or of Brussels? It is incredible that a whole civil population can tranquilly permit such outrage, and such grotesque outrage, to be committed in its name.

It is indeed very much as though the owner of Raffaeles and Titians tore them up into tatters and bought chromo-lithographs and olegraphs to hang in their places.

Oftentimes the populace itself is pained and mortified to see its old heirlooms torn down and its old associations destroyed, but the populace has no power; the whole civic power is vested in the bureaucracy, and civic electoral rights are wholly misunderstood and practically unused by the masses of the people. It is for the most part the smug and self-complacent *bourgeoisie* which rules, and which finds a curious delight in the contemplation of everything which can destroy the cities of the Renaissance, and the records of classic Latium, to replace them with some gimcrack and brand-new imitation of a third-rate modern French or Belgian town, glaring with plate-glass, gilding, dust, smoke, acres of stucco, and oceans of asphalt.

The modern Italian has not the faintest conception of the kind of religious reverence with which the English, the German, the American scholar visits the cities of Italy. Such an emotion seems to the son of the soil wholly inexplicable and grotesquely sentimental. If the Englishman praise a monster hotel or a torpedo-boat, or the German the march of a regiment, or the American the shafts of a factory, then, and then only, will the Italian regard the travellers with complacency. And what is done in the cities is repeated in the small towns, of which the municipalities think it grand and 'advanced' to imitate the innovations of larger ones, and where the house-owners and owners of the soil are just as greedy as their town councillors, and just as eager to sacrifice any classic beauty or mediæval memory for gain.

Could Dante come to life, no curse that he ever breathed upon his countrymen would be one-half so fierce and deep as that with which he would devote the Italian of the close of the nineteenth century to the vengeance of the offended gods. But Dante's self would say his curses to deaf ears, wadded close with the wool of vanity and greed.

Meanwhile the taxation of all these towns is so high that tradespeople are ruined in them, as the country proprietors are ruined in hundreds and thousands by the imposts on land and all that land produces. Against blind cupidity the gods themselves are impotent.

THE FAILURE OF CHRISTIANITY

Very soon, as the history of the world counts time, Christianity will have completed its two thousand years of existence. In some shape or other its doctrines dominate the civilised portions of Europe and America and Australasia; and even in Asia and in Africa its representatives and its missionaries are busied in the endeavours to diffuse them into the dark places of the earth. Whether we accept it as what is called a revealed or supernatural religion, or whether we more rationally consider it an offspring of the older and similar myths of Asia united to Judaism, the fact remains the same of the immense area of its adoption by the human race, and especially by the Aryan race. Islamism is widespread, but has no continuous power of proselytism similar to Christianity; and Judaism, though inexorably potent on the Jewish tribes, whatever country they inhabit, can claim little or no power of attracting strangers within its fold; does not, indeed, seek to attract any.

To live and spread as it has done, Christianity must have some vital force within itself superior to those possessed by other creeds. It must be suited to the human race in some manner which the religion of Mohammed and that of Israel have alike missed. Indeed, the whole history of the acquisition of its dominion is very singular, and has probably been due to the socialistic element contained in it; for the gospels are a breviary intimately dear to the heart of every communist. Mohammedanism is aristocratic; so is Judaism, so were the Greek and Latin religions; but Christianity is the religion of democracy, of universal equality, of the poor man consoled for privation on earth by his belief that such privation is surely the narrow gate by which heaven alone can be reached. Even in the moment when Christianity most nearly approached an aristocratic worship, it still contained the germs of democracy; it still held out hope to the poor man, hope both spiritual and material; in the feudal ages, when it was the war-cry of knights and ruling power of great kings and arrogant priests, it still whispered in the ear of the swineherd and the scullion, — 'Take my tonsure and my habit, and who knows that thou mayest not live to earn the triple crown?'

Because Socialism is for a great part atheistic, it has been wholly forgotten how socialistic have been the influences on society of Christianity. The evangels are essentially the dream of a poor man; the vision of a peasant asleep after a day of toil, and seeing in his vision the angels come for him, whilst they spurn the rich man on whose fields he has laboured. 'Come to Me, all ye who sorrow and are heavy-laden, and I will give you rest.' It is the invitation to the poor; not to the rich. The disciples are fishermen for the most part; Christ is himself a carpenter; the whole dream is a passion-play of peasants as entirely as that which represented it last year in Ammergau; and in it power, intellect and law are all subverted and proved wrong when Pilate gets down from the judgment-seat, and the watching fishers believe that they behold the resurrection. This socialistic influence the doctrines of Christianity have had, and have gradually made felt throughout many ages, and are making felt more sharply and rudely in this our own than in any other age. The most 'pious' of all sects are also always the most democratic; the Nonconformists and the Wesleyans are always the most intent on levelling the barriers and irregularities of social life. Protestantism was the democratic daughter of the Papacy, but the Papacy was also a democrat when it made it possible for a swineherd to hold the keys of St Peter, and for a Becket to rule a Plantagenet, for a Wolsey to rule a Tudor.

Again and again the humble vassal lived to thunder excommunication upon monarchs, and the timid scribe who dared not lift his eyes from his scroll became the most powerful, the most arrogant, the most inexorable of churchmen. It was this hope contained within it for the lowliest, this palm held out by it to the poorest, which made the enormous influence of Christianity from the days of Basil and Augustine to the days of Richelieu and Wolsey. The feudal lords who shouted Christian war-cries, and the despotic kings who swore by the Holy Rood and by Our Lady, were wholly unconscious that in the creed they cherished there were the germs of the democratic influences which would in time to come undermine thrones and make aristocracy an empty name; they did not know that in Clement Marot's psalm-books and in Wycliffe's Bible there lay folded that which would in time to come bring forth the thesis of Bakounine and the demands of the Knights of Labour.

If we meditate on and realise the essentially socialistic tendencies of the Christian creed, we may wonder that the '*grands de la terre*' ever so welcomed it, or ever failed to see in it the death-germs of their own order; but we shall completely understand why it fascinated all the labouring classes of mankind and planted in them those seeds of communism which are now bearing forth full fruit. But what is almost equally certain is that Christianity will be wholly powerless to restrain the results of what it has inspired.

For of all absolutely powerless things on earth Christianity is the most powerless, even though sovereigns are still consecrated, multitudes still baptised, parliaments and tribunals still opened, and countless churches and cathedrals still built in its name. It has become a shibboleth, a husk, a robe with no heart beating within it, a winged angel carved in dead wood. It has said that it is almost impossible for the rich man to be just or inherit the kingdom of heaven: the Anarchists insist that it is utterly impossible, and will, if they can, cast the rich man into hell on earth.

Christianity has opened the flood-gates to Socialism; but it will not have any power in itself to close them again. For nothing can be in more complete contradiction than the prevalence of the profession of Christianity with the impotency of that profession to colour and control human life. The Buddha of Galilee has not one-thousandth part of the direct influence on his professional disciples that is possessed by the Buddha of India. Christianity is professed over the whole earth wherever the Aryan race exists and rules, but all the kingdoms and republics which make it their state creed are, practically, wholly unaffected by its doctrines, except in so far as their socialistic members derive precedent and strength from them.

Take, for instance, that which governs states and prescribes the duties of men—the majesty of the law, as it is termed—the science and the practice of legislation. Side by side with the religion enjoined by the state there exists a code of legislation which violates every precept of Christianity, and resembles only the *lex talionis* of the old Hebrew law, which the Christian creed was supposed to have destroyed and superseded.

A savage insistence on having an eye for an eye and a tooth for a tooth is the foundation of all modern law. The European, or the American, or the Australasian, goes on Sunday to his church and says his formula, 'Forgive us our trespasses as we forgive those who trespass against us,' and then on the Monday morning prosecutes a boy who stole a ball of string, or a neighbour who has invaded a right of way, or an enemy whose cow has strayed, or whose horse has kicked, or whose dog has bitten, and exacts for one and all of these offences the uttermost penalty that the law will permit him to demand. It may be said that such law is absolutely necessary in civilised states: it may be so: but then the empty formula of the Christian forgiveness of trespasses should be in honesty abandoned.

Mr Ruskin never writes on Venice without dwelling on the vital influence of the Christian creed on the men of the middle ages, and contrasting the religious spirit of those whose cry was St Mark, and whose admiration was St Jerome, with those of modern times, when these names mean nothing on the ears of men. But, in truth, the influence was architectural and artistic rather than moral; the memory neither of St Mark nor St Jerome ever prevented the blinding of the eyes of doges who had displeased the people, the treachery and brutality of their inexorable decrees, the torture of the Foscari, the betrayal of Carracciolo, the sale of slaves, or any one of the awful cruelties and tyrannies of the Council of Ten.

As it was in the Venice of the middle ages, so has it been and is wherever Christianity is nominally dominant. The cross is embroidered on banners and its psalter is carried to churches in pious hands, but its real influence on the life of nations is as slight as that of Mark and Jerome on the Council of Ten. The whole practical life of nations lives, breathes and holds its place by creeds and necessities which are the complete antithesis of the Christian; they are selfish in their policies, bloodthirsty in their wars, cunning in their diplomacy, avaricious in their commerce, unsparing in their hours of victory. They are so, and, alas! they must be so, or they would be pushed out of their place amongst nations, and parcelled out, like Joseph's coat, amongst their foes.

The capitalist who makes millions by the manufacture of rifled cannon sees no inconsistency in murmuring in his seat at Catholic mass or Protestant service, 'Return good for evil,' 'If one cheek be smitten, turn the other,' and all the rest of the evangelical injunctions to peace and forbearance: were any to suggest to him the inconsistency of his conduct, such an one would speak to deaf ears; that his whole life was a violation of the precepts he professed would be an unintelligible reproach to him: his soul would take refuge, smug and safe, in his formulas. Yet who can deny that, if the commands of Christianity had in the least penetrated beneath the surface of human life, to make weapons of destruction would be viewed as a crime so frightful that none would dare attempt it? Some writer has said that 'singing psalms never yet prevented a grocer from sanding his sugar.' This rough joke expresses in a grotesque form what may be said in all seriousness of the impotency of Christianity to affect modern national life.

Christianity is a formula: it is nothing more. The nations in which daily services in its honour are said in thousands and tens of thousands of cathedrals and churches, sell opium to the Chinese, cheat and slay red Indians, slaughter with every brutality the peaceful natives of Tonquin and Anam, carry fire and sword into central Asia, kill Africans like ants on expeditions, and keep a whole populace in the grip of military service from the Spree to the Elbe, from the Zuider Zee to the Tiber, from the Seine to the Neva. Whether the nation be England, America, France, Russia, Italy, or Germany, the fact is the same; with the gospels on its reading-desks and their shibboleth on its lips, every nation practically follows the lusts and passions of its human greeds for possession of territory and increase of treasure. Not one amongst them is better in this matter than another. Krupp guns, shrapnel shells, nitro-glycerine and submarine torpedoes are the practical issues of evangelicism and Catholicism all over the civilised world.

And the nations are so sublimely unconscious of their own hypocrisy that they have blessings on their warfare pronounced by their ecclesiastics, and implore the Lord of Hosts for his sympathy before sending out armoured cruisers.

This is inevitable, is the reply: in the present state of hostility between all nations, the first one to renounce the arts of war would be swallowed up by the others. So it would be, no doubt; but if this be the chief fruit of Christianity, may not this religion justly be said to have failed conspicuously in impressing itself upon mankind? It has impressed its formulas; not its spirit. It has sewn a phylactery on the hem of humanity's robe: it has never touched the soul of humanity beneath the robe. It has produced the iniquities of the Inquisition, the egotism and celibacy of the monasteries, the fury of religious wars, the ferocity of the Hussite, of the Catholic, of the Puritan, of the Spaniard, of the Irish Orangeman and of the Irish Papist; it has divided families, alienated friends, lighted the torch of civil war, and borne the virgin and the greybeard to the burning pile, broken delicate limbs upon the wheel and wrung the souls and bodies of innocent creatures on the rack: all this it has done, and done in the name of God.

But of mercy, of pity, of forbearance, of true self-sacrifice, what has it ever taught the world?

A while ago there was published an account of the manufacture of the deadliest sort of dynamite on the shores of Arran. Full in the front of the great sea, with all the majesty of a rock-bound and solitary shore around them, these hideous works raise their blaspheming face to Nature and pollute and profane her most solemn glories; and there, on this coast of Arran, numbers of young girls work at the devilish thing in wooden huts, with every moment the ever-present risk of women and huts being blown into millions of atoms if so much as a shred of metal, or even a ray of too warm sunshine, strike on the foul, sickly, infernal compound which their fingers handle. A brief while since two girls were thus blown into the air, and were so instantaneously and utterly annihilated that not a particle of their bodies or of their clothing could be recognised; and all the while the sea-gulls were circling, and the waves leaping, and the clouds sailing, and deep calling to deep, 'Lo! behold the devil and all his works.' And there is no devil there at all except man—man who makes money out of this fell thing which blasts the beauties of Nature, and scars the faces of the hills, and has made possible to civilisation a fashion of wholesale assassination so horrible, so craven, and so treacherous that the boldness of open murder seems almost virtue beside it.

The manufactory of nitro-glycerine on the Arran shore is the emblem of the world which calls itself Christian. No doubt the canny Scots who are enriched by it go to their kirk religiously, are elders of it, very likely, and if they saw a boy trundle a hoop, or a girl use a needle on the Sabbath day, would think they saw a crime, and would summon and chastise the sinners. Pontius Pilate was afraid and ashamed when he had condemned an innocent man; but the modern followers of Christ have neither fear nor shame when they pile up gold on gold in their bankers' cellars through the death which they have manufactured and sold, indifferent though it should strike down a thousand innocent men.

Even of death Christianity has made a terror which was unknown to the gay calmness of the Pagan and the stoical repose of the Indian. Never has death been the cause of such craven timidity as in the Christian world, to which, if Christians believed any part of what they profess, it would be the harbinger of glad tidings, the welcome messenger of a more perfect life. To visionaries like Catherine of Siena, it may have been so at times, but to the masses of men and women professing the Christian faith, death has been and is the King of Terrors, from whose approach they cower in an agony which Petronius Arbiter would have ridiculed, and Socrates and Seneca have scorned. The Greek and the Latin gave dignity to death, and awaited it with philosophy and peace; but the Christian beholds in it innumerable fears like a child's terror of ghosts in darkness, and by the manner of the funeral rites with which he celebrates it contrives to make grotesque even that mute majesty which rests with the dead slave as much as with the dead emperor.

Christianity has been cruel in much to the human race. It has quenched much of the sweet joy and gladness of life; it has caused the natural passions and affections of it to be held as sins; by its teaching that the body should be despised, it has brought on all the unnamable filth which was made a virtue in the monastic orders, and which in the Italian, the Spanish, the Russian peoples, and the poor of all nations is a cherished and indestructible habit. In its permission to man to render subject to him all other living creatures of the earth, it continued the cruelty of the barbarian and of the pagan, and endowed these with what appeared a divine authority—an authority which Science, despising Christianity, has yet not been ashamed to borrow and to use.

Let us, also, endeavour to realise the unutterable torments endured by men and maidens in their efforts to subdue the natural desires of their senses and their affections to the unnatural celibacy of the cloister, and we shall see that the tortures inflicted by Christianity have been more cruel than the cruelties of death. Christianity has ever been the enemy of human love; it has forever cursed and expelled and crucified the one passion which sweetens and smiles on human life, which makes the desert blossom as the rose, and which glorifies the common things and common ways of earth. It made of this, the angel of life, a shape of sin and darkness, and bade the woman whose lips were warm with the first kisses of her lover believe herself accursed and ashamed. Even in the unions which it reluctantly permitted, it degraded and dwarfed the passion which it could not entirely exclude, and permitted it coarsely to exist for the mere necessity of procreation. The words of the Christian nuptial service expressly say so. Love, the winged god of the immortals, became, in the Christian creed, a thrice-damned and earth-bound devil, to be exorcised and loathed. This has been the greatest injury that Christianity has ever done to the human race. Love, the one supreme, unceasing source of human felicity, the one sole joy which lifts the whole mortal existence into the empyrean, was by it degraded into the mere mechanical action of reproduction. It cut the wings of Eros. Man, believing that he must no longer love his mistress, woman, believing that she must no longer love her lover, loved themselves, and from the cloisters and from the churches there arose a bitter, joyless, narrow, apprehensive passion which believed itself to be religion, but was in truth only a form of concentrated egotism, the agonised desire to be 'saved,' to ascend into the highest heaven, let who else would wait without its doors or pine in hell. The influence of this is still with the world, and will long be with it; and its echo is still loud in the sibilant voices which hiss at the poet who sings and the poet who glorifies love.

And herein we approach that spurious offspring of Christianity which is called cant.

Other religions have not been without it. The Mosaic law had the Pharisee, who for a pretence made long prayers. The Greek and the Latin had those who made oblations to the gods for mere show, and augurs who served the sacred altars with their tongue in their cheek. But from Christianity, alas! has arisen and spread a systematic hypocrisy more general, more complete, more vain, more victorious than any other. The forms of the Christian religion facilitate this. Whether in the Catholic form of it, which cleanses the sinner in the confessional that he may go forth and sin again freely, or in the Protestant form, which, so long as a man listens to sermons and kneels at sacraments, does not disturb him as to the tenor of his private life, the Christian religion says, practically, to all its professors: 'Wear my livery and assemble in my courts; I ask no more of you in return for the moral reputation which I will give to you.'

Its lip-service and its empty rites have made it the easiest of all tasks for the usurer to cloak his cruelties, the miser to hide his avarice, the lawyer to condone his lies, the sinner of all social sins to purchase the social immunity from them by outward deference to churches.

The Christian religion, outwardly and even in intention humble, does, without meaning it, teach man to regard himself as the most important of all created things. Man surveys the starry heavens and hears with his ears of the plurality of worlds; yet his religion bids him believe that his alone out of these innumerable spheres is the object of his master's love and sacrifice. To save his world—whose common multitudes can be no more in the scale of creation than the billions of insects that build up a coral-reef beneath the deep sea—he is told that God himself took human shape, underwent human birth, was fed with human food, and suffered human pains. It is intelligible that, believing this, the most arrogant self-conceit has puffed up the human crowd, and that with the most cruel indifference they have sacrificed to themselves all the countless suffering multitudes which they are taught to call 'the beasts which perish.' It is this selfishness and self-esteem which, fostered in the human race by Christianity, have far outweighed and overborne the humility which its doctrines in part strove to inculcate and the mercy which they advocated.

It is in vain that the human race is bidden to believe that its Creator cares for the lilies of the field and for the birds of the air: it is the human race alone for which its God has suffered and died, so it believes, and this solitary selection, this immense supremacy, make it semi-divine in its own sight. It is the leaven of egotism begotten by the Christian creed which has neutralised the purity and the influence of its teachings. Here and there saintly men and women have been guided by it solely in the ways of holiness and unselfishness; but the great majority of mankind has drawn from it chiefly two lessons—self-concentration and socialism. 'Rock of ages, cleft for *me*,' sighs the Christian; and this 'immense Me' is, as Emerson has said of it, the centre of the universe in the belief of the unconscious egotist.

Christians repeat like a parrot's recitative the phrase that no sparrow falls uncounted by its Creator, and they go to their crops and scatter poison, or load fowling-pieces with small shot to destroy hundreds of sparrows in a morning. If they believed that their God saw the little birds of the air fall, would they dare to do it? Of course they would not; but they do not believe: it only suits them to use their formula, and they are never prevented by it from strewing bird-poison or setting bird-traps.

Behold their priests taking on themselves the vows of poverty, of chastity, and of renunciation, and whether they be the Catholic cardinal, stately, luxurious and arrogant, or whether they be the Protestant bishop, with his liveried servants, his dinner parties, and his church patronage, what can we see more widely removed in unlikeness from all the precepts of the creed which they profess to obey? What fiercer polemics ever rage than those which wrangle about the body of religion? What judge would not be thought a madman who should from the bench counsel the man who has received a blow to bear it in meekness and turn the other cheek? What missionary would be excused for leaving his wife and children chargeable on parish rates because he pointed to the injunction to leave all that he had and follow Christ?

What attempt on the part of any community to put the precepts of Christianity into practical observance would not cause them to be denounced to magistrates as communists, as anarchists, as moonstruck dreamers, as lunatics? There are sects in Russia which endeavour to do so, and the police hunt them down like wild animals. They are only logically trying to carry out the precepts of the gospels, but they are regarded therefore as dangerous lunatics. They can have no place in the conventional civilisation of the world. What judge who should tell the two litigants in any lawsuit concerning property that they were violating every religious duty in wrangling with each other about filthy lucre would not be deemed a fool, and worse? The French Republic, in tearing down from its courts of law and from its class-rooms the emblems of Christianity, has done a rough, but sincere and consistent, act, if one offensive to a great portion of the nation; and it may be alleged that this act is more logical than the acts of those nations who open their tribunals with rites of reverence towards a creed with which the whole legislature governing these tribunals is in entire and militant contradiction. 'Religion is one thing; law is another,' said a lawyer once to whom this strange discrepancy was commented on; but so long as law is founded on assumptions and principles wholly in violence with those of religion, how can such religion be called the religion of the state? It is as absurd a discrepancy as that with which the Italian nation, calling itself Catholic, drove out thousands of Catholic monks and Catholic nuns from their religious houses and seized their possessions by the force of the secular arm. It is not here the question whether the suppression of the male and female monastic orders was or was not right or necessary; what is certain is that the state, enforcing this suppression, can with no shadow of sense or of logic continue to call itself a Catholic state; as it still does continue to call itself in the person of its king and in its public decrees.

How is it to be accounted for—this impotence of Christianity to affect the policies, politics, legislation and general life of the nations which think their salvation lies in the profession of its creed? How is it that a religion avowedly making peace and long-suffering of injury the corner-stone of its temple has had as its principal outcome war, both the fanaticism of religious war and the avarice of civil war; a legislation founded on the *lex talionis* and inexorable in its adherence to that law; and a commerce which all the world over is saturated with the base desire to overreach, outwit and outstrip all competitors?

It is chiefly due to the absolutely 'unworkable' character of its injunctions; and partly due to the Jewish laws entering so largely into the creeds of modern Christians: also it is due to the fact that even in the purer creeds of the evangelists there is so much of egotism. 'What shall it profit a man if he gain the whole world and lose his own soul?' 'His own' — that throughout is to be the chief thought of his existence and its constant end. The greatest of the Christian martyrs were but egotists when they were not matoïdes. Their fortitude and constancy were already rewarded, in their belief, by every sweetness of celestial joys and glories. It may be doubted whether they even felt the scourge, the torch, the iron, or the rods, so intensely in their exaltation was their nervous system strung up to ecstasy. What could the poor offer of earthly life seem worth to those who believed that by thus losing it they would enter at once and forever into the exquisite consciousness of a surpassing beatitude? An intense, though innocent, selfishness was at the root of all the martyrdoms of the early Christian Church. There was not one amongst them which approached for unselfishness the death of Antinous. And it is surely this egotism which is an integral part of the Christian creed, and which has been at once its strength and its weakness; its strength in giving it dominion over human nature, and its weakness in allying it with baser things. The alloy has made the gold more workable, but has destroyed its purity.

Meanwhile, although the majority of Christian nations profess the Christian faith more or less sincerely, and give it at least the homage of hypocrisy, all the intellectual life of the world is leaving its folds without concealment. There is in its stead either the hard and soulless materialism of the scientist, or the sad, vague pantheism and pessimism of the scholar and the poet. Neither will ever suffice for the mass of mankind in general. The purely imaginative and intellectual mind can be content to wait before the immense unexplained enigma of life; it accepts its mystery, and sees the marvel of it, in the changing cloud, the blossoming weed, the wistful eyes of the beasts of burden, as much as it sees it in humanity itself. To such a mind the calmness and sadness of patience, and the kind of universal divinity which it finds in nature, can suffice: and to it the complacent conceit of science over the discovery of a new poison, or a hitherto unsuspected action of the biliary duct in mammals, must seem as childish and as narrow as does the belief in the creeds of the Papist, the Evangelical, or the Baptist. This is the only mental attitude which is at once philosophic and spiritual; but it must ever remain the privilege of the few; it can never be the possession of the multitude. The multitude will be forever cast into the arms of science, or of faith, either of which will alike flatter it with the assurance that it is the chief glory of creation, before which all the rest of creation is bound to lie subject in bonds and pain.

It is this selfishness and self-admiration which have neutralised in man the good which he should have gained from the simple benevolence of the Sermon on the Mount. A religion which is founded on the desire of men to attain eternal felicity will be naturally seductive to them, but the keynote of its motive power can never be a lofty one. The jewelled streets of the New Jerusalem are not more luxuriously dreamed of than the houris of the Mohammedan paradise. Each form of celestial recompense is anticipated as reward for devotion to a creed. And as all loyalty, all loveliness, all virtue *pêchent par la base* when they are founded on the expectation of personal gain, so the Christian religion has contained the radical defect of inciting its followers to obedience and faithfulness by a bribe—a grand bribe truly—nothing less than eternal life; such life as the soul of man cannot even conceive; but still a bribe. Therefore Christianity has been powerless to enforce its own ethics on the world in the essence of their spirit, and has been perforce contented with hearing it recite its formulas.

What will be its future? There is no prophet of vision keen enough to behold. The intellect of mankind is every year forsaking it more utterly, and the ever-increasing luxury which is possible with riches, and the ever-increasing materialism of all kinds of life into which mechanical labour enters, are forces which every year drive the multitudes farther and farther from its primitive tenets. In a small, and a poor, community Christianity may be a creed possible in its practical realisation, and consistent in its simplicity of existence; but in the mad world of modern life, with its overwhelming wealth and its overwhelming poverty, with its horrible satiety and its horrible hunger, with its fiendish greed and its ghastly crimes, its endless lusts and its cruel bitterness of hatreds, Christianity can only be one of two things—either a nullity, as it is now in all national life, or a dynamic force allied with and ruling through socialism, and destroying all civilisation as it, at present, stands.

Which will it be? There is no prophet to say. But whichever it be, there will be that in its future which, if it remain dominant, will make the cry of the poet the sigh of Humanity:

'Thou hast triumphed Opale Gallilean,
And the world has grown grey with Thy breath!'

THE PASSING OF PHILOMEL

Will there ever be a world in which the voice of Sappho's bird will be no longer heard?

I fear it.

For thrice a thousand years, to our knowledge, that divine music, the sweetest of any music upon earth, has been eloquent in the woods and the gardens of every springtime, renewing its song as the earth her youth. The nightingale has ever been the poet's darling; is indeed poetry incarnated; love, vocal and spiritual, made manifest. Nothing surely can show the deadness, dulness, coarseness, coldness of the human multitude so plainly as their indifference to this exquisite creature. Do even people who call themselves cultured care for the nightingale? How do they care? They rise from their dinner-table and stroll out on to a terrace or down an avenue, and there in the moonlight listen for a few moments, and say 'How charming!' then return to their flirtations, their theatricals, their baccarat or their bézique within doors. Bulbul may sing all night amongst the roses and the white heads of the lilies; they will not go out again. They prefer the cushioned lounge, the electric light, the tumbler of iced drink, the playing cards, the spiced *double entendre*. Here and there a woman may sit at her open casement half the night, or a poet walk entranced through the leafy lanes till dawn, but these listeners are few and far between.

When Nature gave this gift to the world she might well have looked for some slight gratitude. But save when Sappho has listened, or Meleager, or Shakespeare, or Ford, or Musset, or Shelley, or Lytton, who has cared? Not one.

Possibly, if the nightingale had been born once in a century, rarity might have secured for it attention, protection, appreciation. But singing everywhere, as it has done, wherever the climate was fit for it, through so many hundreds and hundreds of years, it has been almost wholly neglected by the soulless and dull ears of man.

A slender, bright and agile bird, the nightingale is neither shy nor useless, as it is said that most poets and musicians are. It eats grubs, worms, lice, small insects of all kinds, and hunts amongst the decaying leaves and grass for many a garden pest, with active energy and industry, qualities too often lacking to the human artist. It builds a loose, roomy nest, often absolutely on the ground, and always placed with entire confidence in man's good faith. It is a very happy bird, and its song is the most ecstatic hymn of joy. I never can imagine how it came to be associated with sorrow and tragedy, and the ghastly story of Procne and Itys. For rapturous happiness there is nothing to be compared to the full love-song of the nightingale. All other music is harsh, cold, dissonant, beside it. But, alas! the full perfection of the song is not always heard. For it to sing its fullest, its richest, its longest, it must have been in peace and security, it must have been left untroubled and unalarmed, it must have its little heart at rest in its leafy home. Where the nightingale is harassed, and affrighted, and disturbed, its song is quite different to what it is when in happiness and tranquillity; where it feels alarmed and insecure it never acquires its full song, the note is shorter and weaker, and the magnificent, seemingly unending, trills are never heard, for the bird sings as though it were afraid of being heard and hunted—which, indeed, no doubt it is.

When entirely secure from any interference, year after year in the same spot (for, if not interfered with, it returns unerringly to the same haunts), many families will come to the same place together, and the males call and shout to each other in the most joyous emulation day and night. Under these conditions alone does the marvellous music of the nightingale reach its full height and eloquence. No one who has not heard the song under these conditions can judge of it as it is in its perfection: the strength of it, the rapture of it, the long-sustained, breathless tremulo, the wondrous roulades and arpeggios, the exquisite liquid sweetness, surpassing in beauty every other sound on earth.

In one spot, dearer to me than any upon earth, where the old stones once felt the tread of the armoured guards and the cuirassed priests of the great Countess Matilda, the nightingales have nested and sung by dozens in the bay and arbutus of the undergrowth of the woods, and under the wild roses and pomegranates fringing the meadows. On one nook of grass land alone I have seen seven close together at daybreak, hunting for their breakfasts amongst the dewy blades, in amicable rivalry. Here they have come with the wild winds of March ever since Matilda's reign, and for many ages before that, when all which is now the vale of Arno was forest and marsh. Here, because long protected and beloved, they sing in the most marvellous concert, challenging and answering each other in a riot of melody more exquisite than any orchestra created by man can produce; the long ecstasy pouring through the ardours of full noonday, or across the silver radiance of the moon; saluting the dawn with joyous *Io triomphe!* or praising the starry glories of the night with a rapturous *Salve Regina!*

The hawks sweep through the sun rays, the owls flash through the shadows, but the nightingales sing on, fearless and unharmed; it is only man they dread, and man cannot hurt them here.

Naturalists state that the nightingale does not attain to the uttermost splendour of its voice until the eighth or ninth year of its life, and that the songsters of that age give lessons to the younger ones. To the truth of this latter fact I can vouch from personal observation, but I doubt so many years being required to develop the song to perfection. I think its perfection is dependent, as I have said, on the peace and security which the singer enjoys; on its familiarity with its nesting haunts, and on the sense of safety which it enjoys. This may be said, in a measure, of the song of all birds; but it is especially true of the nightingale, which is one of the most sensitive and highly organised of sentient beings, and one, moreover, with intense affections, devoted to its mate, its offspring and its chosen home.

It will be objected to me that nightingales sing in captivity. They do so; but the song of the caged nightingale is intolerable to the ear which is used to the song of the free bird in wood and field and garden. It is not the same song; it has changed its character: it sounds like one long agonised note of appeal, and this indeed we may be certain that it is.

I confess that I hold many crimes which are punishable by the felon's dock less infamous than the caging of nightingales, or indeed the caging of any winged creatures. Migratory birds, caged, suffer yet more than any, because, in addition to the loss of liberty, they suffer from the repression of those natural instincts of flight at certain periods of the year, which denial must torture them to an extent quite immeasurable by us. The force of the migratory instinct may be imagined by the fact that it is intense and dominant enough to impel a creature so small, so timid, and so defenceless as a song-bird to incur the greatest perils, and wing its unprotected way across seas and continents, mountains and deserts, from Europe to Asia or Africa, in a flight which is certainly one of the most marvellous of the many marvels of Nature to which men are so dully and so vain-gloriously indifferent. The intensity of the impelling power may be gauged by the miracle of its results; and the bird in whom this instinct is repressed and denied must suffer incredible agonies of longing and vain effort, as from unfit climate and from unchanged food. No one, I am sure, can measure the torture endured by migratory birds from these causes when in captivity. Russian women of the world are very fond of taking back to Russia with them nightingales of Southern Europe, for which they pay a high price: these birds invariably die after a week or two in Russia, but the abominable practice continues unchecked. Nightingales are captured or killed indiscriminately with other birds in all the countries where they nest, and no one seems alive to the shameless barbarity of such a sacrifice.

With every year their chosen haunts are more and more invaded by the builder, the cultivator, the trapper, the netter. Nightingales will nest contentedly in gardens where they are unmolested, but their preference is for wild ground, or at least for leafy shrubberies and thickets: the dense hedges of clipped bay or arbutus common to Italy are much favoured by them. Therefore the nudity characteristic of high farming is fatal to them: to Philomel and her brood shadow and shelter are a necessity.

Where I dwell, much is still unaltered since the days of Horace and Virgil. The 'silvery circle' of the reaping-hook still flashes amongst the bending wheat. The oxen still slowly draw the wooden plough up and down the uneven fields. The osiers still turn to gold above the flag-filled streamlets; the barefooted peasants run through the flower-filled grass; the cherries and plums tumble uncounted amongst the daisies; the soft, soundless wings of swallow and owl and kestrel fan the air, as they sweep down from the old red-brown tiles of the roofs where they make their homes; the corn is threshed by flails in the old way on the broad stone courts; the vine and ash and peach and maple grow together, graceful and careless; the patient ass turns in the circular path of the stone olive-press; the huge, round-bellied jars, the amphoræ of old, stand beside the horse-block at the doors; the pigeons flash above the bean-fields and feast as they will; the great walnut trees throw their shade over the pumpkins and the maize; men and women and children still work and laugh, and lounge at noon amongst the sheaves, thank the gods, much as they did when Theocritus ate honey by the fountain's brink. But how long will this be so? How long will the Italy of Virgil and Horace be left to us?

Under the brutality of chemical agriculture the whole face of the world is changing. The England of Gilbert White and Thomas Bewick is going as the England of the Tudors went before it; and the France of the Bourbons is being effaced like the France of the Valois. The old hedgerow timber is felled. The cowslip meadows are turned into great grazing grounds. The high flowering hedges are cut to the root, or often stubbed up entirely, and their place filled by galvanised wire fencing. The wildflowers cannot blossom on the naked earth; so disappear. The drained soil has no longer any place for the worts and the rushes and the fennels and the water spurges. Instead of the beautiful old lichen-grown orchard trees, bending to the ground under the weight of their golden or russet balls, there are rows of grafts two feet high, bearing ponderous, flavourless prize fruits, or monotonous espaliers grimly trimmed and trained, with shot bullfinches or poisoned blackbirds lying along their ugly length.

The extreme greed which characterises agriculture and horticulture, as it characterises all other pursuits in modern times, will inevitably cause the gradual extermination of all living things which it is considered possible may interfere with the maximum of profit. In the guano-dressed, phosphate-dosed, chemically-treated fields and gardens of the future, with their vegetables and fruits ripened by electric light, and their colouring and flavouring obtained by the artificial aids of the laboratory, there will be no place for piping linnet, rose-throated robin, gay chaffinch, tiny tit, or blue warbler; and none amidst the frames, the acids, the manures, the machines, the hydraulic engines, for Philomel. The object of the gardener and the farmer is to produce: the garden and the farm will soon be mere factories of produce, ugly and sordid, like all other factories.

The vast expanses of unbroken corn lands and grazing lands, to be seen in modern England, have no leafy nooks, as the fields of Herrick, of Wordsworth, of Tennyson's earlier time had for them. In Italy and in France the acids, phosphates, sublimates, and other chemicals, poured over vineyards and farm lands drive away the nightingale, which used to nest so happily under the low-growing vine leaves, or amongst the endive and parsley. 'The lands are never left at peace,' said a peasant to me not long ago; and the peace of the birds is gone with that of the fields: the fates of both are intimately interwoven and mutually dependent. Where the orchard and the vineyard are still what they were of old—green, fragrant, dusky, happy places, full of sweet scents and of sweet sounds—there the birds still are happy. But in the newfangled fields, acid-drenched, sulphur-powdered, sulphate-poisoned, stripped bare and jealously denuded of all alien life, winged and wild animals, hunted and harassed, can have no place. Scientific husbandry has sacrificed the simple joys of rural life, and with them the lives of the birds. 'What shall it profit a man if he gain the whole world and lose his own soul?' has been asked by the wisdom of old. The song of the birds is the voice of the soul of Nature, and men stifle it for sake of avarice and greed.

Three or four years ago the village of San Domenico, on the highway to Fiesole, was a green nest which in spring was filled with the music of nightingales; the fields, with the wild-rose hedges, were one paradise of song in springtime and early summer. The old villa, which stands with its big trees between the little streams of Africa and Mensola, where Walter Savage Landor lived and where he wished to be allowed to die, was hidden away under its deep cedar shadows, and the nightingales day and night sang amongst its narcissi and its jonquils. An American came, bought and ruined. He could let nothing alone. He had no sentiment or perception. He built a new glaring wing, spoiling all the symmetry of the old tenement, daubed over with new stucco and colour the beautiful old hues of the ancient walls, cut down trees by the old shady gateway, and built a porter's lodge after the manner beloved of Hampstead and of Clapham. He considers himself a man of taste; he is (I am ashamed to say) a scholar! It would have been less affront to the memory of Landor, and to the spirits haunting this poetic, historic, legendary place, to have razed the house to the ground, and have let the grass grow over it as over grave.

Higher up, but quite near, on the same hillside as the villa of Landor, there stood a stone house, old, solid, coloured with the beautiful greys and browns of age; it had at one side a stone staircase leading up to a sculptured and painted shrine, before it were grass terraces with some bamboos, some roses, some laurels and beneath these a lower garden which joined the fields and blended with them. It was quite perfect in its own simple, ancient way. A year ago the dreadful hand of the improver seized on it, daubed it over with staring stucco, painted and varnished its woodwork, stuck vulgar green *persiennes* in its old casements, and, in a word, made it as nearly as possible resemble the pert, paltry, staring, gimcrack structure of a modern villa. It is now a blot on the hillside, an eyesore to the wayfarer, an offence to the sight and to the landscape; and the nightingales, which were so eloquent on its grass terraces, go to its rosebushes and bamboos no more.

Such treatment as this of secluded places scares away the little brown lover of the moon: where there are brought all the pother and dust of masons', carpenters' and painters' work, the voice of Philomel cannot be heard; the sweet solitude of the rose thicket is invaded by uncouth din and vulgar uproar; the cedar shadows lie no more unbroken on the untrodden sward; the small scops owl flits no more at evening through the perfumed air, the big white owl can nest no more beneath the moss-grown tiles and timbers of the roof; all the soft, silent, shy creatures of fur and feather, which have been happy so long, are startled, terrified, driven away for ever, and the nightingale dare nest no more. It is impossible to measure the injury done to the half-wild, half-tame denizens of the woods and gardens by the mania for restoration and innovation which characterises the purchasers and the tenants of the present day.

One such ghastly renovation as this, which has vulgarised and ruined the Landor villa and its neighbour, causes an amount of havoc to the creatures of the brake and bush which can never be repaired. Once frightened and driven out, they never come back again. They are the youth of the world; and, like all youth, once gone, they are gone for ever.

The builder who desecrated these places, the people who live in them, do not perceive the abomination which they have wrought; and if they were called to account, would stare at their accuser, understanding nothing of their sin. Are there not an admirably grained and varnished hall door, and window shutters of the brightest pistachio green? What matter if Philomel nest no more under the cuckoopint and burdock? Is there not the scream of the tramway whistle? What matter if the Madonna's herb grow no longer on the old stone steps and the swallow build no more under the hanging eaves? Are there not the painted boards declaring, in letters a foot long, that the adjacent land is to be let or sold for building purposes?

By the increase of bricks and mortar, and the sterility and nudity which accompany scientific agriculture, the nightingale is everywhere being driven higher into the hills, where it may still hope to nest unmolested, but where the temperature is unsuited to it. Its breeding grounds become, with every season, fewer and more difficult to find. It is sociable, and would willingly be at home in the gardens even of cities; but men will not leave it in peace there. Its nests are taken and its feeding grounds are destroyed by the over-sweeping and over-weeding of the modern gardener. The insensate modern practice of clearing away all leaves as they fall from the soil of shrubberies and avenues starves the nightingales, as it starves the roots of the trees. When the leaves are left to lie through the winter the trees rejoice in their warmth and nourishment, and the returning birds find a rich larder in the spring. A carpet of golden leaves is a lovely and useful thing; but the modern gardener does not think so, and his intolerable birch broom, and yet more intolerable mechanical sweeper, tears away the precious veil which Nature's care would spread in preservation over the chilly earth.

Starved, hunted, robbed of its nest, and harassed in its song, the nightingale must therefore inevitably grow rarer and rarer every year.

The vile tramways, which have unrolled their hideous length over so many thousands of miles all over Europe, bring the noise, the glare, and the dirt of cities into the once peaceful solitude of hill and valley. They are at this moment being made through the beautiful forest roads of the Jura!

The curse of the town is being spread broadcast over the face of the country, as the filth of urban cesspools is being carried out over rustic fields. The sticks, the guns, the nets, the traps, the birdlime of the accursed bird destroyer, are carried by train and tram into the green heart of once tranquil wolds and woods. The golden gorse serves to shelter the grinning excursionist, the wild hyacinths are crushed under the wine flasks and the beer bottles. The lowest forms of human life leave the slums and ravage the virgin country; ten thousand jarring wheels carry twenty thousand clumsy, greedy hands to tear down the wild honeysuckle and pull to pieces the bird's nest, to tear up the meadow-sweet and strangle the green lizard. The curse of the town mounts higher and higher and higher every year, and clings like a vampire to the country, and sucks out of it all its beauty, and stifles in it all its song.

Soon the hiss of the engine and the bray of the cad will be the only sounds heard throughout Europe. It is very probable that the conditions of human life in the future will be incompatible with the existence of the nightingale at all. It is almost certain that all natural beauty, all woodland solitude, all sylvan quiet, will be year by year more and more attacked, diminished, and disturbed, until the lives of all creatures which depend on these will come altogether to an end.

Let us imagine what the world was like when Sappho heard the nightingales of Greece, and we can then measure by our own present loss what will be the probable loss of future generations; the atmosphere was then of a perfect purity; no coal smoke soiled the air or blurred the sea; no engine hissed, no cogwheel whirred, no piston throbbed; the sweet wild country ran to the very gates of the small cities; there was no tread noisier than the footfall of the ox upon the turf; there was no artificial light harsher than the pale soft gleam of the olive oil, the temples were white as the snow on Ida, and the brooks and the fountains were clear as the sparkling smile of the undimmed day. In such a world every tuft of thyme and every bough of laurel had its nest, and under the radiant skies the song of the nightingales must have been eloquent over all the plains and hills in one unbroken flood of joy.

Let us picture the fairness of the world as it was then, with undimmed skies, unpolluted waters, untouched forests, and untainted air; and we must realise that what is called civilisation has given us nothing worth that which it has taken, and will continue to take away from us, forever.

THE ITALY OF TO-DAY

Cavallotti[C] has written, in his letter of protest against the arrest of the Sicilian deputy, De Felice, a sentence which deserves to be repeated all over the land: one of those sentences, *multum in parvo*, which resume a whole situation in a phrase: he has written: 'Invece che del pane si da il piombo.' Instead of bread to the suffering and famished multitudes there is offered lead, the lead of rifle bullets and of cannon-balls. That is the only response which has as yet been given to demands which are in the main essentially just. Is the English public aware that the Italian city of Caltanissetta has been, the first week of the year, bombarded by Italian artillery, and that in that town alone six hundred arrests have been made in one day? If this were taking place in Poland the English public and its press would be convulsed with rage.

The attitude of the press in England towards the present Italian struggle against overwhelming fiscal burdens is so singular that it can only be attributed to one of two things: Bourse interests or German influence. All that is said in the English press concerning Italian affairs is at all times marked by singular ineptitude and inaccuracy; but at the present crisis it is conspicuous for a resolute and unblushing concealment of facts. The unfortunate flattery which has been poured out on Italy by the German press and Parliament for their emperor's ends, and by the English press and Parliament out of hatred of France, has been taken for gospel truth by the Quirinale, the Palazzo Braschi, and every deputy and editor from Alps to Etna, and has fed the natural vanity of the Italian disposition, until, in a rude awakening, the whole nation finds itself on the brink of bankruptcy and anarchy.

To all conversant with the true state and real needs of the country ever since the death of Victor Emmanuel, the language of the German and English press and Parliaments has seemed almost insane in its optimism, as it has been most cruel in its fulsome falsehood. Much of the present woe may be attributed to it; for if Berlin and London had not taken, or pretended to take, Messer Francesco Crispi for a statesman, it is very possible that that ingenious lawyer might never have dragged his sovereign into the meshes of the Triple Alliance and the Slough of Despond of a bottomless debt. That unintelligent and interested flattery is as injurious to nations as to individuals and gives them vertigo, is a truth too frequently forgotten or purposely disregarded.

Perhaps one of the oddest and least admirable traits in the public opinion of the latest half of this century is its absolute unconsciousness of its own caprices and inconsequence; its entire ignorance of how flatly its assertions of to-day contradict those of yesterday and will be contradicted by those of to-morrow. History has accustomed us to such transmogrifications, and we know that power is potent to turn the insurgent into the reactionist, but certainly the drollest and most picturesque episode in connection with the Sicilian revolution is the arrest of the deputy De Felice, for inciting to civil war, coupled with the fact that the last deputy arrested for precisely the same cause was Francesco Crispi at the time of Aspromonte! History, in all its length and breadth, does not furnish us with any droller antithesis than that of Crispi as arrested and Crispi as arrester. The Italian press has contented itself with merely stating the circumstances, and letting them speak for themselves; the European press does not appear even to be aware of them. For the European press, with the exception of the French, the Crispi of Aspromonte is dead and buried, as the Crispi of Montecitorio and the Quirinale would desire that he should be. The prostration of the English press in especial before the latter is infinitely comical to those who know the real career of the fortunate Sicilian notary who began life as a penniless republican, and is ending it as a plutocrat, a reactionist, and a Knight of the Order of the Association. It is probable that Europe on the whole knows but little of the Crispi of Aspromonte; it is possible that De Felice and his friends will cause it to know more. Falstaff abjuring cakes and ale, and putting two mirthful roysterers in the pillory, would present the only companion picture worthy of comparison with the Crispi of Montecitorio gravely defending the seizure of the leader of the Fasci on the score that the offence of the latter is *lesa alla patria*. Why is revolutionary effort in '93 and '94 treason to the country when revolutionary effort in '59 and '48 was, we are taught by all Italian text-books, the most admirable patriotism? It is a plain question which will never be honoured by an answer. Crispi of Montecitorio does not condescend to reason; he finds it easier to use cannon and bayonets, as they were used against that Crispi of Aspromonte of whom he considers it ill-bred in anyone to remind him. Crispi understands the present era; he knows that it does not punish, or even notice, such inconsistencies, at least when they are the inconsistencies of successful men.

Were the national sense of humour as quick as it was in the days of Pulci and Boiardo this circumstance would be fatal to the dictatorship of the ex-revolutionist.

In the national litany of Italy the chief of gods invoked are Mazzini, Ugo Foscolo, Garibaldi, Manini, and a score of others of the same persuasion, and all the present generation (outside what are termed Black Society and Codini Circles) are reared in religious veneration of such names. Now, it does not matter in the least whether this veneration be well or ill founded, be wise or unwise; it has been taught to all the present youth and manhood of all liberal-minded Italian families as a duty, a pleasure, and a creed in one. What sense is there in blaming this multitude if they carry out their own principles to a logical conclusion, and refuse to see that the opinions which were noble and heroic in their fathers become treason and crime in themselves? The House of Savoy, by a lucky chance for itself, drew the biggest prize in the lottery of national events in 1859; but it was not to place the House of Savoy on the Italian throne that Garibaldi fought, and Mazzini conspired, and a host of heroes died in battle or in exile. To all those whose names are like trumpet-calls to us still, the merging of their ideal of United Italy into a mere royal state must have seemed bathos, must have caused the most cruel and heartbreaking disillusion. They accepted it because at the time, rightly or wrongly, they considered that they could do no less; but they suffered, as all must suffer who have cherished high and pure dreams and behold what is called the realisation of them in the common clay of ordinary circumstance.

No one can pretend that the chief makers of the union of the country were monarchical. They were Red; and were hunted, imprisoned, exiled, shot for the colour of their opinions, precisely in the same manner as the leaders of the Fasci and the deputies of the Extreme Left are being dealt with now. Measures of this kind are excusable in absolute or arbitrary governments, such as Russia or Prussia; but in a State which owes its very existence to revolutionary forces, they are an anomaly. It is truly the sad and sorry spectacle of the son turning on and strangling the father who begat him.

At the present date Italy is a military tyranny. It is useless to deny the fact. Many parts of the country are in a state of siege, as though actually invaded and conquered; and although recent events are alleged in excuse for this, it is by no means the first time that the army has been used for the suffocation of all public expression of feeling. Arbitrary and unexplained arrest has always been frequent; and when the sovereigns visit any city or town the gaols thereof have always been filled on the vigil of the visit with crowds of persons suspected of democratic or dangerous tendencies. A rigid censorship of telegrams has long existed, as inquisitorial as any censorship of an *ancien régime*; and at the present moment telegrams from Sicily are absolutely forbidden to be despatched. Wholesale invasion of the privacy of private houses takes place at the pleasure of the police, and seizure of private letters and papers follows at the caprice of the Questura.

Where is there any pretext of liberty? In what does the absolutism of 1894 differ from that of the Bourbon, or of the Este-Lorraine? In what sense can a Free Italy be said to exist? The Gallophobia now so general amongst English political speakers and writers may account for the determination in them to applaud the Italian Government, alike when it is wrong as when it is right; but it is quite certain that, whatever be the motive, the English press has, with very few exceptions, combined to hide from the English public the true circumstances and causes of a revolution which, however to be deplored in its excesses, is not a whit more blameable, or less interesting and excusable than the other revolutions of Italy which filled England with such delight and sympathy. The kingdom of Italy was created by revolution. As the life of a nation counts, it was but yesterday that Garibaldi's red shirt was pushed through the gates of Stafford House, narrowly escaping being torn to rags by the admiring and enthusiastic crowds of London. To the philosophic observer there is something extremely illogical in the present denunciation of men who are now doing nothing more than Garibaldi did with the applause of Europe and America. To set up statues in every public square to Garibaldi, and imprison Garibaldi Bosco, and charge with high treason De Felice Giuffrida, is a nonsense to which it is difficult to render homage.

It is well known that the King, unconstitutionally, refused to accept the Zanardelli Ministry because it would have led to reduction of the army, and, as a necessary consequence, to withdrawal from the German incubus. He is possessed with a mania for German influences; influences, of all others, the most fatal to public freedom and political liberty. Nothing in the whole world could have been so injurious to Italy as to fall, as she has done, under the mailed hand of the brutal Prussian example and exactions.

Germany has always been fatal to Italy, and always will be. The costly armaments which have made her penniless are due to Germany. Her army and navy receive annual and insulting inspection by Prussian princes. The time will probably come when German troops will be asked to preserve 'social order' in the cities and provinces of Italy. So long as the German alliance continues in its present form, so long will this danger for Italy always exist, that, in the event of the Italian army proving insufficient, or unwilling, to quell revolution, the timidity or despotism of Italian rulers may beg the aid of Germany to do so.

In the manifesto of the Extreme Left, after the fall of Giolitti, the state of the country was described in language forcible but entirely true.

'Commerce is stagnant, bankruptcy general, savings are seized, small proprietors succumb under fiscal exactions, agriculture languishes, stifled under taxation, emigration is increased in an alarming proportion to the population, the municipalities squander and become penniless; the country, in taxes of various kinds, pays no less than seventy per cent., *i.e.*, four or five times as much as is paid by rich nations. The material taxable diminishes every day, because production is paralysed in its most vital parts, and misery has shrunken consumption; in a word, the whole land is devoured by military exactions and the criminal folly of a policy given over to interests and ambitions which totally ignore the true necessities of the people. The hour is come to cry, "Hold, enough!" and to oblige the State not to impose burdens, but to make atonement.'

There is nothing exaggerated in these statements; they are strictly moderate, and understate the truth. The Extreme Left may or may not be Socialistic, but in its manifesto it is entirely within the truth, and describes with moderation a state of national suffering and penury which would render pardonable the greatest violence of language.

The Extreme Left affirms with the strictest truth that its members have never contributed to bring about the present misery, and are in no degree responsible for it. The entire responsibility lies with corrupt administration, and with military tyranny and extravagance.

When a people are stripped bare, and reduced to destitution, can it be expected, should it be dreamed, that they can keep their souls in patience when fresh taxes threaten them, and the hideous Juggernauth of military expenditure rolls over their ruined lives?

Italians have been too long deluded with the fables of men in office; and many years too long, patient under the intolerable exactions laid upon them. It is not only the imperial, but the municipal tyrannies which destroy them; they are between the devil and the deep sea; what the State does not take the Commune seizes. The most onerous and absurd fines await every trifling sin of omission or commission, every insignificant, unimportant, little forgetfulness leads to a penalty ridiculously disproportioned to the trifling offence—a little dust swept on to the pavement, a dog running loose, a cart left before a door, a guitar played in the street, a siesta taken under a colonnade, a lemon or a melon sold without permit to trade being previously purchased and registered, some infinitesimal trifle—for which the offender is dragged before the police and the municipal clerks, and mulcted in sums of three, five, ten, twenty, or thirty francs. Frequently a fine of two francs is quite enough to ruin the hapless offender. If he cannot pay he goes to prison.

The imperial tax of *ricchezza mobile* is levied on the poorest; often the bed has to be sold or the saucepans pawned to pay it. The pawning institutes are State affairs; their fee is nine per cent., and the goods are liable to be sold in a year. In France the fee is four per cent., and the goods are not liable to be sold for three years. When a poor person has scraped the money together to pay the fees, the official (*stimatore*) often declares that the article is more worthless than he thought, and claims a *calo* of from ten to a hundred francs, according to his caprice; if the *calo* be not paid the object is sold, though the nine per cent. for the past year may have been paid on it. The gate-tax, *dazio consumo*, best known to English ears as *octroi*, which has been the especial object of the Sicilian fury, is a curse to the whole land. Nothing can pass the gates of any city or town without paying this odious and inquisitorial impost. Strings of cattle and of carts wait outside from midnight to morning, the poor beasts lying down in the winter mud and summer dust. Half the life of the country people is consumed in this senseless stoppage and struggle at the gates; a poor old woman cannot take a few eggs her hen has laid, or a bit of spinning she has done, through the gates without paying for them. The wretched live chickens and ducks, geese and turkeys, wait half a day and a whole night cooped up in stifling crates or hung neck downwards in a bunch on a nail; the oxen and calves are kept without food three or four days before their passage through the gates, that they may weigh less when put in the scales. By this insensate method of taxation all the food taken into the cities and towns is deteriorated. The prating and interfering officers of hygiene do not attend to this, the greatest danger of all to health, *i.e.*, inflamed and injured carcasses of animals and poultry sent as food into the markets.

The municipalities exact the last centime from their prey; whole families are ruined and disappear through the exactions of their communes, who persist in squeezing what is already drained dry as a bone. The impious and insensate destruction of ancient quarters and noble edifices goes on because the municipal councillors, and engineers, and contractors fatten on it. The cost to the towns is enormous, the damage done is eternal, the debt incurred is incalculable, the loss to art and history immeasurable, but the officials who strut their little hour on the communal stage make their profits, and no one cares a straw how the city, town, or village suffer.

If the Italian States could have been united like the United States of America, and made strictly neutral like Belgium, their condition would have been much simpler, happier, and less costly. As a monarchy, vanity and display have ruined the country, while the one supreme advantage which she might have enjoyed, that of keeping herself free to remain the courted of all, she has wilfully and stupidly thrown away, by binding herself, hand

and foot, almost in vassalage, to Prussia. For this, there can be no doubt, unfortunately, that the present King is mainly responsible; and, strange to say, he does not even seem to be sensible of the magnitude of the evil of his act.

It is as certain as any event which has not happened can be, that nothing of what has now come to pass would have occurred but for the disastrous folly which has made the Government of Italy strain to become what is called a Great Power, and conclude alliances of which the unalterable condition has been a standing army of as vast extent as the expenditure for its maintenance is enormous. There is nothing abnormal in the present ruin of the country, nothing which cannot easily be traced to its cause, nothing which could not have been avoided by prudence, by modesty, and by renunciation. As the pitiful vanity and ambition to reach a higher grade than that which is naturally theirs beggars private individuals, so the craze to be equal with the largest empire, and to make an equal military and naval display with theirs, has caused a drain on the resources of the country, a pitiless pressure upon the most powerless and hopeless classes, which have spread misery broadcast over the land.

It might be deplorable, unwise, possibly thankless, if the country dismissed the House of Savoy; but in so doing the country would be wholly within its rights. The act would be in no sense whatever *lesa alla patria*; it might, on the contrary, be decided on, and carried out, through the very truest patriotism. The error of the House of Savoy is the same error as that of the House of Bonaparte; they forget that what has been given by a plebiscite, a later plebiscite has every right and faculty to withdraw. The English nation, when it put William of Orange on the throne, would have been as entirely within its rights and privileges had it put him down from it. When a sovereign accepts a crown from the vote of a majority, he must in reason admit that another larger and later majority can withdraw it from his keeping. A plebiscite cannot confer Divine Right. It cannot either confer any inalienable right at all. It is, therefore, entirely illogical and unjust to visit the endeavour and desire to make Italy a republic as a crime of high treason. An Italian has as much right to wish for a republican form of government, and to do what he can to bring it about, as the Americans of the last century had to struggle against the taxation of George III. And if the Casa Savoia be driven from the Quirinale, it will owe this loss of power entirely to its own policy, which has impoverished the nation beyond all endurance. The present King's lamentable and inexplicable infatuation for the German alliance, and all the frightful expenditure and sacrifice to which this fatal alliance has led, have brought the country to its present ruin.

At the moment at which these lines are written, the flames of revolution are destroying the public buildings of the city of Bari; before even these lines can be printed, who shall say that these flames may not have spread to every town in the Peninsula? Of course, the present revolts may be crushed by sheer armed force; but if a reign of terror paralyse the movement for awhile, if a military despotism crush and gag the life out of Palermo and Naples and Rome, as it has been crushed and gagged by similar means in Warsaw and in Moscow, the causes which have led to revolution will continue to exist, and its fires will but die down awhile, to break forth in greater fury in a near future. The Crispi of Montecitorio is now busy throwing into prison all over the country a large number of citizens, for doing precisely the same things as the Crispi of Aspromonte did himself, or endeavoured to do. But in the present age a man may abjure and ignore his own past with impunity. As it is always perfectly useless to refute Mr Gladstone's statements by quotations from his own earlier utterances, so it would be quite useless to hope to embarrass the Italian premier by any reminder of his own younger and revolutionary self. Renegades always are impervious to sarcasm, and pachydermatous against all reproach.

Crispi is very far from a great man in any sense of those words, *Au pays des aveugles le borgne est roi*, and he has had the supreme good fortune to have outlived all Italian men of eminence. If Cavour and Victor Emmanuel were living still, or even Sella and Minghetti and La Marmora, it is extremely probable that the costly amusement of making Crispi of Aspromonte First Minister of the Crown would never have been amongst the freaks of fate. He has had 'staying power,' and so has buried all those who would have kept him in his proper place. It is possible that if he had adhered to his earlier creeds he might have been by this time President of an Italian Republic, for his intelligence is keen and versatile, and his audacity is great and elastic. But he has preferred the more prosperous and less glorious career of a minister and a *maire du palais*. He has emerged with amazing insolence from financial discredit which would have made any other man ashamed to face the social and political worlds; and, *mirabile dictu!* having dragged his King and country into an abyss of poverty, shame and misery, he is still adored by the one and suffered to domineer over the other.

Successful in the vulgar sense of riches, of decorations, of temporary power, and of overweening Court favour, the Sicilian man of law is; successful in the higher sense of statesmanship, and the consolation of a suffering nation, he never will be. And that he has been permitted to return to power is painful proof of the weakness of will and the moral degradation of the country. There is no great man in Italy at the present hour, no man with the magnetism of Garibaldi, or the intellect of D'Azeglio, or even the rough martial talent of Victor Emmanuel, and in the absence of such the sly, subtle, fox-like lawyers, by whom the country is overrun, come to the front, and add one curse more to the many curses already lying on the head of Leopardi's beloved Mater Dolorosa. It is possible that, for want of a man of genius who would be able to gather into one the scattered forces, and fuse them into irresistible might by that magic which genius alone possesses, the cause of liberty will be once more lost in Italy. If such a leader do not appear, the present movement, which is not a revolt but a revolution in embryo, will probably be trampled out by armed despotism, and the present terror of the ruling classes of Europe before the bugbear of anarchy will be appealed to in justification of the refusal to a ruined people of the reforms and the atonement which they have, with full right, demanded.

January 1894.

BLIND GUIDES

Amongst the famous gardens of the world, the Orti Oricellari[D] must take a foremost place, alike for sylvan beauty and for intellectual tradition. Second only to the marvellous gardens of Rome, they were first, for loveliness and for association, amongst the many great and carefully-cultured gardens which once adorned Tuscany. Under the Rucellai their superb groves and glades sheltered the most intellectual meetings which Florence has ever seen. The Società Oricellari (which continued that imitation of the Platonic Academy created by Cosimo and Lorenzo) assembled here under the shade of the great forest trees. Here Machiavelli read aloud his Art of War, and here Giovanni Rucellai composed his Rosamunda. The house built for Bernardo Rucellai by Leon Battista Alberti was a treasure-house of art, ancient and contemporary; and learning, literature and philosophy found their meet home under the ilex and cedar shadows, and in the fragrant air of the orange and myrtle boughs. High thoughts and scholarly creation were never more fitly housed than here. Their grounds, covered with trees, plants, fruits and flowers, were then known as the Selva dei Rucellai, and must have been of much larger extent in the time of Machiavelli than they had become even in the eighteenth century; for when Palla Rucellai fled in fear of being compromised in the general hatred of all the Medici followers and friends, he left the Selva by a little postern door in its western wall which opened on to the Porta Prato and the great meadow then surrounding that gateway. Therefore they must then have covered all the space now occupied by the detestable modern streets called Magenta, Solferino, Montebello, Garibaldi, etc., and I have myself indeed conversed with persons who remember, in their youth, the orchards appertaining to these gardens existing where there are now the ugly boulevards and the dirt and lumber of the railway and tramway works.

On this unfortunate flight of Palla in 1527, the populace broke into the gardens, and destroyed the statues, obelisks and temples which ornamented them, but the woods and orchards they appear to have spared; for, some thirty years later, the park seems to have been in its full perfection still, when Ferdinand, in the height of a violent and devoted passion, gave it to his Venetian mistress as her *casin de piacere*, and Bianca brought a mode of life very unlike that of the grave and scholarly Rucellai into its classic groves; for although her fate was tragic, and her mind must have been ever apprehensive of foul play, she was evidently of a gay, mirthful, pleasure-loving temperament.

The jests and pranks, the sports and pastimes, the conjuring and comedy, the mirth and music, the dances and mummeries, which pleased the taste of Bianca and her women, replaced the 'noble sessions of free thought' and the illustrious fellowship of the Academicians. The gravity and decorum of the philosophical society departed, but the floral and sylvan beauty remained. At the time when she filled its glades with laughter and song and the beauty of her women, the Selva was what was even then called an English garden, with dense woods, wide lawns, deep shade, and mighty trees which towered to the skies. But when it passed into the hands of Giancarlo de' Medici that Cardinal decorated it with a grotto, a giant, and other *gentilezze*, and changed it into an Italian garden, with many sculptural and architectural wonders, and plants and flowers from foreign countries, employing in his designs Antonio Novelli, who, amongst other feats, brought water to it from the Pitti, and built up an artificial mountain in its midst. He must have done much to disfigure it, more than the mob of 1527 had done; but soon after these ill-considered works were completed the gardens passed to the Ridolfi, who, preserving the rare flowers and fruits, with which the Cardinal had planted it, allowed the woodland growth to return to its freedom and luxuriance. Of him who ultimately restricted the park to its present limits, and robbed the house of all its treasures of art and admirable ornament, there is, I believe, no record. From the Ridolfi it went to a family of Ferrara, of the name of Canonici, and from them to the Stiozzi, who sold it in our own time to Prince Orloff, by whose heir it has once more been put up for sale. Amidst all these changes the beauty of the park, though impaired, has existed much as it was when it was celebrated in Latin and Italian prose and verse, although diminished in size and shorn of its grandeur, invaded on all sides by bricks and mortar, and cruelly violated, even in its inmost precincts. The house has been miserably modernised, and the gardens and glades miserably lopped, yet still there is much left; and many of their historic trees still lift their royal heads to morning dawn and evening stars. Enough remains to make a green oasis in the desert of modern bricks and stucco; enough remains for the student to realise that he stands beneath boughs of cedar and ilex which once sheltered the august brows of Leone X. and cast their shade on the gathered associates of that literary society of which no equal has ever since been seen. The gardens, even in their shrunken and contracted space and verdure, are still there, priceless in memories and invaluable to the artist, the student and the lover of nature and of history.

It seems scarcely credible, yet such is the fact, that these treasures of natural beauty and storehouses of historical association should have already once been invaded to build the ordinary modern house called Palazzo Sonnino, and that now the municipality is about to purchase half of them — for what purpose? — *to cut the trees down and cover the ground with houses for the use of its own office-holders*, those multitudinous and pestilent *impiegati* who are the curse of the public all over Italy, and feed on it like leeches upon flesh. That the destruction of such gardens as these for such a purpose can even be for an instant spoken of is proof enough of the depths of degradation to which public indifference and municipal vandalism have sunk in the city of Lorenzo. It can only be equalled by the destruction of the Farnesina and Ludovisi gardens. Few places on earth have such intellectual memories as the Oricellari gardens; yet these are disregarded as nought, and the cedars and elms which shaded the steps of philosophers and poets, of scholarly princes and mighty Popes, are to be felled, as though they were of no more value than worm-eaten mill-posts.

That a people can be *en masse* so utterly dead to memory, to greatness, to beauty, and to sense, makes any serious thinker despair of its future. There are waste grounds (grounds already deliberately laid waste) yawning by scores already, in the town and around it, on which any new buildings which may be deemed necessary might be raised. There is not one thread or shadow of excuse for the abominable action now contemplated by the Florence Municipality, and certain to be consummated unless some opposition, strong and resolute, arise. Even were the Orti Oricellari a mere ordinary park, without tradition, without heritage, without association, it would be imbecility to cover the site with bricks and mortar, for Maxime du Camp has justly written that whoever fells a tree in a city commits a crime. 'Chaque fois qu'un arbre tombe dans une ville trop peuplée cela équivaut à un meurtre et parfois à une épidémie. On a beau multiplier les squares, ils ne remplaceront jamais la ceinture de forêt qui devrait entourer toute capitale et lui verser l'oxygène, la force, et la santé.' These are words salutary and true, which would be well inscribed in letters of gold above the council chamber of every municipality. When towns are desperately pinched for space, hemmed in on every side, and at their wits' end for lodging-room, there may be some kind of credible excuse for the always mistaken destruction of gardens, trees and groves. But in all the cities of Italy there is no such excuse; there are vast unoccupied lands all around them; and in their midst more, many more, houses than are occupied. In Rome and Florence the latter may be counted by many thousands. There is not the feeblest, flimsiest pretext for such execrable destruction as has already overtaken so many noble gardens in the former city, and now menaces the Orti Oricellari in the latter.

Nor is this Selva, although the most famous, the only garden which is being destroyed in Florence, whilst many beautiful glades and lawns have been, in the last ten years, ruthlessly ruined and effaced that the wretched and trumpery structures of the jerry-builders may arise in their stead. The Riccardi garden in Valfonda was once like that of the Oricellari, a marvel of loveliness; and its lawns, its avenues, its marbles, its deep, impenetrable shades, its sunlit orange-walks and perfumed pergolate, surrounded a house which was a temple of art and contained many choice statues of ancient and contemporary masters. Talleyrand once said that no one who had not lived before the great revolution could ever know how perfect life could be. I would say that none can know how perfect it can be who did not live in the Italy of the Renaissance. Take the life of this one man, Riccardo, Marchese Riccardi, who spent most of his existence in this exquisite pleasure-place, which he inherited from its creator, the great scholar and *dilettante*, Romolo Riccardi, and where he resided nearly all the year round. In the contemporary works of Cinelli on the *Bellezze di Firenze*, his house and gardens are described; they are alluded to by Redi, —

'Nel bel giardino

Nei bassi di gualfondo inabissato

Dove tieni il Riccardi alto domino.'

They are spoken of in admiration by Baldinucci, and, in the description of the festival of Maria de' Medici's marriage by proxy to Henri Quatre, they are enthusiastically praised by the younger Buonarotti. The court of the Casino was filled with ancient marbles, busts, statues and inscriptions, Latin and Greek; the exterior was decorated in fresco and tempera, with many rare sculptures and paintings and objects of art, whilst, without, a number of avenues led in all directions from the house to the gardens and the woods, where, in shade of ilex and cypress, marble seats and marble statues gave a sense of refreshing coolness in the hottest noon. Here this elegant scholar and accomplished noble passed almost all his time, receiving all that was most learned and illustrious in the society of his epoch; and occasionally giving magnificent entertainments like that with which he bade farewell to Maria de' Medici. Of this delicious retreat a few trees alone remain now; a few trees, which raise their sorrowful heads amongst the bricks and mortar, the theatres and photographic studios, around them, are all that are left of the once beautiful and poetic retreat of the scholars and courtiers, the ambassadors and *illuminati*, of the family of the Riccardi. Why has not such a place as this once was been religiously preserved through all time, for the joy, health and beauty of the city?

It would be scarcely possible for so beautiful and precious a life as this of the Riccardi to be led in our times, because it is scarcely possible, lock our gates as we may, to escape from the detestable atmosphere of excitation and worry which is everywhere around. The mania of senseless movement is now in the human race, as the saltatory delirium seized on the Neapolitan peasants and hurried them in crowds into the sea.

Riccardo Riccardi living now would be ashamed to dwell the whole year round in his retreat of Valfonda; would waste his time over morning newspapers, cigars and ephemeral telegraphic despatches; would probably spend his money on horse-racing; would send his blackletter folios, his first copies, and his before-letter prints to the hammer, and would make over his classic marbles to the Louvre, the Hermitage, or to his own government. He and his contemporaries had the loveliness of leisure and the wisdom of meditation; they knew that true culture is to be gained in the library, not in the rush of a *pérégrinomanie*; and being great, noble and rich, judged aright that the best gifts given by high position and large fortune are the liberty which they allow for repose, and the power which such repose confers to enjoy reflection and possession. In modern life this faculty is almost wholly lost, and the wit and the fool are shaken together in the vibration of railway trains, and jostled together in the eating-houses of the world, till, if the fool thus obtain a varnish of sharpness, the wit has lost all individuality and grace.

Not long since, I said to an Englishman who has filled high posts and attained high honours, whilst public life is always repugnant to his tastes and temperament, that he would have been wiser to have led his own life in his own way, under his own ancestral roof-tree in England; and he answered, 'I would willingly have done so, but they would have said that I had nothing in me!' Characteristic nineteenth century reply! Romolo and Riccardo Riccardi did not trouble themselves in their different generations what their contemporaries thought of them. They led their own lives in their own leafy solitude, and only called their world about them when they were themselves disposed to entertain it.

The gardens of the Gaddi were equally and still earlier renowned, and in them the descendants of Taddeo Gaddi had a pleasure-house wondrous and lovely to behold, while the rich gallery of pictures annexed to it was situated next to the Valfonda, and covered what is now the new Piazza di S. M. Novello. These descendants had become great people and eminent in the church, many cardinals and monsignori amongst them, and also celebrated *letterati*, of whom Niccolo, son of Senibaldo, was the most illustrious. He, as well as a scholar and patron of letters and arts, was, like the Riccardi, a botanist, and, as may be seen in the pages of Scipione Ammirato, was foremost for his culture of sweet herbs and of lemons and citrons. Whilst he filled worthily the post of ambassador and of collector of works of art for the Medici, he never forgot his garden and his herb-garden, and was the first to make general in Tuscany the Judas-tree, the gooseberry, the strawberry, the Spanish myrtle, the northern fir and other then rare fruits and shrubs. So fragrant and so fair were his grounds, that the populace always called them, and the vicinity perfumed by them, Il Paradiso dei Gaddi. This beautiful retreat has for centuries been entirely destroyed and forgotten; and all which is left of the rich collections of the Gaddi are those thousand manuscript folios which Francis I. of Austria purchased and gave to the libraries of Florence, where to this day they remain and can be read.

The director of the Gaddi gardens bore the delightful name of Messer Giuseppe Benincasa Fiammingo; and a contented life indeed this worthy and accomplished student must have led, working for such a patron, and passing the peaceful seasons and fruitful years amidst the cedar-shadows and the lemon-flower fragrance of this abode of the Muses and of Flora and Pomona.

We dwell too much upon the strife and storm, the bloodshed and the internecine feuds of the passed centuries; we forget too often the many happy and useful lives led in them, which were spent untroubled and consecrated to fair studies and pursuits, and which let the clangour of battle go by unheard, and mingled not with camp or court or council.

We forget too often the placid life of Gui Patin under his cherry trees by the river, or of the Etiennes, in the learned and happy seclusion of their classic studies and noble work, even their women speaking Latin as their daily and most natural tongue; we only have ear for the fusillades of the Fronde, or the war-cries of Valois and Guise. In like manner we are too apt only to dwell upon the daggers and poison powders, the factions and feuds, the conspiracies and the city riots of the Moyenage and Renaissance, and forget the many quiet, useful, happy persons clad in doublet and hose, like Messer Benincasa, and the many learned and noble gentlemen clothed in velvet and satin, like Niccolo Gaddi, his master, who passed peacefully from their cradle to their grave.

In the fifteenth century, according to Benedetto Varchi, who himself saw them, there were no less than a hundred and thirty of these magnificent demesnes in the city; and whatever may have been the sins of the earlier and the follies of the later Medici, that family, one and all, loved flowers, woods and lawns, and fostered tenderly 'il gusto del giardinaggio' in their contemporaries. This taste in their descendants has entirely disappeared. They are bored by such of the magnificent gardens of old as still exist in their towns and around their villas; they abandon them without regret, grudging the care of keeping them up, and letting them out to nursery gardeners or to mere peasants whose only thought is, of course, to make profit out of them.

The Latins were at all times celebrated for their beautiful gardens; all classic records and all archæological discoveries prove it. The Romans and the Tuscans, the Venetians and the Lombards, in later mediæval times, inherited this elegant taste, this art, which is twin child itself with Nature; but in our immediate epoch it has vanished; the glorious legacies of it are supported with indifference or done away with without regret. How is this to be explained? I know not unless the reason be that there has come from without a contagion of vulgarity, avarice and bad taste which the Italian temperament has been too weak to resist, and with which it has become saturated and debased. The modern Italian will throw money away recklessly on the Bourses or at the gaming-tables; he will spend it frivolously at foreign baths and fashionable seaports; he will let himself be ruined by a pack of idle and good-for-nothing hangers-on whom he has not the courage to shake off; but he grudges every penny which is required for the maintenance of woodland and garden, and he will allow his trees to be felled, his myrtles, bays and laurels to vanish, his fountains to be choked up by sand or weed, and his lawns to degenerate into rough pasture, without shame or remorse.

Almost all these noble gardens enumerated by Varchi still existed in Florence before 1859. Now but few remain. Even the Torrigiani gardens (which for many reasons one would have supposed would have been kept intact by that family) have been almost entirely destroyed within the last year, and the site of them is being rapidly covered with mean and ugly habitations. The magnificent Capponi garden, so dear to the blind statesman and scholar, Gino Capponi, has been more than half broken up by his heirs. The renowned Serristori garden was cut in two and shorn of half of its beauty when the first half of the Via dei Bardi was destroyed. The Guadagni garden is advertised as building ground. The Guicciardini gardens are still standing, but as they and their palace have been given over to amalgamated railway companies, the respite accorded to them will probably be of brief duration. The bead roll of these devastated pleasure-grounds and historic groves could be continued in an almost endless succession of names and memories, and the immensity of their irreparable loss to the city is scarcely to be estimated. When we reflect, moreover, that before 1859 the whole of the ground from the Carraia Bridge westward was pasture and garden and avenue, where now there are only bricks and mortar and a network of ugly streets, we shall more completely comprehend the senseless folly which built over such green places, or, where it did not build, made in their stead such barren, dusty, featureless, blank spaces as the Piazza degli Zuavi and its congeners.

Ubaldino Peruzzi (who has been buried with pomp in Santa Croce!) was the chief promoter and leader of this mania of demolition. It was at his instigation that the Ponte alle Grazie and the chapel of the Alberti were pulled down; that the Tetto dei Pisani was destroyed to make way for an ugly bank; that the noble trees at the end of the Cascine were felled to make way for a gaudy, gingerbread bust and a hideous guardhouse; that the beautiful Stations of the Cross leading to San Miniato al Monte were destroyed to give place to vulgar eating-houses and trumpery villas; and that old palaces, old gardens and old churches were laid waste to create the bald and monotonous quays called severally the Lung Arno Serristori and Torrigiani. Peruzzi began, and for many years directed, the destruction of the beauties of the city, and only stopped when, having brought the town to the verge of bankruptcy, funds failed him, and he retired perforce from municipal office.

But if it may be feared that the good we do does perish with us, it is certain that the evil we do does long survive us, and flourishes and multiplies when we are dust. The lessons which Peruzzi taught his fellow-citizens in speculation and spoliation will long remain, whilst his bones crumble beneath a lying epitaph. His dead hand still directs the scrambling haste with which the historic centre of the city is being torn down, in order that glass galleries, brummagem shops, miserable statues, and a general reign of stucco and shoddy, may, as far as in them lies, bring the Athens of Italy to a level with some third-rate American township.

Except with a few rare exceptions, Italians are wholly unable to comprehend the indignation with which their callousness fills the cultured observer of every other nationality. Anxiety to get ready-money, an ignorance of their true interests, and a babyish love of new things, however vulgar or barbarous, have completely extinguished, in the aristocracy and bureaucracy, all sentiment for the arts and all reverence for their inheritance and for the beauty of Nature. It would seem as if a kind of paralysis of all perception had fallen on the whole nation. A prince of great culture, refinement and reputed taste having occasion this year to repair his palace, has stuccoed and coloured it all over a light ochre yellow! A great noble sold his ancestral gardens last year to a building company, and his family clapped their hands with delight as the first ilex trees fell beneath the axe! To make a *paven* street in Venice, unneeded, incongruous, vulgar, abhorrent to every educated eye and mind, Byzantine windows, Renaissance doorways, admirable scrollworks, enchanting façades, marbles, and mosaics, of hues like the sea-shell and the sea-mouse, are ruthlessly torn down and pushed out of sight for ever. Ruskin in vain protests, his tears scorched up by his rage, and both alike powerless. Gregorovius died recently, his last years embittered and tortured by the daily destruction of the Rome so sublime and sacred to him. I remember well the day when the axe was first laid to the immemorial groves of the Farnesina: a barbarous and venal act, done to gratify private spleen and greed, leaving a mere mass of mud and dirt where so late had been the gracious gardens which had seen Raffaelle and Petrarca pace beneath their shade. The Spanish Duke, Ripalda, whose passionate love for his Farnesina was known to all Rome, died of the sorrow and fever brought on by seeing its desecration, died actually of a broken heart. 'I shall not long survive them,' he said to me, the tears standing in his proud eyes, as he looked on the ruin of his avenues and lawns, which had so late been the chief beauty of the Tiber, facing their sponsor and neighbour, the majestic Farnese Palace.

To the student, the artist, the archæologist, to live in Rome now is to suffer inexpressibly every hour, in mind and heart.

Who does not know the piazza of San Giovanni Laterano as it was? The most exquisite scene of earth stretched around the most beautiful basilica of the world! Go there now: the horizon is closed and the landscape effaced, vile modern erections, crowded, paltry, monstrous in their impudence and in their degradation, shut out the green plains, the azure hills, the divine, ethereal distance, and close around the spiritual beauty of the great church, like bow-legged ban-dogs round a stag at bay. The intolerable outrage of it, the inconceivable shame of it, the crass obstinacy and stupidity which make such havoc possible, should fill the dullest soul with indignation. Yet such things are being done yearly, daily, hourly, ceaselessly, and with impunity all over Italy, and no voice is raised in protest. Whenever any such voice is raised, it is seldom that of an Italian; it is that of Ruskin, Story, Yriarte, Taine, Vernon Lee, Augustus Hare, or it is my own, to the begetting of ten thousand enemies, to the receiving of twice ten thousand maledictions.

Nor is it only in the great cities that such ruin is wrought. In every little hamlet, on every hill and plain there is the same process of destruction going on, which I have before compared to the growth of lupus on a human face. Rapidly, in every direction, the beauty, the marvellous, the incomparable, natural, and architectural beauty of the country is being destroyed by crass ignorance and still viler greed.

Along those famous hillsides, which rise above Careggi, there was, until a few months ago, a landmark dear to all the countryside, a line of colossal cypresses which had been planted there by the hand of the Pater Patriæ, Cosimo de' Medici himself. These grand and noble trees were lately sold, with the ground on which they stood, to a native doctor of Florence, who *immediately felled them*. Yet if before this unpardonable action, in looking on the fallen giants, anyone is moved to see the pity of it and curse the stupid greed which set the axe at their sacred trunks, he who does so mourn is never the prince, the noble, the banker, the merchant, the tradesman; it is some foreign painter or scholar, or some peasant of the soil who remembers the time when one vast avenue connected Florence and Prato.

Within one mile of each other there are, near Florence, a green knoll, crowned with an ancient church, and a river, shaded by poplar trees; the beauty of the hill was an historic tower, dating from the year 1000, massive, mighty, very strong, having withstood the wars of eight centuries; at its foot was a stately and aged stone pine. The beauty of the river was a wide bend, where the trees and the hills opened out from the water, and a graceful wooden bridge spanned it, chiefly used by the millers' carts and the peasants' mules. In the gracious spring-time of last year, the old tower was pulled down to be used for building materials, for which it was found that it could not be used, and the stone pine was felled, because its shade prevented a few beans to the value of, perhaps, two francs growing beneath it. On the river the white wooden bridge has been pulled down, and a huge, red, brick structure, like a ponderous railway bridge, hideous, grotesque, and shutting out all the sylvan view up stream, has been erected in its stead, altogether unfitted for the slender rural traffic which alone passes there, and costing a heavy price, levied by taxation from a rural, and far from rich, community. Thus are two exquisite landscapes wantonly ruined; no one who has known those scenes, as they were a year ago, can endure to look at them as they are. There was no plea or pretext of necessity for such a change; the one was due to private greed, the other to municipal brutishness and speculation; some persons are a few pounds the heavier in purse, the country is for ever so much the poorer.

There is, within another mile, an old castellated villa with two mighty towers, one at either end, and within it chambers panelled with oak carvings of the Quattro Cento, of great delicacy and vigour of execution; it stands amidst a rich champagne country, abounding in vine and grain and fruits, and bears one of the greatest names of history. *It is now about to be turned into a candle manufactory!* In vain do the agriculturists around protest that the filthy stench of the offal which will be brought there, and the noxious fumes of the smoke, which will pour from the furnace chimney about to be erected amongst its fir-trees, will do infinite harm to the vineyards and orchards around. No one gives ear to their lament. Private cupidity and communal greed run hand in hand; and the noble building is doomed beyond hope. Who can hold their soul in patience or seal their lips to silence before such impiety and imbecility as this?

When this kind of destruction is going on everywhere, in every city, town, village, province, commune, all over Italy, who can measure the ultimate effects upon the face of the country? What, in ten years' time, will be left of it as Eustace and Stendahl saw it? What, in twenty years' time, will be left of it as we now know it? Every day some architectural beauty, some noble avenue, some court or loggia or gateway, some green lawn, or shadowy ilex grove, or sculptured basin, musical with falling water, and veiled with moss and maidenhair, is swept away for ever that some jerry-builder may raise his rotten walls or some tradesman put up his plate-glass front, or some dreary desert of rubble and stones delight the eyes of wise modernity.

It is impossible to imagine any kind of building more commonplace, more ugly, and less suitable to the climate than the modern architecture, or rather masons' work, which has become dear to the modern Italian mind. It is the kind of house which was built in London twenty or thirty years ago, and now in London is despised and detested. The fine old hospital of Santa Lucia, strong as a rock, and sound as an oak, has recently been knocked down by a man who, returning with a fortune made in America, desired to be able to name a street after himself. (Streets used to be named after heroes who dwelt in them; they are now named after *rastaqouères*, who pull them down and build them up again.) Instead of the hospital, there are erected some houses on the model of London houses of thirty years ago, with narrow, ignoble windows and façades of the genuine Bayswater and Westbourne Grove type. There has not been one opposing voice to their erection, and any censure of them is immediately answered by a reference to the brand-new dollars of their builder. In the suburbs it is the hideous cottage (here called *villino*), which, having disgraced the environs of London and Paris, is now rapturously set up in the neighbourhood of Italian towns. Both these types of house-building (for architecture it is absurd to call it) are as degraded as they can possibly be; and, whereas the London and Paris suburban cottages have frequently the redeeming feature of long windows down to the ground, modern Italian houses have narrow windows of the meanest possible kind, affording no light in winter and no air in summer. The horrible English fashion of putting a window on each side of a narrow doorway is considered beautiful in Italy, and slavishly followed everywhere, whilst the climbing roses and evergreen creepers which in England and France so constantly cover the poorness of modern houses, are, in Italy, only conspicuous by their absence. The noble loggias, and balconies, and colonnades of old Italian mansions were in the old time run over with the tea rose, the glycine and the banksia; but the wretched modern Italian 'villino' is, in all its impudence, naked and not ashamed.

These dreadful modern constructions, with flimsy walls, slate roof, pinched doorway, mean windows, commonness, cheapness and meanness staring from every brick in their body, are disgracing the approach of every Italian city; they are met with climbing the slope of Bellosguardo, beside the hoary walls of Signa, behind the cypresses of the Poggio Imperiale, on the road to the Ponte Nomentana, outside the Porta Salara, on the way to the baths of Caracalla, close against the walls of the Colosseum, above the green canal water of Venice, in front of the glad blue sea by Santa Lucia, anywhere, everywhere, insulting the past, making hideous the present, suited to no season and absurd in every climate, the rickety offspring of a century incapable of artistic procreation.

It is impossible to enter into the minds of men who actually consider it a finer thing, a prouder thing, to be a third-rate, mediocre, commercial city than to be the first artistic, or the noblest historic, city of the world. Yet this is what the modern Italian, the Italian who governs in ministry, bureaucracy, municipality, and press, deliberately does prefer. He thinks it more glorious, and worthier, to be a feeble imitation of a shoddy American city than to be supreme in historic, artistic and natural beauty. He will sell his Tiziano, his Donatello, his Greek and Roman marbles, and his Renaissance tapestries without shame; and he will pant and puff with pride because he has secured a dirty tramway coaling-yard, has befouled his atmosphere with mephitic vapours and coal-tar gas, and has reduced his lovely *verzaja*, so late green with glancing foliage and fresh with rippling water, into a howling desert of iron rails, shot rubbish, bricks and mortar, unsightly sheds, and smoke-belching chimneys. To the educated observer the choice is as piteous and as grotesque as that of the South Sea Islander greedily exchanging his pure, pear-shaped, virgin pearl for the glass and pinchbeck of a Birmingham brooch.

Not many years ago there was in these gardens of the Oricellari of which I have spoken a neglected statue lying unnoticed in a darksome place. It was the Cupid of Michaelangelo, which, being discovered by the sculptor Santerelli, there and then was sold to the South Kensington Museum, where it may be seen to-day. This will ere long be the fate of all the sculptures and statues of Italy, and the 'modern spirit' now prevailing in the country will consider it best that it should be so.

The empty word of 'progress' which is repeated by all nations in this day, as if they were parrots, and has as much meaning in it as if it were only 'poor poll,' is continually used to cover, or feign to excuse, all these barbarous enormities; but most insincerely, most vainly. To turn a rich agricultural country into a fourth-rate manufacturing one can claim neither sagacity nor prudence as its defence. To demolish noble, ancient and beautiful things, in order to reproduce the modern mushroom-growths of a dreary and dusty 'western township,' can allege neither sense nor shrewdness as its excuse; it is simply extremely silly; even if inspired by greed it is both silly and short-sighted. Yet it is the only thing which the Italian municipal councils consider it excellent to do; they have, after their manner, sufficiently paid tribute to the arts when they have chipped a Luca Della Robbia medallion out of an ancient wall and put it away in a glass case in some gallery, or when they have taken an altar (as they have just taken the silver altar out of San Giovanni) and locked it up in some museum where nobody goes.[E]

To the arguments of common sense that an altar is as safe, and as visible, in the baptistery as in a museum, and that five centuries have passed over Luca's out-of-door work without wind or weather, heat or frost, impairing it in the least, no one in the municipal council of any town would for a moment attend. They do not want reason or fitness; they only want the vaporous, fussy, greedy, braggart 'modern tone.'

Everyone who has visited Florence knows the house fronting the gate of San Pier Gattolino (Porta Romana), on the front of which are found remnants of an almost wholly damaged fresco, through which a window has been cut. The house was once radiant with the frescoes of Giovanni di San Giovanni, which Cosimo dé Medici caused to be painted on its façade, because fronting the gateway by which all travellers came from Rome, 'it was to be desired, for the honour of the city, that the first impression of all such travellers should be one of joy and beauty, to the end that such strangers might receive pleasure therein and tarry willingly.' This wise and hospitable reasoning has been utterly lost sight of by those who rule our modern cities, and the approaches to all of them are defiled and disfigured, so that the heart of the traveller sinks within his breast. Instead of Cosimo's gay and gracious fresco-pageantry upon the walls, there are only now, by the Romano gate, a steam tramway belching filthy smoke, a string of carts waiting to be taxed, and a masons' scaffolding where lately towered the Torrigiani trees!

Reflect for a moment what the rule of—we will not say an Augustus, but merely of a Magnifico, of a Francois Premier—might have made in these thirty years of modern Italy. Marvellous beauty, incomparable grandeur of form, surpassing loveliness of Nature, entire sympathy of the cultured world and splendour immeasurable of tradition and example, all these after the peace of Villafranca, as after the breach of Porta Pia, lay ready to the hand of any ruler of the land who could have comprehended their meaning and their magnificence, their assured opportunity and their offered harmony.

But there was no one; and the moment has long passed.

The country has been guided instead into the trumpery and ephemeral triumphs of what is called modern civilisation, and an endless expenditure has gone hand in hand with a mistaken policy.

Whenever a royal visit is made to any Italian town, the preparations for it invariably include some frightful act of demolition, as when at Bologna, on the occasion of the late state visit of the sovereigns, the noble Communal Palace of that city was bedaubed all over with a light colouring, and its exquisitely picturesque and irregular casements were altered, enlarged, and cut about into the mathematical monotony dear to the municipal mind, no one present having sense to see that all the harmony and dignity of its architecture were ruthlessly obliterated. Some similar action is considered necessary in every town, big or little, before the reception of any prince, native or foreign. The results are easily conceived. It is said that William of Germany did not conceal his ridicule of the colossal equestrian statues in *pasteboard* which were set up in the station entrance at Rome in his honour; but as a rule the royal persons in Europe appear not to have any artistic feeling to offend. The only two who had any were hurled in their youth, by a tragic fate, out of a world with which they had little affinity. Those who remain have no sympathy for tradition or for the arts. The abominations done daily in their names and before their eyes leave them wholly unmoved. Nay, it is no secret that they do constantly approve and urge on the vandalism of their epoch.

The Italian people would have been easily led into a higher and wiser form of life. (I speak of the Italian people as distinguished from the Italian bureaucracy and borghesia, which are both of a crass and hopeless philistinism.) The country people especially have an artistic sense still latent in them, and they remain often artistic in their attire, despite the debasing temptations of cheap and vulgar modern clothing. Their ear for music is generally perfect, they detect instantly the false note or the faulty chord which many an educated hearer might let pass unnoticed. Their national songs, serenades, and poems are admirable in purity and grace, and although now, alas! comparatively rarely heard on hillside and by seashore, they remain essentially the verse of the people. Unfortunately this part of the nation is absolutely unrepresented. The noisy agitator, the greedy office-seeker, the unscrupulous politician, the pert, unhealthy lawyer crowd to the front and screech and roar until they are esteemed both at home and abroad to be the sole and indivisible 'public,' whilst their influence, by intrigue and bustle, does most unhappily predominate in all spheres municipal and political; and the entire press, subsidised by them, justifies them in all they do and pushes their selfish and soulless speculations down the throats of unwilling and helpless men.

'Mi son meco,' says Benedetto Varchi, 'molte volte stranamente maravigliato com' esser posso che in quelli uomini i quali son usati per piccolissimo prezzo, insino della prima fanciullezza loro, a portare le balle della Lana in guisi di facchini, e le sporte della Seta a uso di zanaiuoli, ed in somma a star poco meno che schiavi tutto il giorno, e gran pezza della notte alla Caviglia e al fuso, si ritrovi poi in molti di loro, dove e quando bisogna, tanta grandezza d'anima e cosi nobili e alti pensieri, che sappiamo, e osino non solo di dire ma di fare quelle tante e si belle cose, ch' eglino parte dicono, e parte fanno.'[F]

A people of whom this was essentially, and not merely rhetorically, true, would have been with little difficulty kept within the fair realm of art and guided to a fine ideal, in lieu of being given for their guides the purchased quill-men of a venal journalism, and bidden to worship a dirty traction-engine, a plate-glass shop front, and a bridge of cast-iron, painted red.

If through the last thirty years a sovereign with the cultured tastes of a Leonello d'Este or a Lorenzo del Moro, had been dominant in the councils of Italy, he would have made his influence and his desires so felt that the municipalities and ministries would not have dared to commit the atrocities they have done. Constitutional monarchs may be powerless in politics, but in art and taste their power for good and for evil is vast. Alas! in no country in Europe is any one of them a scholar or a connoisseur. They have no knowledge of the one field in which alone their influence would be unhampered, and might be salutary. They think themselves forced to pat and praise the modern playthings of war and science, and of beauty they have no conception, of antiquity they have merely jealousy.

It is to be deplored, not only as a national, but as a world-wide, loss that Modern Italy has entirely missed and misconceived the way to true greatness and to true prosperity. In other centuries she was the light of the world; in this she deliberately prefers to be the valet of Germany and the ape of America. Had there been men capable of comprehending her true way to a new life, and capable of leading her varied populations in that way, she might have seen a true and a second Renaissance. But those men are not existing, have not existed, within recent times for her; her chiefs have all been men who, on the contrary, knew nothing of art and cared nothing for nature; a statesman like Cavour, a conspirator like Mazzini, a free-lance like Garibaldi, a soldier like Victor Emmanuel were none of them men to understand, much less to re-create, the true genius of the nation; their eyes were fixed on political troubles, on social questions, on acquisition of territory, on quarrels with the Pope, and alliances with reigning houses. Since their death lesser people have taken their places, but have all followed in the same tracks, have all misled the nation to imagine that her *risorgimento* lies in copying American steam-engines and keeping ironclads ready for a signal from the potentate of Berlin.

Italy might be now, as she was in the past, the Muse, the Grace, the Artemis and the Athene of the world; she thinks it a more glorious thing to be only one amongst a sweating mob of mill-hands.

Italy, beautiful, classic, peaceful, wise with the wisdom inherited from her fathers, would have been the garden of the world, the sanctuary of pure art and of high thought, the singer of immortal song. Instead, she has deliberately chosen to be the mere imitator of a coarse and noisy crowd on the other side of the Atlantic, and the mere echo of the armed bully who dictates to her from the banks of the Spree.

L'UOMO FATALE

If there were any free speech or free action in matters political permitted in what is known as Free Italy, it would be at once interesting and useful to ask of its Government under what *régime* they govern? Is it under a constitutional monarchy, a dictatorship, a military despotism, or what? The reply would probably be that it is still a constitutional monarchy with popular parliamentary representation. But the counter reply would be: Then why are all the restraints limiting a constitutional sovereign broken through and all the privileges appertaining to, and creating the purpose of, parliamentary representation violated or ignored? When the king of a constitutional Italy violated the Constitution in refusing the Zanardelli Cabinet because it did not promise acquiescence in his own views, the country should have protested, and insisted on the Zanardelli Cabinet being placed in power for the sake of the constitutional principle therein involved. It was the first step towards absolutism. If it had been promptly stopped and punished there would have been no more similar steps. It was allowed to pass unchastised, and the result has been that every succeeding week which has since passed has seen worse and continual violations of the Constitution and the Code.

'*L'uomo fatale*,' as the Italian people call Crispi, was summoned to rule, and the result has been, what everyone cognisant of his character knew would be inevitable, namely, the abolition of all liberties and safeguards of the body politic, and the substitution of secret, irresponsible, and absolutely despotic, tribunals, and secret agencies, worked by the will of one man. The revolutionary movement has been crushed by military force with a brutality and injustice which, were the scene Russia or Austria, would cause monster meetings of indignation in London. Led by *The Times*, *The Post*, and other journals, English opinion is deaf and blind to the tyrannies which it would be the first to denounce in any other nation. English opinion does not choose to understand, and does not desire to be forced to understand, that Italy is at the present time as completely ruled by an unscrupulous despotism, and by sheer use of the sabre and musket, as is Poland at this hour, or as Austrian Venetia was earlier in the century; and that Italy presents the same spectacle of prisoners, purely political, being hustled through the towns manacled by handcuffs and chained to one another by a long iron fetter; lawyers, landowners, merchants, editors, men of education, probity and honourable life being yoked with the common criminal and the hired bravo. It is difficult to comprehend how and why this shameful outrage upon decency and liberty is viewed with indifference by the rest of Europe. That it may give pleasure to the foes of Italy is easily understood; but how can it fail to give pain and alarm to her friends? How is it that unanimous protest and unanimous censure do not arise from all those who profess to recognise the necessity of freedom for national well-being?

The extreme gravity of the fact that the Italian sovereign chooses and caresses a minister who is permitted to set aside at will all ordinary provisions and protections of the law, does not appear to excite any astonishment or apprehension outside Italy. In Italy itself the people are paralysed with fear; the steel is at their throats, and the army, which they have been ruined to construct and maintain, crushes them into silence and exhaustion.

Let the English people picture to themselves what would have been the verdict of Europe if England had dealt with Ireland as Sicily has been dealt with; let them imagine Lord Wolseley acting like General Morra; let them imagine a cordon drawn around the whole island, ingress and egress forbidden under pain of arrest, telegrams destroyed, approaching vessels fired upon, the whole population forcibly disarmed, no news—save such as might be garbled by superior order—permitted to be despatched from the interior to the world at large, thousands of men thrust into prison on suspicion whilst their families starved, absolute secrecy, absolute darkness and mystery covering irresponsible despotism; let the English public imagine such a state as this in Ireland, and then ask themselves what would be the verdict of Europe and America upon it. Sicily contains two millions of persons, and this vast number has been given over to the absolute will of a single brutal soldier, who is screened by ministerial protection from any ray of that daylight of publicity which is the only guarantee for the equity of public men.

We are told that the island is pacified. So is a garotted and blindfolded creature pacified; so is a murdered corpse pacified. The most merciless reprisals have followed on the attempts of the peasantry to save themselves from the grinding extortions of their usurers and the pitiless taxation of their communes; and the reign of terror which has been established is called tranquillity. The same boast of 'peace when there is no peace' is made in the Lunigiana.

There is not even the gloss of affected legality in the countless arrests which have filled to overflowing the prisons of Italy. The charges by which these arrests are excused are so wide that they are a net into which all fish, big and little, may be swept. The imputation of 'inciting to hatred between the classes' is so vague that it may include almost any expression of social or political opinion. It is an accusation under which almost every great writer, thinker or philosopher would be liable to arrest, and under which Jesus Christ and Jean Jacques Rousseau, Garibaldi and John Milton, Washington and Brahma, Tolstoï and St Paul would be all alike condemned as criminals.

Equally vague is the companion accusation of inciting to civil war. As I pointed out in my article of last month, Italy owes her present existence entirely to civil war. Civil war may be a dread calamity, but it may be also an heroic remedy for ills far greater than itself. What is called authority in Italy is so corrupt in itself that it cannot command the respect of men, and has no title to demand their obedience. The creator itself of civil war and disturbance, such authority becomes ridiculous when draping itself in the toga of an intangible dignity. Moreover, it is now incarnated in the person of a single unscrupulous opportunist. Why should the nation respect either his name or his measures? The King of Italy, always servilely copying Germany, has decreed the name and measures of the lawyer Crispi sacred, as Germany has sent to prison many writers and printers for having expressed opinions hostile to the acts or speeches of German public men. Under the state called *piccolo stato d'assedio* military tribunals judge civil offences, or what are considered offences, and pass sentences of imprisonment varying in duration from six months to thirty years. The infamous sentence of twenty-three years' imprisonment, of which three are to be passed in solitary confinement, passed on the young advocate Molinari, for what is really no more than an offence of opinions, has forced a cry of surprise and disgust even from the German press. The monstrous iniquity of this condemnation has made even the blind and timid worm of Italian public feeling turn writhing under the iron heel which is crushing it, and this individual sentence is to be carried for appeal into the civil courts, where it is fervently to be hoped it may be altered if not cancelled.[G] Hundreds of brutal sentences have been passed for which there is no hope or chance of appeal, and vast numbers of men, in the flower of youth or the prime of manhood, are being flung into the hell of Italian prisons, there to be left to rot away in unseen and unpitied suffering, till death releases them or insanity seizes them. Insanity comes quickly in such torture as Italian prison-life is to its victims.

A journal called *L'Italia del Popolo* contained a spirited and eloquent article proving that Crispi was neither courageous nor honest, as a Socialist deputy had in a moment of flattery called him: this perfectly legitimate and temperate article caused the confiscation of the paper! 'If Crispi be Almighty God, let us know it!' said the *Secolo* of Milan, a courageous and well-written daily newspaper which has itself been frequently confiscated for telling the truth.

As specimens of other sentences passed in the month of February of the present year, take the following examples:

In Siena the proprietor of the journal *Martinello del Calle* was condemned to thirty-five days of prison for having called the deputy Piccarti 'violent and grotesque.'

The journal *Italia del Popolo* was seized because it contained quotations from the Memoirs of Kossuth.

The *Secolo* of Milan was seized for protesting against the condemnation to *twenty years'* imprisonment of the soldier Lombardino, although he had completely proved his innocence of the offence attributed to him.

The barber, Vittorio Catani, having been heard, in the Piazza S. Spirito of Florence, to say that the revolts in Sicily were due to hunger and distress, was condemned to three months' imprisonment and fifty francs fine.

At San Giuseppe, in Sicily, an old peasant surrendered one gun; confessed to having a better one, and showed where he had put it; he was sentenced to a year's imprisonment.

A day-labourer, Stefano Grosso, went to visit his father who was dying; a revolver being found in the cottage, during his visit, he was condemned to six months of prison for owning it, although there was no proof of his ownership.

The brothers Di Gesù, herdsmen, accustomed to sleep in a building where many other persons slept also, were sentenced to a year and a half of prison because an old rusty gun, quite useless, was found in a cupboard, although there was no evidence whatever that they owned, or knew of its existence.

These are a few typical instances of sentences passed by the hundred, and tens of hundreds, at the present hour in the unhappy kingdom of Italy. Everyone suspected however slightly, accused however indirectly, is arrested and removed from sight. Oftentimes, as in Molinari's case, the sentence embraces periods of solitary confinement, that infernal mental torture under which the strongest intellect gives way. What is the rest of Europe about that it views unmoved such suffering and such tyranny as this? Let it be remembered that the vast majority of these prisoners have no crime at all on their consciences. Molinari, sentenced in his youth to twenty-three years of prison, has committed no sin except that of being a Socialist. The term Anarchist is constantly used by the tribunals to describe men who are merely guilty of such opinions as are held by your Fabian Society in England.

There has been no actual *coup d'état*, but there has been what is worse, because less tangible, than a *coup d'état*, namely, the insidious and secretive alteration of a constitutional Government into a despotic one, the unauthorised and illegitimate suppression of free discussion and of lawful measures, and the substitution for them of arbitrary methods and secret-police investigation. The change has been quite as great as that which was wrought in Paris by the canon of the Tenth of December, but it has been made by means more criminal, because less open and as yet unavowed. The King of Italy, having mounted the throne under an engagement to hold inviolate the Constitution, has violated it as violently as Louis Napoleon his oath to the French Republic; but he has done so more insidiously and less courageously, having never dared to announce to his people his intention to do so. His decree postponing the assembling of the Chambers because 'public discussion would be prejudicial' was a virtual declaration that parliamentary government was at an end, but the fact was covered by an euphemism. In like manner, Crispi has said that he will 'ask' for irresponsible powers to be given him, but he defers the day of asking, and *ad interim* takes those powers and uses them as he chooses. The Italian Chambers are to be allowed to meet, but it is intimated to them that unless they vote for the 'full powers' they will be dissolved, and a more obedient Parliament elected under the military law of the existing reign of terror. 'La camera sapra quelle che si deve sapere,' Crispi stated the other day; that is, he will tell them as much as he chooses them to know. The amount of the financial deficit is to be put before the Chambers as one half only of what it really is. If there be any exposure made, or hostility shown, he has his weapon ready to his hand in dissolution. A new chamber elected under his docile prefects and his serried bayonets will not fail to be the humble spaniel he requires. If the present deputies, when the decree proroguing their assembly was proclaimed, had all met in Rome, and, without distinction of party or group, had insisted on the opening of Parliament, and compelled the monarch to keep his engagement to the Constitution, it is possible that both he and his minister would have submitted. But Italian deputies are poor creatures, and the few men of mark and strength who are amongst them are swamped under the weight of the invertebrate numbers. Hence we are scandalised by the spectacle of a whole body of the elected representatives of a nation being muzzled and set aside, and their discussion of opinion and action declared prejudicial to the interests of their country. It would be simpler and more candid to sweep away Parliament and Senate altogether than to make of them a mere mechanical dummy, pushed aside as useless lumber whenever there is any agitation or danger before their country. Umberto of Savoia would hesitate to proclaim himself an absolute sovereign, but *de facto*, though not *de jure*, he has made himself one. The text of the Treaty of the Triplice has never been made known to the country. Rumours have been heard that there are private riders attached to it which personally bind the House of Savoy to the House of Hohenzollern, and cause the otherwise inexplicable, and in every event culpable, obstinacy of the Italian sovereign in insisting on the inviolability of the military *cadres*. Be this as it may, the engagements of the treaty are kept a profound secret, and such secrecy is probably one of the clauses. Now, if the will and signature of one man suffice to pledge a nation in the dark to the most perilous obligations none can predict the issue, what is this except an absolute monarchy? What pretence can there still be of a constitutional Government?

Let the English nation figure to itself their Queen binding them secretly to the most onerous engagements which might cause in the end the total exhaustion and even extinction of their country, and they will then comprehend what Italians are enduring, and have long endured, from the secret pact of their sovereign, of which they have no means to measure the dangers or the responsibilities, although the burden and terror of these lie upon them. It is only by means of the military gag that the sovereign can keep mute the popular anxiety, curiosity and alarm.

The only reforms which would be of the slightest practical use would be the abolition of the hated gate-tax, and salt-tax,[H] and the reduction of the military and naval expenditure. There is no ministry of any party who dares propose these, the only possible, alleviations of the national suffering.

The formation of the Kingdom of Italy has been aggrandisement, gain and rejoicing to the Piedmontese and Lombard States, but it has been only oppression, loss and pain to the country south of the Appenines. Even in the Veneto, if the gauge of felicity be prosperity, the province must miserably regret the issue of its longed-for liberation. 'Piû gran' miseria non c'è sulla terra che n' l'è la nostra,' says a gondolier of Venice to me in this ninety-fourth year of the century. The magnificent and hardy race of gondoliers is slowly and wretchedly perishing, under the grinding wheels of communal extortion, and the ignoble rivalry of the dirty steamboats and the electric launches. But there is greater misery still than theirs, such misery as makes the worst hell of Dante's heaven by comparison—the misery of the children in Sicily, little white slaves sold for a hundred, or a hundred and fifty francs each, to brutal blows, smarting wounds, incessant labour, and absolutely hopeless bondage.

Court-martial is substituted for civil law at the mere will of the monarch and his minister. There has been nothing in the recent events which can justify the establishment of it, and its abominable and irresponsible decrees, in which the torture of solitary confinement so largely figures. Local dissensions and jealousies find vent in accusations and condemnations, and the barbarity of the soldier and the gendarme to the civilian is regarded as a virtue and rewarded. What can be said of a Government which confounds the political writer with the brigand of the hills, the peaceful doctrinaire with the savage assassin, the harmless peasant with the poisoner or strangler, and chains them all together, and pushes them all together into prison-cells, fœtid, pestilent, wretched, already overcrowded? What will be done with all these thousands? What will be made of all this loss and waste of life? Miserable as is the existence of Italian felons, they must eat something, however scanty. The cost to the country of their useless, stagnant, fettered lives will be immense, whilst their own anguish will be unspeakable. Many of them, I repeat, are guilty of no offence whatever except of desiring a republic, or professing Socialist doctrines. I have no personal leaning towards Socialism, and regard it as unworkable, and believe that it would be pernicious if it could be brought to realisation. But it is no crime to be a Socialist. Socialism is an opinion, a doctrine, a creed, an idea; and those who hold it have every right to make a propaganda when they can. It is monstrous that, at the pleasure of a monarch or a minister, an idea can be treated as a capital crime. The young advocate Molinari is guilty of nothing except of inculcating revolutionary doctrines. What sin is this? It is one shared by Gautama and Christ.

Maxime du Camp has just died, a member of the Academy of France. He was once one of the Thousand of Marsala. What is now bringing intellectual and gifted youths to the felon's dock in Italy is precisely such a creed as drove the late Academician to enrol himself under Garibaldi. Who shall affirm that there may not be in these young men, thus infamously judged and sentenced to-day, such brilliant intelligence and critical acumen as have made Maxime du Camp the admired of all who can appreciate scholarship, style, perception and true philanthropy, whether they may or may not agree with his arguments or endorse his deductions?

It would be impossible for any generous or unselfish nature not to burn with indignation before the poverty entailed on Italy by military madness, and the suffering caused to the poor and harmless by the fiscal and municipal tyrannies and the hired spies and extortioners of the Government.[I] Jules Simon said the other day that pity is the mark of great souls. In Italy it is considered the mark of the malefactor. A young nobleman of the Lunigiana, Count Lazzoni, has now a price set upon his head because he has espoused and taught the doctrines of Mazzini. He was rich, gifted, fortunate; his family insisted that he should give up either his doctrines or themselves, and, with themselves, his estates and title. He chose to abandon the last, not without great personal affliction, because he was tenderly attached to his relatives. This young hero is now being hunted by soldiery, and when found will be tried by court-martial under the convenient charge of 'exciting to class-hatreds.' Yet what are such young men as these but the very salt and savour of a country? It is not they who are the criminals, but the egotists who dance and dine, and gamble and smoke, and bow at the Quirinale, and the Vatican, and pay court to the favourites of the hour, and care nothing what ruin hangs over their country, nor what suffering is entailed on their countrymen, so long as they get a rosette for their buttonhole, or rear the favourite for a race in their stables. They are the true criminals; not the youths, like Molinari and Lazzoni, not the men like De Felice and Barbato, who think and feel and dare.

Why are not the young Princes of the House of Savoy amongst the suffering peasantry of Sicily, seeing with their own eyes, hearing with their own ears, doing something to aid, to mitigate, to console, instead of spending their lives in leading cotillons, driving tandem, trying on new uniforms, and shooting in all seasons of the year? Why do they not go and live for a month in the sulphur-mines, carry the creels of sulphur on their bare backs, and feel the stinging smart of it in their blinded eyes and dried-up throats and excoriated lips? They would then, at least, know something of how a portion of their people live and die. It would be more useful than dressing up in plumes and armour to amuse William of Prussia.

Lockroy, in writing to the French newspaper *L'Eclair*, says that Italy is served well by her public servants, and possesses unlimited resources and marvellous genius. In what way is she well served by her public servants? She is stripped bare by all who pretend to serve her, and everyone who enters her service, high and low, seeks only to advantage and enrich himself. Corruption, like dry-rot in a tree, permeates the whole public organisation of Italy, from the highest to the lowest official. All the municipalities are rotten and rapacious. Nothing is done without *mancia*; or, as it is called further East, *backsheesh*. The law courts are swarming hotbeds of bribery and perjury.

Her natural resources may be great, but they are so burdened by impost and tax, so strained, fettered, prematurely harvested and spent, that they are exhausted ere they are ripe. Of her genius there is but little fruit in these days; there is no originality in modern Italian talent; in art, literature, science, architecture, all is imitation, and imitation of an ignoble model; the national sense of beauty, once so universal, so intense, is dead; the national grace and gaiety are dying; the accursed, withering, dwarfing, deforming spirit of modernity has passed like a blast over the country and made it barren.

In the people there are still beauty of form and attitude, charm and elegance of manner, infinite patience, infinite forbearance, infinite potentialities of excellence as of evil. But they need a saviour, a guide, a friend; they need a Marcus Aurelius, a Nizahualcoytl, a St Louis, a Duke Frederic of Montefeltro, a ruler who would love them, who would raise them, who would give them food bodily and mental, and lead them in the paths of peace and loveliness. Instead of such, what have they? Men who set their wretched ambition on the approving nod of a Margrave of Brandenburg; who deem it greatness to turn a whole starving peasantry into a vast ill-ordered, ill-equipped, and ill-fed army; who, for pomp, parade, and windy boast seize the last coin, the last crust, the last shirt; who find a paltry ideal in an American machine-room, an elevated railway, and an electric gun; and who deem an ignoble vassalage to the German Emperor meet honour and glory for that Italy which was empress of the earth and goddess of the arts when the German was a forest-brute, a hairy boor, a scarce human Caliban of northern lands.

As events have moved within the last few weeks it is wholly within the bonds of possibility, even of probability, that if the Crown and its chief counsellor see greater danger to themselves threaten them in the coming year, they may appeal for armed help to their ally, who is almost their suzerain, and a fence of Prussian bayonets may be placed around the Quirinale and the House of Assembly. Who shall say that the secret and personal treaty does not provide for such protection?

So far as a public opinion can be said to exist in Italy (for in a French or English sense of the words it does not as yet exist), it is stirring to deep uneasiness and indignation at the subserviency of the tribunals to the ferocity of the Government in what is compared to the Bloody Assize of the English Jeffreys. It is becoming every day more and more alarmed at the absolutism of a King, all criticism of whose acts is made penal, yet whose personal interference and obstruction is every day becoming more obvious, more galling, and more mischievous. A new place of deportation for the condemned of Massa-Carrara is being prepared on the pestilential shore of the Southern Maremma. This new *ergastolo* may prove not only a tomb for those confined in it; but it may very possibly become a pit in which the Italian monarchy will be buried. If the next election should return, as it may do, two hundred of the Extreme Left, *'l'uomo fatale'* may be the cause of a revolution as terrible as that of 1789.

Foreign speakers and writers of the present hour predict the success of Crispi. What is meant by the word? What success is there possible? The enforced acceptance of additional taxation? The placing of the last straw which breaks the camel's back? The quietude which in the body politic, as in the physical body, follows on drainage of the blood and frequently presages the faintness of death? The reduction of parliamentary representation to a mere comedy and formula? The passive endurance of martial tyranny by a frightened nation, whose terror is passed off as acquiescence? The increase of debt, the enlargement of prisons, the paralysis of the public press?

These are the only things which can be meant by the success of Francesco Crispi, or can be embodied in it.

He is the brummagen Sylla of an age of sham, but he has all the desire of Sylla to slay his enemies and to rule alone.

In this sense, but only in this sense, he may succeed. Around the sham Sylla, as around the real Sylla, there may be laid waste a desolated and silent country, in which widows will mourn their dead, and fatherless children weep for hunger under burning roofs. Such triumph as this he may obtain. Italy has seen many triumph thus, and has paid for their triumph with her tears and with her blood.

March 1894.

THE NEW WOMAN

It can scarcely be disputed, I think, that in the English language there are conspicuous at the present moment two words which designate two unmitigated bores: The Workingman and the Woman. The Workingman and the Woman, the New Woman, be it remembered, meet us at every page of literature written in the English tongue; and each is convinced that on its own special W hangs the future of the world. Both he and she want to have their values artificially raised and rated, and a status given to them by favour in lieu of desert. In an age in which persistent clamour is generally crowned by success they have both obtained considerable attention; is it offensive to say much more of it than either deserves?

A writer, signing the name of Sarah Grand, has of late written on this theme; and she avers that the Cow-Woman and the Scum-Woman, man understands; but that the New Woman is above him. The elegance of these choice appellatives is not calculated to recommend them to educated readers of either sex; and as a specimen of style forces one to hint that the New Woman who, we are told, 'has been sitting apart in silent contemplation all these years' might in all these years have studied better models of literary composition.

We are farther on told 'that the dimmest perception that you may be mistaken, will save you from making an ass of yourself.' It appears that even this dimmest perception has never dawned upon the New Woman.

We are farther told that 'thinking and thinking,' in her solitary, sphinx-like contemplation, she solved the problem and prescribed the remedy (the remedy to a problem!); but what this remedy was we are not told, nor did the New Woman apparently disclose it to the rest of womankind, since she still hears them in 'sudden and violent upheaval' like 'children unable to articulate whimpering for they know not what.' It is sad to reflect that they might have been 'easily satisfied at that time' (at what time?), 'but society stormed at them until what was a little wail became convulsive shrieks;' and we are not told why the New Woman who had 'the remedy for the problem,' did not immediately produce this remedy. We are not told either in what country or at what epoch this startling upheaval of volcanic womanhood took place in which 'man merely made himself a nuisance with his opinions and advice,' but apparently did quell this wailing and gnashing of teeth since it would seem that he has managed still to remain more masterful than he ought to be.

We are further informed that women 'have allowed him to arrange the whole social system, and manage, or mismanage, it all these ages without ever seriously examining his work with a view to considering whether his abilities and his methods were sufficiently good to qualify him for the task.'

There is something comical in the idea thus suggested, that man has only been allowed to 'manage or mismanage' the world because woman has graciously refrained from preventing his doing so. But the comic side of this pompous and solemn assertion does not for a moment offer itself to the New Woman sitting aloof and aloft in her solitary meditation on the superiority of her sex. For the New Woman there is no such thing as a joke. She has listened without a smile to her enemy's 'preachments'; she has 'endured poignant misery for his sins;' she has 'meekly bowed her head' when he called her bad names; and she has never asked for 'any proof of the superiority' which could alone have given him a right to use such naughty expressions. The truth about everything has all along been in the possession of woman; but strange and sad perversity of taste! she has 'cared more for man than for truth, and so the whole human race has suffered!'

'All that is over, however,' we are told, and 'while on the one hand man has shrunk to his true proportions' she has, during the time of this shrinkage, been herself expanding, and has in a word come to 'fancy herself' extremely, so that he has no longer the slightest chance of imposing upon her by his game-cock airs.

Man, 'having no conception of himself as imperfect' (what would Hamlet say to this accusation?) will find this difficult to understand at first; but the New Woman 'knows his weakness,' and will 'help him with his lesson.' '*Man morally is in his infancy.*' There have been times when there was a doubt as to whether he was to be raised to her level, or woman to be lowered to his, but we 'have turned that corner at last and now woman holds out a strong hand to the child-man and insists upon helping him up.' The child-man (Bismarck? Herbert Spencer? Edison? Gladstone? Alexander III.? Lord Dufferin? the Duc d'Aumale?)—the child-man must have his tottering baby steps guided by the New Woman, and he must be taught to live up to his ideals. To live up to an ideal, whether our own or somebody else's, is a painful process; but man must be made to do it. For, oddly enough, we are assured that despite 'all his assumption he does not make the best of himself,' which is not wonderful if he be still only in his infancy; and he has the incredible stupidity to be blind to the fact that 'woman has self-respect and good sense,' whilst he has neither, and that 'she does not in the least intend to sacrifice the privileges she enjoys on the chance of obtaining others.'

I have written amongst other *pensées éparses* which will some day see the light, the following reflection:—

L'école nouvelle des femmes libres oublie qu'on ne puisse pas à la fois combattre l'homme sur son propre terrain, et attendre de lui des politesses, des tendresses, et des galantéries. Il ne faut pas au même moment prendre de l'homme son chaire à l'Université et sa place dans l'omnibus; si on lui arrâche son gagne-pain on ne peut pas exiger qu'il offre aussi sa parapluie.

The whole kernel of the question lies in this. The supporters of the New Woman declare that she will not surrender her present privileges, *i.e.*, though she may usurp his professorial seat, and seize his salary, she will still expect the man to stand that she may sit; the man to get wet through that she may use his umbrella. Yet surely if she retain these privileges she can only do so by an appeal to his chivalry, *i.e.*, by a confession that she is weaker than he. But she does not want to do this; she wants to get the comforts and concessions due to feebleness, at the same time as she demands the lion's share of power due to superior force alone. It is this overweening and unreasonable grasping at both positions which will end in making her odious to man and in her being probably kicked back roughly by him into the seclusion of a harem.

The New Woman declares that man cannot do without woman. It is a doubtful postulate. In the finest intellectual and artistic era of the world women were not necessary to either the pleasures or passions of men. It is possible that if women make themselves as unlovely and offensive as they appear likely to become, the preferences of the Platonic Age may become acknowledged and dominant, and women may be relegated entirely to the lowest plane as a mere drudge and child-bearer.

Before me at the moment lies an engraving from an illustrated journal of a woman's meeting; whereat a woman is demanding, in the name of her sovereign sex, the right to vote at political elections. The speaker is middle-aged and plain of feature; she wears an inverted plate on her head, tied on with strings under her double-chin; she has balloon-sleeves, a bodice tight to bursting, a waist of ludicrous dimensions in proportion to her portly person; her whole attire is elaborately constructed so as to conceal any physical graces which she might possess; she is gesticulating with one hand, of which all the fingers are stuck out in ungraceful defiance of all artistic laws of gesture. Now, why cannot this orator learn to gesticulate properly and learn to dress gracefully, instead of clamouring for a franchise? She violates in her own person every law, alike of common-sense and artistic fitness, and yet comes forward as a fit and proper person to make laws for others. She is an exact representative of her sex as it exists at the dawn of the twentieth century.

There have been few periods in which woman's attire has been so ugly, so disfiguring and so preposterous as it is in this year of grace (1894) at a period when, in newspaper and pamphlet, on platform and in dining-room, and in the various clubs she has consecrated to herself, woman is clamouring for her recognition as a being superior to man. She cannot clothe herself with common sense or common grace, she cannot resist the dictates of tailors and the example of princesses; she cannot resist the squaw-like preference for animals' skins, and slaughtered birds, and tufts torn out of the living and bleeding creature; she cannot show to any advantage the natural lines of her form, but disguises them as grotesquely as mantua-makers bid her to do. She cannot go into the country without making herself a caricature of man, in coat and waistcoat and gaiters; she apes all his absurdities, she emulates all his cruelties and follies; she wears his ugly pot hats, his silly, stiff collars; she copies his inane club-life and then tells us that this parody, incapable of initiative, bare of taste and destitute of common sense, is worthy to be enthroned as the supreme teacher of the world!

Woman, whether new or old, leaves immense fields of culture untilled, immense areas of influence wholly neglected. She does almost nothing with the resources she possesses, because her whole energy is concentrated on desiring and demanding those she had not. She can write and print anything she chooses; and she scarcely ever takes the pains to acquire correct grammar or elegance of style before wasting ink and paper. She can paint and model any subjects she chooses, but she imprisons herself in men's *atéliers* to endeavour to steal their technique and their methods, and thus loses any originality she might possess in art. Her influence on children might be so great that through them she would practically rule the future of the world; but she delegates her influence to the vile school boards if she be poor, and if she be rich to governesses and tutors; nor does she in ninety-nine cases out of a hundred ever attempt to educate or control herself into fitness for the personal exercise of such influence. Her precept and example in the treatment of the animal creation might be of infinite use in mitigating the hideous tyranny of humanity over them, but she does little or nothing to this effect; she wears dead birds and the skins of dead creatures; she hunts the hare and shoots the pheasant, she drives and rides with more brutal recklessness than men; she watches with delight the struggles of the dying salmon, of the gralloched deer; she keeps her horses standing in snow and fog for hours, with the muscles of their heads and necks tied up in the torture of the bearing rein; when asked to do anything for a stray dog, a lame horse, a poor man's donkey, she is very sorry, but she has so many claims on her already; she never attempts by orders to her household, to her *fóurnisseurs*, to her dependents, to obtain some degree of mercy in the treatment of sentient creatures and in the methods of their slaughter, and she continues to trim her court gowns with the aigrettes of ospreys.

The immense area for good influence which lies open to her in private life is almost entirely uncultivated, yet she wants to be admitted into public life. Public life is already overcrowded, verbose, incompetent, fussy and foolish enough without the addition of her in her sealskin coat with the dead humming bird on her hat. Women in public life would exaggerate the failings of men, and would not have even their few excellencies. Their legislation would be, as that of men is too often, the offspring of panic or prejudice; and women would not put on the drag of common-sense as men frequently do in public assemblies. There would be little to hope from their humanity, nothing from their liberality; for when they are frightened they are more ferocious than men, and, when they gain power, more merciless.

'Men,' says one of the New Women, 'deprived us of all proper education and then jeered at us because we had no knowledge.' How far is this based on facts? Could not Lady Jane Grey learn Greek and Latin as she chose? Could not Hypatia lecture? Was George Sand or Mrs Somerville withheld from study? Could not in every age every woman choose a Corinna or a Cordelia as her type? become either Helen or Penelope? If the vast majority have not the mental or physical gifts to become either, that is Nature's fault, not man's. Aspasia and Adelina Patti were born, not made. In all eras and all climes a woman of great genius or of great beauty has done very much what she chose; and if the majority of women have led obscure lives, so have the majority of men. The chief part of humanity is insignificant whether it be male or female. In most people there is very little character indeed, and as little mind. Those who have much of either never fail to make their mark, be they of which sex they may.

The unfortunate idea that there is no good education without a college curriculum is as injurious as it is erroneous. The college education may have excellencies for men in its friction, its preparation for the world, its rough destruction of personal conceit; but for women it can only be hardening and deforming. If study be delightful to a woman, she will find her way to it as the hart to water brooks. The author of *Aurora Leigh* was not only always at home, but she was also for many years a confirmed invalid; yet she became a fine classic, and found her path to fame. A college curriculum would have done nothing to improve her rich and beautiful mind; it might have done much to debase it.

It would be impossible to love and venerate literature of the highest kind more profoundly than did Elizabeth Barrett Browning, yet she was the most retiring of women and chained by weakness to her couch until her starry-eyed and fiery suitor descended on her and bore her away to Italy. It is difficult to see what the distinction of being called a wrangler can add to the solid advantage and the intellectual pleasure of studying mathematics; or what the gaining of a college degree in classics can add to the delightful culture of Greek and Latin literature as sought *per se*.

The perpetual contact of men with other men may be good for them, but the perpetual contact of women with other women is very far from good. The publicity of a college must be injurious to a young girl of refined and delicate feeling, whilst the adoration of other women (as in the late chairing of a wrangler by other girl graduates) is unutterably pernicious. Nor can I think the present mania for exploration and incessant adventure beneficial either to the woman or the world.

When a young and good-looking girl chooses to ride or walk all alone through a wild and unexplored country, it must be admitted that, if the narrative of her adventures be not sheer fable, she must have perpetually run the risk of losing what women have hitherto been taught to consider dearer than life. It is nothing short of courting abuse of her maiden person to explore all alone mountainous regions and desert plains inhabited by wild and fierce races of men. One such young traveller describes, amongst other risky exploits, how she came one night in the Carpathians upon a deep and lonely pool, made black as the mouth of Avernus by its contrast with the moonlit rocks around, and of how, tempted by this blackness, she got down from her saddle, stripped, plunged and bathed! The stars alone, she says, looked down on this exploit, but how could this Susannah be sure there were no Elders? And common sense timidly whispers, how, oh how, did she manage to dry herself?

Personally, I do not in the least believe in these stories any more than in those of the noted Munchausen; but they are put into print as sober facts, and as such we are requested and expected to receive them.

The 'Scum-Woman' and the 'Cow-Woman,' to quote the elegant phraseology of the defenders of their sex, are both of them less of a menace to humankind than the New Woman with her fierce vanity, her undigested knowledge, her overweening estimate of her own value, and her fatal want of all sense of the ridiculous.

When scum comes to the surface it renders a great service to the substance which it leaves behind it; when the cow yields pure nourishment to the young and the suffering, her place is blessed in the realm of nature;

but when the New Woman splutters blistering wrath on mankind she is merely odious and baneful.

The error of the New Woman (as of many an old one) lies in speaking of women as the victims of men, and entirely ignoring the frequency with which men are the victims of women. In nine cases out of ten the first to corrupt the youth is the woman. In nine cases out of ten also she becomes corrupt herself because she likes it.

When Leonide Leblanc, scorning to adopt the career of a school teacher, for which her humble family had educated her, walked down the hill from Montmartre to seek her fortunes in the streets of Paris, she did so because she liked to do so, which was indeed quite natural in her. Neither Mephistopheles nor Faust led her down from Montmartre, and its close little kitchen and common little bedchamber; neither Mephistopheles nor Faust was wanted, Paris and the boulevards were attraction enough, and her own beauty and ambition were spurs sufficiently sharp to make her leave the unlovely past and seek the dazzling future. The accusation of seduction is very popular with women, and they excuse everything faulty in their lives with it; but the accusation is rarely based on actual facts. The youth and the maiden incline towards each other as naturally as the male and female blossoms of trees are blown together by the fertilising breeze of spring. An attraction of a less poetic, of a wholly physical kind, brings together the boy and girl in the garrets, in the cellars, in the mines, on the farm lands, in the promiscuous intercourse of the streets. It is nature which draws the one to the other; and the blame lies less on them than with the hypocritical morality of a modern world which sees what it calls sin in Nature.

It is all very well to say that prostitutes were at the beginning of their career victims of seduction; but it is not probable and it is not provable. Love of drink and of finery, and a dislike to work, are the more likely motives and origin of their degradation. It never seems to occur to the accusers of man that women are just as vicious and as lazy as he is in nine cases out of ten, and need no invitation from him to become so.

A worse prostitution than that of the streets, *i.e.*, that of loveless marriages of convenience, are brought about by women, not by men. In such unions the man always gives much more than he gains, and the woman in almost every instance is persuaded or driven into it by women: her mother, her sisters, her acquaintances. It is rarely that the father interferes to bring about such a marriage.

A rich marriage represents to the woman of culture and position what the streets represent to the woman of the people. But it is none the less a loveless sale of self, because its sale is ratified at St Paul's Knightsbridge or at S. Philippe du Roule.

In even what is called a well-assorted marriage, the man is frequently sacrificed to the woman. As I wrote long ago, Andrea del Sarte's wife has many sisters; Correggio, dying of the burden of the family, has many brothers. Men of genius are often pinned to earth by their wives. They are continually dwarfed and dulled by their female relations, and rendered absurd by their sons and daughters. In our own day a famous statesman is made very ridiculous by his wife. Frequently the female influences brought to bear on him render a man of great and original powers and disinterested character, a time-server, a conventionalist, a mere seeker of place. Woman may help man sometimes, but she certainly more often hinders him. Her self-esteem is immense and her self-knowledge very small. I view with dread for the future of the world the power which modern inventions place in the hands of woman. Hitherto her physical weakness has restrained her in a great measure from violent action; but a woman can make a bomb and throw it, can fling vitriol, and fire a repeating revolver as well as any man can. These are precisely the deadly, secret, easily handled modes of warfare and revenge, which will commend themselves to her ferocious feebleness.

Jules Rochard has written:

'J'ai professé de l'anatomie pendant des longues années, j'ai passé une bonne partie de mavie dans les amphithéâtres, mais je n'en ai pas moins éprouvé un sentiment pénible en trouvant dans toutes les maisons d'education des squelettes d'animaux et des mannequins anatomiques entre les mains des fillettes.'

I suppose this passage will be considered as an effort 'to withhold knowledge from women,' but it is one which is full of true wisdom and honourable feeling. When you have taken her into the physiological and chemical laboratories, when you have extinguished pity in her, and given weapons to her dormant cruelty, which she can use in secret, you will be hoist with your own petard—your pupil will be your tyrant, and then she will meet with the ultimate fate of all tyrants.

In the pages of an eminent review a physician has recently lamented the continually increasing unwillingness of women of the world in the United States to bear children, and the consequent increase of ill-health; whilst to avoid child-bearing is being continually preached to the working classes by those who call themselves their friends.

The elegant epithet of Cow-Woman implies the contempt with which maternity is viewed by the New Woman, who thinks it something fine to vote at vestries, and shout at meetings, and lay bare the spine of living animals, and haul the gasping salmon from the river pool, and hustle male students off the benches of amphitheatres.

Modesty is no doubt a thing of education or prejudice, a conventionality artificially stimulated; but it is an exquisite grace, and womanhood without it loses its most subtle charm. Nothing tends so to destroy modesty as the publicity and promiscuity of schools, of hotels, of railway trains and sea voyages. True modesty shrinks from the curious gaze of other women as from the coarser gaze of man. When a girl has a common bedchamber and a common bathroom with other girls, she loses the delicate bloom of her modesty. Exposure to a crowd of women is just as nasty as exposure to a crowd of men.

Men, moreover, are in all, except the very lowest classes, more careful of their talk before young girls than women are, or at least were so until the young women of fashion insisted on their discarding such scruples. It is very rarely that a man does not respect real innocence; but women frequently do not. The jest, the allusion, the story which sullies her mind and awakes her inquisitiveness, will much oftener be spoken by women than men. It is not from her brothers, nor her brother's friends, but from her female companions that she will understand what the grosser laugh of those around her suggests. The biological and pathological curricula complete the loveless disflowering of her maiden soul.

Everything which tends to obliterate the contrast of the sexes, like the mixture of boys and girls in American common schools, tends also to destroy the charm of intercourse, the savour and sweetness of life. Seclusion lends an infinite seduction to the girl, whilst the rude and bustling publicity of modern life robs woman of her grace. Packed like herrings in a railway carriage, sleeping in odious vicinity to strangers on a shelf, going days and nights without a bath, exchanging decency and privacy for publicity and observation, the women who travel, save those rich enough to still purchase seclusion, are forced to cast aside all refinement and delicacy.

It is said that travel enlarges the mind. There are many minds which can no more be enlarged, by any means whatever, than a nut or a stone. What have their journeys round the world and their incessant gyrations done for the innumerable princes of Europe? The fool remains a fool, though you carry him or her about over the whole surface of the globe, and it is certain that the promiscuous contact and incessant publicity of travel, which may not hurt the man, do injure the woman.

Neither men nor women of genius are, I repeat, any criterion for the rest of their sex; nay, they belong, as Plato placed them, to a third sex which is above the laws of the multitude. But even whilst they do so they are always the foremost to recognise that it is the difference, not the likeness, of sex which makes the charm of human life. Barry Cornwall wrote long ago,—

> As the man beholds the woman,
> As the woman sees the man;
> Curiously they note each other,
> As each other only can.
> Never can the man divest her
> Of that mystic charm of sex;
> Ever must she, gazing on him,
> That same mystic charm annex.

That mystic charm will long endure, despite the efforts to destroy it of orators, in tight stays and balloon sleeves, who scream from platforms, and the beings so justly abhorred of Mrs Lynn Lynton who smoke in public carriages and from the waist upward are indistinguishable from the men they profess to despise.

But every word, whether written or spoken, which urges the woman to antagonism against the man, every word which is written or spoken to try and make of her a <u>hybrid,</u> self-contained opponent of men, makes a rift in the lute to which the world looks for its sweetest music.

The New Woman reminds me of an agriculturist who, discarding a fine farm of his own, and leaving it to nettles, stones, thistles and wire-worms, should spend his whole time in demanding neighbouring fields which are not his. The New Woman will not even look at the extent of ground indisputably her own, which she leaves unweeded and untilled.

Not to speak of the entire guidance of childhood, which is certainly already chiefly in the hands of woman (and of which her use does not do her much honour), so long as she goes to see one of her own sex dancing in a lion's den, the lions being meanwhile terrorised by a male brute; so long as she wears dead birds as millinery and dead seals as coats, so long as she goes to races, steeplechases, coursing and pigeon matches; so long as she 'walks with the guns'; so long as she goes to see an American lashing horses to death in idiotic contest with velocipedes, so long as she curtsies before princes and emperors who reward the winners of distance-rides; so long as she receives physiologists in her drawing-rooms, and trusts to them in her maladies; so long as she invades literature without culture, and art without talent; so long as she orders her court-dress in a hurry, regardless of the strain thus placed on the poor seamstresses; so long as she makes no attempt to interest herself in her servants, in her animals, in the poor slaves of her tradespeople; so long as she shows herself, as she does at present, without scruple at every brutal and debasing spectacle which is considered fashionable; so long as she understands nothing of the beauty of meditation, of solitude, of Nature; so long as she is utterly incapable of keeping her sons out of the shambles of modern sport, and lifting her daughters above the pestilent miasma of modern society; so long as she is what she is in the worlds subject to her, she has no possible title or capacity to demand the place or the privilege of man, for she shows herself incapable of turning to profit her own place and her own privilege.

DEATH AND PITY

Le livre de la Pitié et de la Mort is the latest and, in my estimation, in some respects, the most touching and the most precious of the works of Loti, and I wish that this little volume, so small in bulk, so pregnant with thought and value, could be translated into every language spoken upon earth, and sped like an electric wave over the dull, deaf, cruel multitudes of men. It is not that Loti himself needs a larger public than he possesses. All who have any affinity with him know every line he writes.

Despite the singular absence of all scholarship in his works—for, indeed, he might be living before the birth of Cadmus for any allusion which he ever makes to the art of letters—a perfect instinct of style, like the child Mozart's instinct for harmony, has led him to the most exquisite grace and precision of expression, the most accurate, as well as the most ideal realisations in words alike of scenery and of sentiment.

His earlier works were not unjustly reproached with being *trop décousu*, too impressionist; but in his later books this imperfection is no longer traceable, they are delicately and beautifully harmonious. A sympathetic critic has said, perhaps rightly, that the long night-watches on the sea, the long isolation of ocean voyages, and the removal from the common-place conventional pressure of society in cities and provinces have kept his mind singularly free, original and poetic. But no other sailor has ever produced anything beautiful, either in prose or in verse; and the influence of the Armorican coast and the Breton temperament have probably had more to do with making him what he is than voyages which leave sterile those who with sterile minds and souls go down to the deep in ships, and come back with their minds and their hands empty. He would have been just what he is had he never been rocked on any other waves than the long grey breakers of the iron coast of Morbihan, and, to those whom from the first have known and loved his poetic and pregnant thoughts, even the palm leaves of the first intellectual Academy of the world can add nothing to his merit, nay, they seem scarcely to accord with his soul, free as the seagull's motion, and his sympathy wide as that ocean which has cradled and nursed him.

But it is not of himself that I wish to speak here. It is of this last little book of his which, so small in compass, is yet vast as the universe in what it touches and suggests. All the cultured world has, doubtless, read it; but how little and narrow is that world compared to the immeasurable multitudes to which the volume will for ever remain unknown, and also to that, alas! equally great world to which it would be, even when read, a dead letter: for to those who have no ear for harmony the music of Beethoven is but as the crackling of thorns under a pot. He knows this, and in his preface counsels such as these to leave it alone, for it can only weary them.

Indeed, the book is in absolute and uncompromising opposition to the modern tone of his own times, and to the bare, dry, hard temperament of his generation. It is in direct antagonism with what is called the scientific spirit and its narrow classifications. It is full of altruism of the widest, purest and highest kind, stretching out its comprehension and affection to those innumerable races which the human race has disinherited, driven into bondage, and sacrificed to its own appetites and desires. To its author the ox in the shambles, the cat in the gutter is as truly a fellow creature as the mariner on his deck, or the mother by his hearth; the nest of the bird is as sacred as the rush hut of the peasant, and the cry of the wounded animal reaches his heart as quickly as the wail of the fisherman's widow. No one can reproach him, as they reproach me (a reproach I am quite willing to accept), with thinking more of animals than of men and women. His charities to his own kind are unceasing and boundless; he is ever foremost in the relief of sorrow and want. It cannot be said either that he is what is scornfully called a 'mere sentimentalist.' He is well known as a daring and brilliant officer in his service, and he has shown that he possesses moral as well as physical courage, and that he is careless of censure and indifferent to his own interests and prospects when he is moved to indignation against the tyrannies of the strong over the weak. Here is no woman who has dreamed by her fireside or in her rose garden until her sentiment has overshadowed her reason, but a *brave des braves,* a man whose life is spent by choice in the most perilous contest with the forces of nature, a man who has been often under fire, who has seen war in all its sickly horror, who has felt the lightnings of death playing round him in a thousand shapes. His noble and rashly-expressed indignation at the barbarities shown in the taking of Tonquin led to his temporary banishment from the French navy. He does prove, and has ever proved, in his conduct as in his writings, that to him nothing human can be alien. But he is not hemmed in behind the narrow pale of humanitarianism: he has the vision to see, and the courage to show, that the uncounted, sentient, suffering children of creation for whom humanity has no mercy, but merely servitude and slaughter, are as dear to him as his own kind.

In a century which in its decrepitude has fallen prone and helpless under the fiat of the physiologist and bacteriologist, this attitude needs no common courage. Browning had this courage, Renan had it not. In an age when the idolatry of man is carried to a height which would be ludicrous in its inflated conceit were it not in its results so tragic, it requires no common force and boldness to speak as Loti speaks of the many other races of the earth as equally deserving with their tyrants of tenderness and comprehension; to admit, as he admits, that in the suppliant eyes of his little four-footed companions he can see, as in a woman's or a child's, the soul within speaking and calling to his own.

'She' (she is a little Chinese cat which had taken refuge on board his frigate) 'came out of the shadow, stretching herself slowly, as if to give herself time for reflection. She came towards me with several pauses, sometimes with a Mongolian grace; she lifted one paw in the air before deciding to put it down and take a further step; and all the while she gazed at me fixedly, questioningly. I wondered what she could want with me. I had had her well fed by my servant. When she was quite near, very near, she sat down, brought her tail round her legs, and made a very soft little noise. And she continued to look at me, to look at me *in the eyes*, which indicated that intelligent ideas were thronging through her small head. It was evident that she understood, as all animals do, that I was not a thing, but a thinking being, capable of pity, and accessible to the mute entreaty of a look. Besides, it was plain that my eyes were really eyes to her, that is, they were mirrors in which her little soul sought anxiously to seize some reflection from my own.

'And whilst she thus gazed at me, I let my hand droop on to her quaint little head, and stroked her fur as my first caress. What she felt at my touch was certainly something more than a mere impression of physical pleasure; she had some sentiment, some comprehension of protection and sympathy in her forsaken misery. This was why she had ventured out of her hiding-place in the dark; this was what she had resolved to ask me for with diffidence and hesitation. She did not want either to eat or drink, she only wanted a little companionship in this lonely world, a little friendship.

'How had she learned that such things were, this stray, hunted creature, never touched by a kind hand, never loved by anyone, unless, perhaps, on board some junk, by some poor little Chinese child who had neither caresses nor playthings, sprung up by chance like a sickly plant, one too many in the grovelling yellow crowd, as unhappy and as hungry as herself, and of whom the incomplete soul will at its disappearance from earth leave no more trace than hers? Then one frail paw was timidly laid on my lap, with such infinite delicacy, such exceeding discretion! and, after having lingeringly consulted and implored me through the eyes, she sprang upon my lap, thinking the moment come when she might establish intimate relations with me. She installed herself there in a ball, with a tact, a reserve, a lightness incredible, and always gazing up in my face ... and her eyes becoming still more expressive, still more winning, said plainly to mine,—

'"In this sad autumn day, since we are both alone in this floating prison, rocked and lost in the midst of I know not what endless perils, why should we not give to one another a little of that sweet exchange of feeling which soothes so many sorrows, which has a semblance of some immaterial eternal thing not subjected to death, which calls itself affection, and finds its expression in a touch, a look?"'

In the dying hours of another cat, the charming Moumoutte Blanche, whose frolics we follow, and whose snowy beauty we know so well, the same thought comes to him.

'She tried to rise to greet us, her expression grateful and touched, her eyes showing, as much as human eyes could, the internal presence and the pain of that which we call the soul.

'One morning I found her stiff and cold, with glassy orbs, a dead beast, a thing men cast out on to the dust heap. Then I bade Sylvester dig a little grave in a corner of the courtyard, at the foot of a shrub.... Where was gone that which I had seen shine in her dying eyes, the little, flickering, anxious flame from within: where was it gone?'

And he carries her little lifeless body himself down into the open air.

'Never had there been a more radiant day of June, never a softer silence and warmth crossed by the gay buzzing of summer flies; the courtyard was all blossom, the rose boughs covered with roses; a sweet country calm rested on all the gardens around; the swallows and martins slumbered; only the old tortoise, Suleima, more widely awake the warmer it became, travelled merrily without aim or goal over the old sun-bathed stones. There was everywhere that melancholy of skies too fair, of weather too fine, in the exhaustion of a hot noon-day. All the plants, all the things, seemed to cruelly shout there the triumph over their own perpetual new birth, without pity for the fragile human creatures who heard that song of summer, weighed themselves with the consciousness of their own impending, unavoidable end.

'This garden was and is to me the oldest and most familiar of all the places of the earth, in which all the smallest details have been known to me from the earliest hours of the vague and surprised impressions of infancy. So much so that I am attached to it with all my soul; that I love with a singular force and regard almost as my fetish the venerable plants which grow there, its trellised branches, its climbing jessamines, and a certain rose-coloured diclytra which every month of March displays on the same spot its early-burgeoning leaves, sends out its flowers in April, grows yellow in the suns of June, and at last, burnt up by August, seems to give up the ghost and perish.... And with an infinite melancholy, in this place so gay with the fresh sunlight of a young year, I watched the two beloved figures with white hair and mourning gowns, my mother and Aunt Claire, going and coming, leaning down over a flower border as they had done so many years to see what blossoms were already opening, or raising their heads to look at the buds of the creepers and the roses. And when the two black robes went onward and became farther away in the far perspective of a long green avenue, I saw how much slower was their step, how bent were their forms. Alas for that time too close at hand when in the green avenue which would be ever the same, I should behold their shadows no more! Is it possible that a time will ever come when they shall have left this life? I feel as if they will not entirely depart so long as I myself shall be here, to invoke their benevolent presence, and that in the summer evenings I shall still see their blessed shades pass under the old jessamines and vines, and that something of their spirit will remain to me in the plants which they cherished, in the drooping boughs of the honeysuckle and in the rosy petals of the old diclytra!'

He feels, and feels intensely, the similarity of sentiment between himself and all other forms of sentient life. He is not ashamed to perceive and acknowledge that the emotions of the animal are absolutely the same in substance as our own, and differ from ours only in degree. Could this knowledge become universal it would go far to make cruelty impossible in man, but as yet it has only been realised and admitted by the higher minds of a very few, such as his own, as Tennyson's, as Wordsworth's, as Browning's, as Lecomte de Lisle's, as Sully Prudhomme's; it requires humility and sympathy in the human breast of no common kind; it is the absolute antithesis of the vanity and egotism of what is called the scientific mind, although more truly scientific, that is, more logical, than the bombast and self-worship of the biologist and physiologist.

Loti sees and feels that the little African cat from Senegal, which he brought to his own Breton home, is moved by the same feelings as himself, and in a more pathetic because a more helpless way, and he has remorse for a momentary unkindness to her as though she were living still.

'It was one day when, with the obstinacy of her race, she had jumped where she had been twenty times forbidden to go, and had broken a vase to which I was much attached. I gave her a slap at first; then, my anger not satiated, I pursued her and kicked her with my foot. The slap had only surprised her, but the kick told her that it was war between us; and then she fled as fast as four legs would take her, her tail like a feather in the wind. When safe under a piece of furniture she turned round and cast at me a look of reproach and distress, believing herself lost, betrayed, and assassinated by one beloved, into whose hands she had entrusted her fate; and as my look at her remained hostile and unkind, she gave vent to the great cry of a creature at bay. Then all my wrath ceased in one instant: I called her, I caressed her, I soothed her, taking her on my knees all breathless and terrified. Oh, that last cry of despair from an animal, whether from the poor ox tied to the slaughter-place, or of the miserable rat held in the teeth of a bull-dog—that last cry which hopes nothing, which appeals to no one, which is like a supreme protestation thrown in the face of Nature, an appeal to some unknown pity floating in the air. Now all which remains of my little cat, whom I remember so living and so droll, are a few bones in a hole at the foot of a tree. And her flesh, her little person, her affection for me, her infinite terror that day she was scolded, her great joy, her anguish and reproach—all, in a word, which moved and lived, and had their being around these bones—all have become but a little dust!'

'What a spiritual mystery, a mystery of the soul, that constant affection of an animal, and its long gratitude!' he says in another place; and when, meaning to act mercifully, he gives chloroform to a poor, sick, stray cat, he is haunted by the fear that he has done wrong to end for it that poor little atom of joyless, friendless life, which was all that it could call its own.

This is its story,—

'An old, mange-eaten cat, driven away from its home, no doubt by its owner, for its age and infirmities, had established itself in the street on the doorstep of our house, where a little warmth from a November sun came to comfort it. It is a habit of certain people who call their selfishness sensibility to send out to be purposely lost, the creatures which they will not take care of any longer, and do not desire to see suffer. All the day he had sat there, piteously huddled in a corner of a window, looking so unhappy and so humble! An object of disgust to all the passers-by, threatened by children, by dogs, by continual dangers, every hour more ill and feeble, eating Heaven knows what rubbish, got with difficulty out of the gutter, he dragged out his existence, prolonging it as best he might, trying to retard the moment of his death. His poor head was covered with scabs and sores, and had scarcely any fur left on it, but his eyes remained pretty, and seemed full of thought. He had certainly felt, in all the frightful bitterness of his lot, that last degradation of all, the inability to make his toilette, to polish his coat, to wash and comb himself as all cats love to do so carefully. It hurt me so to see this poor lost animal that, after having sent him food into the street, I approached him and spoke to him gently. (Animals soon understand kind words, and are consoled by them.) Having been so often hunted and driven away, he was at first frightened at seeing me near him; his first look was timid, suspicious, at once a reproach and a prayer! Then soon comprehending that I was there from sympathy, and astonished at so much happiness, he addressed me in his own way: 'Trr! Trr! Trr!' getting up out of politeness, trying, despite his mangy state, to arch his back in the hope that I should stroke him. But the pity I felt for him, though great, could not go as far as that. The joy of being caressed he was never to know again. But in compensation it occurred to me that it would be kind to end his life of pain by giving him a gentle, dreamful death. An hour later, Sylvester, my servant, who had bought some chloroform, drew him gently into our stable, and induced him to lie down on some warm hay in an osier basket which was destined to be his mortuary chamber. Our preparations did not disturb him: we had rolled a card into a cone-shaped form, as we had seen the ambulance surgeon do; he had looked at us with a contented look, thinking he had at last found a lodging and people who had pity on him, new owners who would shelter him.

'Despite the horror of his disease, I stooped over him and stroked him, and, always caressing him, I induced him to lie still, and to bury his little nose in the cone of cardboard; he, a little surprised at first, and sniffing the strange, potent odour with alarm, ended however in doing what I wished with such docility that I hesitated to continue my work. The annihilation of a thinking creature is, equally with annihilation of man, a cruel and responsible thing, and contains the same revolting mystery. And death, besides, carries in itself so much majesty that it is capable of giving grandeur in an instant to the most tiny and finite creatures, as soon as its shadow descends on them. Once he raised his poor head to look at me fixedly; our eyes met, his with an expressive interrogation, an intense anxiety, asked me, "What is it that you do? You whom I know so little, but to whom I trusted—what is it that you do to me?" And I still hesitated; but his throat inclined downwards, and his face rested on my hand, which I did not withdraw; stupefaction had begun to steal over him, and I hoped that he would not look at me again.

'And yet, yes, once again! Cats, as the village people here say, have their lives united to their bodies. In one last struggle for life his eyes met mine; across his mortal semi-sleep he seemed now to perceive and understand: "Ah! it was to kill me, then? Well, I let you do it! It is too late—I sleep!"

'In truth, I feared I had done ill. In this world, where we know nothing surely of anything, it is not even allowed us to let pity take this shape. His last look, infinitely sad, even whilst glazing in death, continued to pursue me with reproach. "Why," it said, "why interfere with my fate? Without you I should have dragged my life on a little longer, had a few more little thoughts. I had still strength to jump up on a window-sill, where the dogs could not reach me; where I was not too cold in the morning, especially if the sun shone there. I still passed some bearable hours watching the movement in the street, seeing other cats come and go, having consciousness of what was doing round me, whilst now there is nothing for me but to rot away for ever into something which will have no memory. *Now I am no more!*" Truly, I should have recollected that the feeblest and poorest things prefer to linger on under the most miserable conditions, prefer no matter what suffering to the terror of being nothing, of *being no more.*'

And he cannot forgive himself an act which was meant out of kindness, but in which the regard of the dying animal makes him see almost a crime. This tenderness for every breathing thing, this sentiment of the infinite, intense pity and mystery which accompany all forms of death is ever present with him, and nothing in its hour of dissolution is too small or too fragile, or too mean or too miserable, in his sight not to arouse this in him.

Read only the story of the *Sorrow of an Old Galley Slave.*

This old man, who has been in prison many times, is at last being sent out to New Caledonia. 'Old as I am, could they not have let me die in France?' he says to our friend Yves (Mon Frére Yves), who is gone with his gunboat to take a band of these prisoners from the shore to the ship in which they are to make their voyage. Encouraged by the sympathy of Yves in his impending exile, the old felon shows him his one treasure; it is a little cage with a sparrow in it.

'It is a tame bird, that knows his voice, and has learnt to sit on his shoulder. It was a year with him in his cell, and with great difficulty he has obtained permission to carry it with him to Caledonia, and, the permission once obtained, with what trouble he has made a little cage for it to travel in, to get the bits of wood and wire necessary, and a little green paint to brighten it and make it look pretty!

'"Poor sparrow!" says Yves to me afterwards when he tells me this tale. "It had only a few crumbs of prison bread such as they give to convicts, but he seems quite happy all the same. He jumps about gaily like any other bird."

'Later still, as the train reaches the transport ship, he, who has forgotten for the moment the old man and the sparrow, passes by the former, who holds out to him the little cage. "Take it," says the old prisoner, in a changed voice. "I give it to you; perhaps you may like to use it."

'"No, no," says Yves, astonished. "You know you are going to take it with you. The bird will be your little comrade there."

'"Ah," answers the old man, "he is no longer in it. Did you not know? He is no longer here."

'And two tears of unspeakable grief rolled down his withered cheeks.

'During a rough moment of the crossing the door of the cage had blown open, the sparrow had fluttered, frightened, and in a second of time had fallen into the sea, his wings, which had been clipped, not being able to sustain him.

'Oh, that moment of horrible pain! To see the little thing struggle and sink, borne away on the tearing tide, and to be unable to do anything to save him! At first, in a natural movement of appeal, he was on the point of crying for help, of begging them to stop the boat, of entreating for pity, for aid; but his impulse is checked by the consciousness of his own personal degradation. Who would have pity on a miserable old man like him? Who would care for his little drowning bird? Who would hearken to his prayer?

'So he keeps silence, and is motionless in his place while the little grey body floats away on the frothing waves, quivering and struggling always against its fate. And he feels now all alone—frightfully alone for evermore, and his tears dull his sight, the slow salt tears of lonely despair, of a hopeless old age.

'And a young prisoner, chained to his side, laughs aloud to see an old man weep.'

Was anything more beautiful than this ever written in any tongue?

Loti stretches to a nobler and a truer scope the *nihil humani a me alienum puto*. To him nothing which has in it the capacity of attachment and of suffering is alien; and it is this sentiment, this sympathy which breathe through all his written pages like the fragrance of some pressed and perfumed blossom. It is these which make his influence so admirable, so precious, in an age which is choked to the throat in suffocating egotisms and vanities, and bound hand and foot in the ligaments of a preposterous and purblind formalism of exclusive self-adoration. Can any reader arise from reading the page which follows without henceforth giving at least a thought of pity to the brave beasts of the pasture who perish that the human crowds may feed?

'In the midst of the Indian Ocean one sad evening when the wind began to rise.

'Two poor bullocks remained of a dozen which we had taken on board at Singapore, to be eaten on the voyage. These last two has been saved for the greatest need, because the voyage was protracted and the ship blown backward by the wicked monsoon.

'They were two poor creatures, weak, thin, piteous to see, their skin already broken about their starting bones by the rude shaking of the waves. They had journeyed thus many days, turning their backs to their native pastures, whither no one would ever lead them again; tied up shortly by the horns, side by side, lowering their heads meekly every time that a wave broke over them and drenched their bodies in its chilly wash; their eyes dull and sad, they munched together at bad hay, soaked and salted; condemned beasts, already struck off the roll of the living, but fated to suffer long before they would be killed—to suffer from cold, from blows, from sickness, from wet, from want of movement, from fear.

'The evening of which I speak was especially melancholy. At sea there are many such evenings, when ugly, livid clouds drag along on the horizon as the light fades, when the wind arises and the night threatens to be bad. Then when one feels oneself isolated in the midst of these infinite waters, one is seized with a vague terror that twilight on shore would never bring with it even in the dreariest places. And these two poor bullocks, creatures of the meadow and its fresh herbage, more out of their element than men on this heaving and rolling desert, and not having like us any hope to sustain them, were forced, despite their limited intelligence, to endure in their manner all this suffering, and must have seen confusedly the image of their approaching death. They chewed the cud with the slowness of sickness, their big, joyless eyes fixed on the sinister distances of the sea. One by one their companions had been struck down on these boards by their side; during two weeks they had lived alone, drawn together by their loneliness, leaning one against another in the rolling of the ship, rubbing their horns against each other in friendship.

'The person charged with provisioning the ship came to me on the bridge, and said to me in the usual formula: "Captain, they are about to kill a bullock."

'I received him ill, though it was not his fault that he came on such an errand. The slaughter of animals took place just underneath the bridge, and in vain one turned away one's eyes or tried to think of other things, or gazed over the waste of waters. One could not avoid hearing the blow of the mallet struck between the horns in the centre of the poor forehead held down so low to the floor by an iron buckle; then the crash of the falling animal, who drops on the bridge with a clashing of bone upon wood. And immediately after it is bled, skinned, cut in pieces; an atrocious, nauseous odour comes from its opened belly, and all around the planks of the vessel, so clean at other times, are soiled and inundated with blood and filth.

'Well, the moment had come to slay one of the bullocks. A circle of sailors was formed round the iron ring to which it was to be fastened for execution. Of the pair they choose the weaker, one which was almost dying and which allowed itself to be led away without resistance.

'Then the other one turned its head to follow its companion with its melancholy eyes, and seeing that its friend was led to the fatal corner where all the others had fallen, *it understood*; a gleam of comprehension came into the poor bowed head, and it lowed loudly in its sore distress. Oh, that moan of this poor, solitary creature! It was one of the most grievous sounds that I have ever heard, and at the same time one of the most mysterious. There were in it such deep reproach to us, to men, and yet a sort of heart-broken resignation, I know not what, of restrained and stifled grief, as if he, mourning, knew that his lament was useless and that his appeal would be heard by none. "Ah, yes," it said, "the inevitable hour has come for him who was my last remaining brother, who came with me from our home far away, there where we used to run together through the grass. And my turn will come soon, and not a living thing in the world will have any pity either for him or me."

'But I who heard had pity.

'I was even beside myself with pity, and a mad impulse came over me to go and take his big, sickly, mangy head to rest it on my heart, since that is our instinctive caress by which to offer the illusion of protection to those who suffer or who perish. But truly indeed he could look for no succour from anyone, for even I, whose soul had thrilled with pain at the intense anguish of his cry, even I remained motionless and impassive in my place, only turning away my eyes. For the despair of a mere animal should one change the direction of a vessel and prevent three hundred men from eating their share of fresh meat? One would be considered a lunatic if one only thought of such a thing for a moment.

'However, a little cabin boy, who, perhaps, was also himself alone in the world, and had found none to pity him, had heard the cry—had heard it and been moved by it like myself to the depths of his soul. He went up to the bullock and very softly stroked its muzzle. He might have said to it, had he thought to do so,—

'"They will all die too, those who are waiting to eat your flesh to-morrow. Yes, all of them, even the youngest and strongest, and maybe their last hour will be more terrible than yours, and with longer pain. Perhaps it would be better for them if they too had a blow of the pole-axe on their foreheads."

'The animal returned affectionately the boy's caress, gazing at him with grateful, kind eyes, and licking his hand.'

The cynic will demur that this compassion for cattle will not prevent the human eater from consuming his *bœuf à la mode*, or his slice from the sirloin, with appetite. But even if cattle must be slaughtered, how much might their torture be alleviated were men not wholly indifferent to it. The frightful infamies of the cattle trade on sea would be ended were none bought after a voyage. The hideous deaths by drought and by cold, all over the plains of South America, would be no more. No longer would a single living bullock endure thirty agonising operations on his quivering body, when fastened down to the demonstrating or experimenting table of veterinary students. It is not so much death itself, when swift, sure, almost painless, which is terrible, as it is the agony, protracted, infinite, frightful, incalculable, which is inflicted for the passions, the pleasure, or the profit of men.

Were such sympathy as breathes through the *Book of Pity and of Death* largely felt, all the needless cruelty inflicted by the human race, that mere carelessness and indifference of which the world is so full, would gradually be reduced until it might in time cease entirely. The cruelty of the rich to horses from mere want of thought alone is appalling. Few know or care how their stables are managed, what is the maximum of work which should be demanded of a horse, and what the torture inflicted by certain methods of breaking-in and harnessing and driving. Frequently are to be seen the advertisements by carriage-makers of 'one-horse broughams, warranted for hill work and to carry four persons, with, if desired, a basket on roof for railway luggage.' That these abominable loads are given to one horse continually there can be no doubt, as these announcements are frequent in all the newspapers, and never seem to elicit any wonder or censure. A shabby and vicious economy constantly gives, in this extravagant and spendthrift generation, a load to one poor horse which would certainly, in a generation earlier, and undoubtedly in a century ago, only have been given to a pair of horses or even to two pairs with postillions. Speed, also, being insisted on, no matter what load is dragged, the race of carriage-horses grows weaker and weaker in build and stamina. What woman, either, in any capital of the world, thinks for a moment of keeping her horses out in rain and snow, motionless for hours, whilst she is chattering in some warm and fragrant drawing-room, or dancing and flirting in some cotillon? No attention is ever given to the preferences, tastes and affections of animals, which yet are undoubtedly of great strength and tenacity in them, not only towards their owners, but often, also, towards their own kind. I am, at the present moment, driving a mare who was always driven with her sister, who died eighteen months ago. She does not forget her sister, and the stable companion given her instead she hates, and endeavours, with all her might, to kick and bite across the pole and in the stalls. I owned also a pony so attached to his comrade that they could live in the same loose-box together, and when the companion died, this pony was miserable, whinnied and neighed perpetually, lost health, and in a few months died also. In life he was the humble and devoted slave of his brother, would fondle him, clean him, follow him about in all directions, and show to him every testimony of affection possible in one creature to another. Yet such feelings as these, although very common in animals, are never remembered or considered for an instant, and animals of all kinds are sold from owner to owner, and hustled from place to place, with no more regard than if they were chairs and tables. What they suffer from strange voices, new homes, and unfamiliar treatment no one inquires, for no one cares. Convenience and profit are all which are considered. There is little or no remembrance of the idiosyncrasy of each creature. The ecstatic, ardent, nervous temperament of the dog; the timid, imaginative, impulsive mind of the horse; the shrinking shyness of the sheep, the attachment to place and people of the wildest or silliest creature when once kindly treated and long domesticated—all these things are never recollected or considered in dealing with them. Hard and fast rules are laid down for them, by which they, in their various ways, are forced to abide. Their natural instincts and desires are treated as crimes, and their longings and preferences are unnoticed or thwarted. Who ever thinks of or cares for the injustice and cruelty concentrated in that single phrase, 'The hounds were whipped off,' or its pendant, 'The fox was broken up,' etc., etc.? They are sentences so common, and so often used, that the horrible cruelty involved in them has altogether passed out of notice. Men and women grow up amidst cruelty, and are so accustomed to it, that they no more perceive it than they do the living organisms in the air they breathe or in the water they drink. Were it otherwise they could not walk down Ludgate Hill or up Montmartre without unbearable pain.

The grief of the ox driven from his pastures, of the cow divided from her calf, of the dog sent away from his master, of the lion torn from his desert or jungle, of the ape brought to die of nostalgia in cold climes, of the eagle chained down in inaction and gloom, of all the innumerable creatures taken from their natural life or their early associations, because the whim, the appetite, the caprice, the pleasure or the avarice of men is gratified or tempted by their pain, never moves anyone to pity. They are 'subject-creatures' in the human code, and what they may suffer, or may not suffer, is of no import; of less import even than the dying out of the Maoris, or the dwindling away of the Red Indian tribes, or the death of African porters on the caravan routes.

It is said that there is less cruelty now than in earlier times, because some public spectacles of cruelty have been put down in many countries. But since this age is the most exacting in small things, the most egotistic, the most silly, and the most nervous which the world has seen, it is probable that its increased interference with animal liberty, and its increased fear of them (not to mention its many increased means of animal destruction and torture, whether for sport or experiment) have diminished their freedom and multiplied their sacrifice. Freedom of choice and act is the first condition of animal as of human happiness. How many animals in a million have even relative freedom in any moment of their lives? No choice is ever permitted to them; and all their most natural instincts are denied or made subject to authority.

If old pictures and old drawings and etchings are any criterion of the modes of life of their own day, there can be no doubt that animals were much freer and much more intimately associated with men in earlier times than they are now. In their representations we see no banqueting scene without the handsome dogs stretched upon the rushes or before the daïs; no village fair without its merry mongrels running in and out between the rustics' legs: no triumph of emperor or ceremonial of cardinal or pope without the splendid retriever and the jewel-collared hound: in the pictures of the Nativity the animals are always represented as friendly and interested spectators; in scenes from the lives of saints the introduction of animals wild and tame are constant; therefore, as we know that all these old painters and etchers depicted invariably what they saw around them, it is certain that they were accustomed to see in their daily haunts animals made part and parcel of men's common life. Those animals were roughly treated, may be, as men themselves then were, but they were regarded as comrades and companions, not as alien creatures to be despised and unremembered except for use and profit. When the knight offered up his falcon his heart was rent, as in parting from a brother most beloved.

It is a fearful thought that were not animals considered to contribute to the convenience, the profit and the amusement of men, they would not be allowed to live for a half-century longer. They would be destroyed as ruthlessly as the buffalo of the United States of America has already been, and all birds would be exterminated as well without remorse. There is no honour, no decency shown in the treatment of animals and birds by men. When Menelek sent, as a gift to Carnot, his two tame young lions, who had been free in his rude African palace, and were only eighteen months old, the receiver of the gift could give them nothing better than a narrow cage in the Jardin des Plantes.

Even the lovely plumage and the great agricultural utility of the thistle-seed-eating goldfinch does not save him from being trapped, shot, poisoned, caged, as the ignorance, greed, or pleasure of his human foes may choose. Nothing is too large or too small, too noble or too innocent, to escape the rapacity, the brutality, and the egotism of men; and in the schools all the world over there is never a syllable said which could by suggestion or influence awaken the minds of the attendant pupils to a wider, gentler, and truer sense of the relations of animals and birds to the human race. Indeed, it would be almost ridiculous to attempt to do so when no princeling makes a royal visit or an Eastern tour without slaughtering, by hundreds and by thousands, tame birds and untamed beasts; when in every market and every shambles the most atrocious suffering is inflicted openly and often needlessly; when the imperial and royal persons find their chief diversion and distraction in rending the tender flesh of hares and pheasants, of elk and chamois with shot and bullet; and when the new scientific lexicons opened to them teach children how to make a white rabbit 'blush' by the severance of certain sensitive nerves, and bid them realise that in the pursuit of 'knowledge,' or even of fantastic conjecture, it is worthy and wise to inflict the most hellish tortures on the most helpless and harmless of sentient creatures. To sacrifice for experiment, or pleasure, or gain, all the other races of creation, is the doctrine taught by precept and example from the thrones the lecture-desks, the gunrooms, and the laboratory-tables of the world. It is not a doctrine which can make either a generous or a just generation. Youth is callous and selfish of itself, and by its natural instincts; and all the example and tuition given from palace, pulpit and professorial chair are such as to harden its callousness and confirm its selfishness.

Even the marvellous sagacity, docility and kindness of the elephant do not protect him from being slain in tens of thousands, either for the mere value of his tusks, or for the mere pleasure and pride taken by men in his slaughter. Even so inoffensive a creature as the wild sheep of the hills of Asia is mercilessly hunted down and shot by European sportsmen, although his carcass is absolutely of no use or value whatever when found, and it is usually lost by the shot creature falling down a precipice or into some inaccessible nullah. Nearer at home the chamois and ibex have been so treated that they will ere long be extinct on the European continent. To wild creatures there is no kind of compassion or of justice ever shown. I have known an officer relate without shame how, when he was once sleeping in a tent on the plains of India, a leopard entered between the folds of the canvas, and as he awoke stood still and looked at him, then quietly turned round and went out again; he stretched out his arm for his revolver, and shot, as it passed out into the air, the creature which had spared him. There is no decency, no common ordinary feeling or conscientiousness, in men in their dealings with animals. They publish their advertisements without compunction of 'geldings' and 'bullocks,' and inflict castration wholesale whenever they deem it to their profit or convenience to do so, whether their prey be a bull or a cock, a colt or a puppy. When the gourmand feels his 'belly with fat capon lined,' the atrocious suffering by which the capon has been swollen to unnatural obesity never troubles him for a moment, nor when he eats his pâté de Strasbourg has he any feelings or remembrance for the geese with their webbed feet nailed down to the boards before the sweltering fires.

England has lately lamented the loss of a young man of royal birth, and of gentle and kindly disposition, who died under circumstances which touched the national sentiment. Yet the Duke of Clarence, of whom it was said that he would not have willingly wronged a living being, passed his last days on earth, the days in which he already felt the chills and languor of impending sickness, in the slaughter of tame birds. There is something shocking in the thought that, during the last hours in which an amiable youth enjoyed the gladness of the air and the freedom of the woods, he should have been solely occupied in taking the life of innocent and happy creatures, reared merely to offer this miserable diversion to him and his. This degraded sport, the curse, the shame and the peril of England, has never had passed on it a commentary more severe, a sarcasm more scathing than the words, 'There will be no shooting until after the royal funeral,' which were announced at, and of, innumerable country-house parties; the sacrifice of the idolised amusement being emphasised as the most complete expression of woe and regret possible to the nation. It would be ridiculous, were it not sickening, that in a land where men prate from morning till night of public duty, and make boast of their many virtues, public and private, no shame is attached to the shameful fact that all its gentlemen of high degree, all its males who have leisure and large means, find no other pursuit or pleasure possible in autumn and winter than the innocent slaughter or maiming of winged creatures, reared merely to furnish them with such diversion.

It is inconceivable that reasonable beings, who claim to exercise preponderance in the influence and direction of public affairs, should not perceive how injurious and debasing as an example is this foolish and cruel pursuit which they have allowed to obtain over them all the force of habit, and all the sanctity of a religion. Common rights are sacrificed, harmless privileges abolished, old paths blocked, pleasant time-consecrated rights of way are forbidden through copse and furze and covert, all wild natural woodland life is destroyed by the traps, poisons and guns of the keepers and their myrmidons, and incessant torture of woodland animals, and incessant irritation of rural populations go on without pause or check, in order that princes, gentlemen and *rastaquouères* may pass week after week, month after month, year after year, in this kind of carnage which is delightful to them, and at which their women unashamed are encouraged to assist. 'Walking with the guns' has now become a favourite and fashionable feminine amusement. In the middle of the day both sexes indulge in those rich dishes and stimulating drinks, which are their daily fare, and carry typhoid fever into their veins; and after luncheon, replete and content, they all return to the organised slaughter in the leafless woodlands, or the heather-covered moors, or the 'happy autumn fields.' The gladiatorial shows of Rome might be more brutal, but were at least more manly than this 'sport,' which is the only active religion of the so-called 'God-serving classes.' It is hereditary, like scrofula; the devouring ambition of the baby-heir of a great house is to be old enough to go out with the keepers; and instinct against such slaughter, if it existed in his childish soul, would be killed by ridicule; example, precept and education are all bent to one end, to render him a slayer of creatures wild and tame. If he make later on the tour of the world, his path over its continents will be littered by dead game, large and small, from the noble elephant to the simple wild sheep, from the peaceful and graminivorous elk to the hand-fed pheasant. There is no escape for him; even if he have little natural taste for it, he will affect to have such taste, knowing that he will otherwise be despised by his comrades, and be esteemed a *lusus naturæ* in his generation. He will not dare to be 'odd'; the gun is the weapon of the gentleman, as in other days was the rapier or the sword; the gunroom is his *Academe*; he is learned in the choice of explosive bullets, and can explain precisely to any fair companion the manner in which they rend and tear the tender flesh of the forest animals.

Read this exploit of sport, printed by a Mr Guillemard, apparently without the slightest sense of shame. He is in the pursuit of 'bighorn' (*ovis nivicola*), animals, perfectly innocent and harmless, living in the wilds of Kamschatka.

'One, which appeared to carry the best horns, was more or less hidden by some rocks, but the other stood broadside on upon a little knoll, throwing up his head from time to time.... Resting my rifle on the ground, I took the easier shot. There was no excuse for missing, and as the bullet *made the well-known sound dear to the heart of the sportsman, I saw that it had broken the shoulder,* and the animal, staggering a yard or two, fell over seawards and was lost to view.'

It is lost irrevocably. The joy of having slaughtered him is not, however, the less.

A little farther on the sportsman suddenly comes upon 'a very much astonished bighorn; a fine old ram of the fifth or sixth year.'

'I fired almost before I was conscious of it, but not a moment too soon, for the beast was in the act of turning as I touched the trigger. It was his last voluntary movement, and the next instant he was rolling down the precipice.... *The fun was not yet over*, for, perched upon a bare pinnacle, stood another of our quarry. The animal had been driven into a corner by some of our party on the cliff above. The next instant, after a vain but desperate effort to save himself, he was whirling through four hundred feet of space.... On going up to him I found one of the massive horns broken short off, and the whole of the hind quarters shattered into a mass of bleeding pulp.... Our decks were like a butcher's shop on Boxing Day.'

And the scene seems so beautiful to him that he photographs it.

This is the tone which is general and which is considered becoming when speaking or writing of the brutal slaughter of harmless creatures. No perception of its disgusting callousness, its foul unseemliness, ever visits writer or reader, speaker or hearer.

When men kill in self-defence it is natural; when they kill for food it is excusable; but to kill for pleasure and for paltry pride is vile. How long will such pleasure and such pride be the rule of the world? They give the strongest justification that Anarchists can claim. If the heart of Tourguenieff could be put into every human breast, the quail would be a dear little feathered friend to all; but as the world is now made, the story of Tourguenieff's quail would be read in vain to deaf ears, or, if heard, would be drowned in peals of inane laughter. Could that sense of solidarity of community between animals and ourselves, which is so strongly realised by Pierre Loti, be communicated to the multitude of men, cruelty would not entirely cease, because men and women are frequently horribly cruel to each other, and to dependents, and to children, and to inferior and subject human races, but cruelty to animals would then be placed on the same plane as cruelty to human beings, would be regarded by society with loathing, and punished by the severity of law, as cruelty in many forms to human creatures is now punished. Whereas, now not only are all punishments of cruelty, other than to man, so slight as to mean hardly anything at all, in fact, totally inefficient and wholly inadequate,[J] but the vast mass of cruelty to animals, the daily continual brutal offences against them of their owners and employers, is placed, perforce, entirely out of reach of any punishment whatsoever.

A man can chain up his dog in filth and misery; the rider may cut his horse to pieces at his caprice; the woman may starve and beat her cat; the landowner may have traps set all over his lands for fur and feather; the slaughterer of cattle may bungle and torture at his pleasure; the lady may wear the dead bodies of birds on her head and on her gown; the mother may buy puppies and kittens, squirrels and marmosets, rabbits and guinea-pigs, to be the trembling plaything of her little children, tormented by these in ignorance and in maliciousness till death releases the four-footed slaves; all these and ten thousand other shapes and kinds of cruelty are most of them not punishable by law. Indeed, no law could in many instances find them out and reach them, for the cruelty often goes on behind the closed doors of house and stable, kennel-yard and cattleshed, nursery of the rich and garret of the poor. No law can reach it in its aggregate; law is indeed, as it stands, poor and meagre everywhere, but cruelty could not, by any alteration of it, be really abolished. To be eradicated, it must become a revolting thing in the eyes of men; it must offend their conscience and their love of justice. It would do this in time, could such a sense of unison with animals as is the inspiring motive of the *Book of Pity and of Death* become general in humanity. There is little hope that it ever will, but the world would be a lovelier dwelling-place if it could be so.

Rome, it is tritely said, had no monument to Pity. Yet it was the Romans by whom the man was stoned who slew the dove which sought refuge in his breast. The multitudes of the present day are, all over the world, below those Romans in sentiment. Their farmers shoot even the swallows which build confidingly beneath the eaves of their roofs. Their gentry cause to be trapped and slain all the innocent birds which shelter and nest in their woods. The down of jays' breasts flutters on the fans of their drawing-room beauties, and *lophophores* and *colibri* sparkle in death upon their hair. If in a mob of Londoners, Parisians, New Yorkers, Berliners, Melbourners, a dove fluttered down to seek a refuge, a hundred dirty hands would be stretched out to seize it, and wring its neck; and if any one with the pity of old Rome tried to save and cherish it, he would be rudely bonneted, and mocked, and hustled amidst the brutal guffaws of roughs, lower and more hideous in aspect and in nature than any animal which lives. There is no true compassion in that crowd of opposed yet mixing races which, for want of a better word, we call the modern world. There is too great a greed, too common a selfishness, for the impersonal and pure feeling to be general in it. Yet, as children are born cruel, but may often be taught, by continual example and perception, kindness and self-sacrifice, so perchance might the multitudes be led to it were there any to teach it as Francis of Assisi taught it in his generation, were there any to cry aloud against its infamy with the force and the fervour of a Bruno, of a Bernard, of a Benedict.

St Francis would have walked with Loti hand in hand, through the olive-trees, with the good wolf between them; and what beautiful things the trio would have said to each other!

But the Churches have never heeded the teaching of Assisi; they have never cared for or inculcated tenderness to the other races of creation in which, whether winged or four-footed, the preacher of Assisi recognised his brethren. They have been puffed up with the paltry pride of human self-admiration; and they are now being outbid and outrun in influence and popularity by the teachers of that still more brutal, more narrow, and more vainglorious creed which calls itself science, in which as many crimes are perpetrated as in the name of liberty.

As all religions reign awhile, then pass and perish, so will the reign of science; but very possibly not before its example and demands will have destroyed on the face of the planet all races except man, who in his turn will become nought on the exhausted surface of a dead earth. Meantime, whilst those whom we call inferior creatures are still with us, while the birds people the air which would be so empty without them, and the beasts live around us with their pathetic eyes, their wise instincts, their long, patient, unrewarded forbearance, we are nearer to the secret mystery of life when we feel, with Francis and with Loti, the common soul which binds ourselves and them, than when we stand aloof from them in a puffed-up and pompous vanity, or regard them as the mere chattels and chores of a bondslave's service.

SHELLEY

Above my head in the starry July night goes with soft, swift, silent movement through the scented air, above the tall leaves of the aloes, and under the green boughs of the acacias, a little brown owl. Families of them live on the roof of this great house, and at sunset they descend and begin hunting for crickets and moths and water-beetles and mice. These owls are called, in scientific nomenclature, the *scops carniola*; to the peasantry they are known as the *chiu*; by Shelley they were called the aziola. I have never found any Italian who called this owl aziola, but I suppose that Mary Godwin did, since she said, 'Do you not hear the aziola cry?' And Shelley made answer, very truly, of this cry, that it was music heard, —

'By wood and stream, meadow and mountain side,
And fields and marshes wide, —
Such as nor voice, nor lute, nor wind, nor bird
The soul ever stirred.'

The note is very far-reaching, deep and sweet, clear and melodious, one single note sounding at intervals of thirty or forty seconds through the still air of the summer night. It is said to be a love call, but I doubt it, for it may be heard long after the pairing season; the bird gives it forth when he is flying as when he is sitting still, and it is unmistakably a note of contentment. Nor do I think it is sad, as Shelley terms it; it has a sound as of pleased meditation in it, and it has a mellow thrill which, once heard, cannot be forgotten ever. For myself, never do I hear the call of the *chiu* (which is often heard from May time until autumn, when these birds migrate to the East) without remembering Shelley and wishing that he lived to hear.

He is more truly a son of Italy than any one of her own poets, for he had the sentiment and passion of her natural beauty, which cannot be said of the greatest of them. Neither he nor Byron can be well comprehended by those who are not intimately acquainted with Italian landscape. The exceeding truthfulness of their observation of, and feeling for, it cannot certainly be appreciated except by those who have lived amongst the sights and sounds which took so close a hold upon their imagination and their heart.

Byron must have often ridden over the firm, smooth, yellow shores of the sea beyond Pisa, for he lived some time in the peaceful city dedicated to

St Ranier, and probably both he and Shelley spent many hours many a time in a wood I know well, which follows the line of the sea for sixteen miles, and is many miles in depth. On the shore, pines, rooted in drifted sand half a mile broad, stand between the deciduous trees and the sea beach, and protect them from the violence of the westerly winds; when you are half a mile inland, you leave the pines and find ilex, acacia, beech, holly, juniper, and many aspen and other forest trees. Here the wood-dove, the goldfinch, the nuthatch, the woodpecker, the jay and the cuckoo dwell; here the grassy paths lead down dusky green aisles of foliage, fringed with dog-roses, where one may roam at pleasure all the day long, and meet nothing living beside the birds, except sometimes a stoat or a fox; here the flag-lily and the sword-rush grow in the reedy pools, and the song of the nightingale may be heard in perfection; its nests are made in numbers under the bracken, amongst the gorse and in the impenetrable thickets of the marucca and the heather. These woods are still entirely wild and natural, and they are rarely invaded except by the oxen or buffaloes drawing waggons to be filled with cut furze and dead branches by the rough and picturesque families who sit aloft on the giddy heights of these sylvan loads. But these invaders are few and far between, and in spring and summer these forest lands are as still and solitary as they certainly were when the poets wandered through them, listening to the sea-breeze sighing through the trees.

No one, I repeat, can fully appreciate the fineness and accuracy of observation and description of both Byron and Shelley who does not know Italy well; not with the pretended knowledge of the social hordes who come to its cities for court, and embassy, and gallery, and tea party, but such knowledge as can alone be gained by long and familiar intimacy with its remote and solitary places.

Few, perhaps, if any, think of Shelley as often as I do; and to me his whole personality seems the most spiritual and the most sympathetic of the age.

The personality of Byron startles, captivates, entrances; he flashes by us like a meteor; lover, noble, man of pleasure and of the world, solitary and soldier by turns, and a great poet always, let the poetasters and sciolists of the moment say what they will in their efforts to decry and to deny him. Shelley's has nothing of this dazzling and gorgeous romance, as he has nothing in his portraits of that haughty and fiery challenge which speaks in the pose of the head and the glance of the eyes in every picture of Byron. Shelley's eyes gaze outward with wistful, dreamy tenderness; they are the eyes of contemplative genius, the eyes which behold that which is not seen by the children of men. That sweetness and spirituality which are in his physiognomy characterise the fascination which his memory, like his verse, must exercise over any who can understand his soul. Nothing is more unfitting to him than those wranglings over his remains which are called studies of his life and letters. The solemnity and beauty of his death and burial should surely have secured him repose in his grave.

In no other country than England would it be possible to find writers and readers, so utterly incapable of realising what manner of nature and of mind his was, that they can presume to measure both by their foot-rule of custom and try to press both into their small pint-pot of conventional mortality. Would he not have said of his biographers, as he wrote of critics, —

'Of your antipathy

If I am the Narcissus, you are free

To pine into a sound with hating me?'

What can his conduct, within the bonds of marriage or without them, matter to a world which he blessed and enriched? What can his personal sorrows or failings be to people who should only rejoice to hearken to his melodious voice? Who would not give the lives of a hundred thousand ordinary women to make happy for an hour such a singer as he?

The greatest duty of a man of genius is to his own genius, and he is not bound to dwell for a moment in any circumstances or any atmosphere which injures, restrains, or depresses it. The world has very little comprehension of genius. In England there is, more than anywhere else, the most fatal tendency to drag genius down into the heavy shackles of common-place existence, and to make Pegasus plough the common fields of earth. English genius has suffered greatly from the pressure of middle-class English opinion. It made George Eliot a hypocrite; it made Tennyson a chanter of Jubilee Odes; it put in chains even the bold spirit of Browning; and it has kept mute within the soul much noble verse which would have had rapture and passion in its cadences. The taint of hypocrisy, of Puritanism, of conventionality, has deeply entered into the English character, and how much and how great has been the loss it has caused to literature none will ever be able to measure.

Shelley affranchised himself in its despite, and for so doing he suffered in his life and suffers in his memory. He was a Republican in a time when republican doctrines were associated with the horrors of the guillotine and the excesses of the mob, then fresh in the public mind. He would now be called an Altruist where he was then called a Jacobin. His exhortation to the men of England, —

'Men of England, wherefore plough

For the lords who lay ye low?

Wherefore weave with toil and care

The rich robes your tyrants wear?' —

would, were it published now, be quoted with admiration by all the good Radicals, with John Morley at their head; indeed, it is astonishing that they have never reprinted it in their manuals for the people. It is wonderful also that 'The Masque of Anarchy' has escaped quotation by the leaders of the Irish opposition, and that the lines written during the Castlereagh administration have not been exhumed to greet the administration of any Tory Viceroy. Shelley in these forgot, as poets will forget, his own law, that the poet, like the chameleon, should feed from air, not earth. But what then was deemed so terrible a political crime in one of his gentle birth and culture would now be thought most generous and becoming, as the democratic principles of Vernon Harcourt and Lord Rosebery are now considered to be by their political party; the odes and sonnets which then drew down on him execration and persecution would now procure him the gratitude of Gladstone and the honour of the *Nineteenth Century*.

'A people starved and stabbed in the untillèd field,'

is a line which has been strangely overlooked by orators for Ireland.

Shelley's political creed — if an impersonal but intense indignation can deserve the name of creed — was born of his hatred of tyranny and a pity for pain which amounted to a passion. But his nature was not one which could long nurture hate; and he says truly that, with him and in all he wrote, 'Love is celebrated everywhere as the sole law which should govern the moral world.'

In politics, had he lived now, he would certainly have fared much better; in moral liberty also he would, I think, have found more freedom. Though the old hypocrisy clings still in so much to English society, in much it has been shaken off, and within the last twenty years there has been a very marked abandonment of conventional opinion. There is much that is conventional still; much to the falsehood of which it is still deemed necessary to adhere. But still there is a greater liberality, a wider tolerance, an easier indulgence; and it may certainly be said that Shelley, if he lived now, would neither be worried to dwell beside Harriet Westbrooke, nor would Mary Godwin be excluded from any society worthy of the name. Society is arriving at the consciousness that for an ordinary woman to expect the monopoly of the existence of a man of genius is a crime of vanity and of egotism so enormous that it cannot be accepted in its pretensions or imposed upon him in its tyranny. Therefore it is wholly out of date, and unfitting to the times, to see critics and authors discussing and embittering the memory of Shelley on account of his relations with women.

These relations are in any man indisputably those which most reveal his character; but they are none the less indisputably those with which the public have least permission to interfere. We have the 'Prometheus Unbound' and 'The Revolt of Islam'; we have the sonnet to England and the ode to the skylark; we have the 'Good-night'; and the 'Song'; and with all these riches and their like given to us by his bounteous and beautiful youth, shall we dare to rake in the ashes of his funeral-pyre and search in the faded lines of his letters to find material for carping censure or for ingenious misconstruction? It adds greater horror to death; this groping of the sextons of the press amongst the dust of the tomb, this unhallowed" searching of alien hands amongst the papers which were written only to be read by eyes beloved. The common mortal is freed from such violation; he has left nothing behind him worth the stealing, he has been a decorous and safe creature, and his signature has been affixed to his weekly accounts, his bank drafts, his household orders, his epistles to his children at school, and not a soul cares to disturb the dust on their tied-up bundles. But the man or woman of genius has no sepulchre buried so deep in earth or barred so strongly that the vampire of curiosity cannot enter to break in and steal; from Heloise to Shelley the paper on which the burning words which come straight from the heart are recorded is the prey of the vulgar, and the soul bared only to one other soul becomes the sport of those who have not eyes to see, nor ears to hear, nor mind to understand.

I have said ere now often, and I shall say it as long as I have power to say anything, that with the private life of the man or woman of genius the world has nothing to do.

What is it to the world who was Allegra's mother, or who was the prototype of Mignon, or who was the Lady of Solitude of the Elysian isles of the 'Epipsychidion'; what matter whether Shakespeare blessed or cursed Anne Hathaway, or whether personal pains and longings inspired the doctrines of the 'Tetrarchordon'? It matters no more than it matters whether Lesbia's sparrow was a real bird or a metaphor, no more than it matters whether the carmen to Cerinthe were written for the poet's pleadings *in propria persona* or for his friend. It matters nothing. We have 'Don Juan' and 'Wilhelm Meister'; we have 'Hamlet' and the 'Lycidas'; we have the songs of Catullus and the elegies of Tibullus; what wants the world more than these? Alas! alas! it wants that which shall pull down the greater stature to the lower; it wants that which shall console it for its own drear dulness by showing it the red spots visible on the lustre of the sun.

The disease of 'documents,' as they are called in the jargon of the time, is only another name for the insatiable appetite to pry into the private life of those greater than their fellows, in the hope to find something therein wherewith to belittle them. Genius may say as it will that nothing human is alien to it, humanity always sullenly perceives that genius *is* genius precisely because it is something other than humanity, something beyond it, above it—never of it; something which stands aloof from it, however it may express itself as kin to it. That the soul of man is divine is a doubtful postulate; but, that whatever there is divine in a human form is to be found in genius, is true for all time. The mass of men dimly feel this, and they vaguely resent it, and dislike genius, as the multitude in India and Palestine disliked Buddha and Christ. When the tiger tears it or the cross bears it the mass of men are consoled for their own inferiority to it. In the world Prometheus is always kept chained; and the fire he brings from heaven is spat upon.

> 'Oh, weep for Adonais!—The quick Dreams,
> The passion-winged Ministers of thought,
> Who were his flocks, whom near the living streams
> Of his young spirit he fed, and whom he taught
> The love which was its music, wander not,
> Wander no more, from kindling brain to brain,
> But droop there, whence they spring; and mourn their lot
> Round the cold heart, where, after their sweet pain,
> They ne'er will gather strength, nor find a home again.
>
> The soul of Adonais, like a star,
> Beacons from the abode where the Eternal are.'

Every line in Shelley's verse which speaks of Italy is pregnant with the spirit of the land. Each line is a picture; true and perfect, whether of day or night, of water or shore, of marsh or garden, of silence or melody. Take this poem, 'Julian and Maddalo,'—

> 'How beautiful is sunset, when the glow
> Of heaven descends upon a land like thee,
> Thou paradise of exiles, Italy!
> As those who pause on some delightful way,
> Though bent on pleasant pilgrimage, we stood
> Looking upon the evening, and the flood
> Which lay between the city and the shore
> Paved with the image of the sky: the hoar

And airy Alps, towards the north, appeared,
Thro' mist, a heaven-sustaining bulwark, reared
Between the east and west; and half the sky
Was roofed with clouds of rich emblazonry,
Dark purple at the zenith, which still grew
Down the steep west into a wondrous hue
Brighter than burning gold, even to the rent
Where the swift sun yet paused in his descent
Among the many-folded hills—they were
These famous Euganean hills, which bear,
As seen from Lido through the harbour piles,
The likeness of a clump of peaked isles—
And then, as if the earth and sea had been
Dissolved into one lake of fire, were seen
Those mountains towering, as from waves of flame,
Around the vaporous sun, from which there came
The inmost purple spirit of light, and made
Their very peaks transparent.'

Whoever knows the lagoons of the Lido and of Murano knows the exquisite justness and veracity of this description. I thought of it not long ago when, sailing over the shallow water on the way to the city from Torcello, I saw the sun descend behind the roseate Euganean hills, whilst the full moon hung exactly opposite, over the more distant chain of the Istrian mountains.

Then this again:

'I see a chaos of green leaves and fruit
Built round dark caverns, even to the root
Of the living stems who feed them; in whose bowers,
There sleep in their dark dew the folded flowers;
Beyond, the surface of the unsickled corn
Trembles not in the slumbering air, and borne
In circles quaint, and ever-changing dance,
Like winged stars the fire-flies flash and glance
Pale in the open moonshine; but each one
Under the dark trees seems a little sun,
A meteor tamed; a fixed star gone astray

From the silver regions of the Milky-way.
Afar the Contadino's song is heard,
Rude, but made sweet by distance;—and a bird
Which cannot be a nightingale, and yet
I know none else that sings so sweet as it
At this late hour;—and then all is still.'

He said, 'which cannot be a nightingale,' because he wrote this on the 1st of July, and nightingales rarely sing after June is past. But I have heard nightingales sing in Italy until the middle of July if the weather were cool and if their haunts, leafy and shady, were well protected from the sun; so that this bird which he heard was most likely Philomel. Blackbirds and woodlarks sing late into the dark of evening, but never in the actual night.

How he heard and studied the nightingale!

'There the voluptuous nightingales
Are awake through all the broad noonday,
When one with bliss or sadness fails,
And through the windless ivy-boughs,
Sick with sweet love, droops dying away
On its mate's music-panting bosom;
Another from the swinging blossom,
Watching to catch the languid close
Of the last strain, then lifts on high
The wings of the weak melody,
Till some new strain of feeling bear
The song, and all the woods are mute;
When there is heard through the dim air
The rush of wings, and rising there
Like many a lake-surrounded flute,
Sounds overflow the listener's brain
So sweet, that joy is almost pain.'

There is not the slightest exaggeration in these lines, for, exquisite as they are, they rather fall below than exceed the rapture and riot of countless nightingales in Italian woods by noon and night, and the marvellous manner in which the stronger singers will take up and develop the broken songs of weaker birds.

'If I were a dead leaf thou mightest bear;

If I were a swift cloud to fly with thee;

A wave to pant beneath thy power, and share

The impulse of thy strength, only less free

Than thou, O uncontrollable! If even

I were as in my boyhood, and could be

The comrade of thy wanderings over heaven,

As then, when to outstrip the skyey speed

Scarce seemed a vision, I would ne'er have striven

As thus with thee in prayer in my sore need.

Oh! lift me as a wave, a leaf, a cloud!

I fall upon the thorns of life! I bleed!

A heavy weight of hours has chained and bowed

One too like thee: tameless, and swift, and proud.

Make me thy lyre, even as the forest is:

What if my leaves are falling like its own!

The tumult of thy mighty harmonies

Will take from both a deep autumnal tone,

Sweet though in sadness. Be thou, spirit fierce,

My spirit! Be thou me, impetuous one!

Drive my dead thoughts over the universe

Like withered leaves to quicken a new birth;

And, by the incantation of this verse,

Scatter, as from an unextinguished hearth

Ashes and sparks, my words among mankind!

Be through my lips to unawakened earth

The trumpet of a prophecy! O wind,

If winter comes, can Spring be far behind?'

In the 'Ode to the West Wind,' written in a wood washed by the Arno waters, how completely his spirit loses itself in and is identified with the forces of Nature! how in every line we feel the sweep and motion of the strong *libeccio* coming from the grey Atlantic, over 'the sapless foliage of the ocean,' to

'waken from his summer dreams

The blue Mediterranean, where he lay,

Lulled by the coil of his crystalline streams,
Beside a pumice isle in Baiæ's bay,
And saw in sleep old palaces and towers
Quivering within the wave's intenser day.'

When that wind sweeps up the broad bed of the Arno, the yellowing canebrakes bend, the rushes thrill and tremble, the summer's empty nests are shaken from the ilex and oak boughs, the great pines bend and tremble, the river, stirred by the breath of the sea, grows yellow and grey and swollen and turgid, the last swallow flies southward from his home under the eaves of granary or chapel, and the nightingales rise from their haunts in the thickets of laurel and bay and go also where the shadows of Indian temples or of Egyptian palm-trees lie upon the sands of a still older world.

In that most beautiful and too little known of poems, 'Epipsychidion,' the whole scene, though called Greek, is Italian, and might be taken from the woods beside the Lake of Garda, or the Sercchio which he knew so well, or the forest-like parks which lie deep and cool and still in the blue shadows of Appenine or Abruzzi.

'There are thick woods where sylvan forms abide;
And many a fountain, rivulet and pond,
As clear as elemental diamond,
Or serene morning air; and far beyond,
The mossy tracks made by the goats and deer
(Which the rough shepherd treads but once a year),
Pierce into glades, caverns, and bowers, and halls
Built round with ivy, which the waterfalls
Illumining, with sound that never fails,
Accompany the noonday nightingales;
And all the place is peopled with sweet airs;
The light clear element which the isle wears
Is heavy with the scent of lemon-flowers,
Which floats like mist laden with unseen showers
And falls upon the eyelids like faint sleep;
And from the moss violets and jonquils peep,
And dart their arrowy odour through the brain,
Till you might faint with that delicious pain.'

In the whole world of poetry Love has never been sung with more beauty than in this great poem.

'Ah me!

I am not thine: I am a part of *thee*.

Pilot of the Fate

Whose course has been so starless! O too late

Beloved! O too soon adored, by me!

For in the fields of immortality

My spirit should at first have worshipped thine,

A divine presence in a place divine;

Or should have moved beside it on this earth,

A shadow of that substance, from its birth;

We—are we not formed, as notes of music are,

For one another, though dissimilar;

Such difference, without discord, as can make

Those sweetest sounds, in which all spirits shake

As trembling leaves in a continuous air?

The day is come, and thou wilt fly with me.

To whatsoe'er of dull mortality

Is mine, remain a vestal sister still;

To the intense, the deep, the imperishable,

Not mine, but me, henceforth be thou united

Even as a bride, delighting and delighted.

The hour is come:—the destined Star has risen,

Which shall descend upon a vacant prison.

The walls are high, the gates are strong, thick set

The sentinels—but true love never yet

Was thus constrained: it overleaps all fence;

Like lightning, with invisible violence

Piercing its continents.

This isle and house are mine, and I have vowed

Thee to be lady of the solitude.

And I have fitted up some chambers there
Looking towards the golden Eastern air.
And level with the living winds which flow
Like waves above the living waves below.
I have sent books and music there, and all
Those instruments with which high spirits call
The future from its cradle, and the past
Out of its grave, and make the present last
In thoughts and joys which sleep, but cannot die,
Folded within their own eternity.
Our simple life wants little, and true taste
Hires not the pale drudge Luxury to waste
The scene it would adorn, and therefore still,
Nature with all her children, haunts the hill.
The ring-dove, in the embowering ivy, yet
Keeps up her love-lament, and the owls flit
Round the evening tower, and the young stars glance
Between the quick bats in their twilight dance;
The spotted deer bask in the fresh moonlight
Before our gate, and the slow silent night
Is measured by the pants of their calm sleep.
Be this our home in life, and when years heap
Their withered hours, like leaves, on our decay,
Let us become the overhanging day,
The living soul of this Elysian isle,
Conscious, inseparable, one. Meanwhile
We two will rise, and sit, and walk together,
Under the roof of Blue Ionian weather,
And wander in the meadows, or ascend
The mossy mountains, where the blue heavens bend
With lightest winds, to touch their paramour;
Or linger, where the pebble-paven shore,
Under the quick faint kisses of the sea,
Trembles and sparkles as with ecstasy, —

Possessing and possest by all that is
Within that calm circumference of bliss,
And by each other, till to love and live
Be one:—or, at the noontide hour, arrive
Where some old cavern hoar seems yet to keep
The moonlight of the expired night asleep,
Through which the awakened day can never peep;
A veil for our seclusion, close as Night's,
Where secure sleep may kill thine innocent lights;
Sleep, the fresh dew of languid love, the rain
Whose drops quench kisses till they burn again.
And we will talk until thought's melody
Become too sweet for utterance, and it die
In words, to live again in looks, which dart
With thrilling tone into the voiceless heart,
Harmonising silence without a sound.
Our breaths shall intermix, our bosoms bound,
And our veins beat together; and our lips
With other eloquence than words, eclipse
The soul that burns between them; and the wells
Which boil under our beings inmost cells,
The fountains of our deepest life, shall be
Confused in passion's golden purity,
As mountain springs under the morning Sun.
We shall become the same, we shall be one
Spirit within two frames, oh! wherefore two?
One passion in twin hearts, which grows and grew
Till like two meteors of expanding flame,
Those spheres instinct with it become the same,
Touch, mingle, are transfigured; ever still
Burning, yet ever inconsumable:
In one another's substance finding food,
Like flames too pure and bright and unimbued
To nourish their bright lives with baser prey,

Which point to Heaven and cannot pass away:
One hope within two wills, one will beneath
Two overshadowing minds, one life, one death,
One Heaven, one Hell, one immortality,
And one annihilation. Woe is me!
The winged words on which my soul would pierce
Into the height of love's rare Universe,
Are chains of lead around its flight of fire, —
I pant, I sink, I tremble I expire!'

No words which were ever written ever expressed more truly that infinite and indefinite yearning which exists in all love that is a passion of the soul as well as of the senses; that nameless longing for some still closer union than any which physical and mental union can bestow upon us; that desire for absolute absorption into and extinction within the life beloved, as stars are lost in the light of the sun, which never can find full fruition in life as we know it here.

Keats, Shelley, Savage Landor, Byron, Browning, and Robert Lytton, have been each and all profoundly penetrated by and deeply imbued with the influence of Italy; and it may be said of each and all of them that their genius has been at its highest when under Italian influences, and has been injured and checked and depressed in its development by all English influences brought to bear upon it.

Shelley most completely of all escapes the latter, not only because he died so early, but because his whole temperament resisted conventional pressure as a climbing plant resists being fastened to the earth; flung it off with impatience, as the shining plumage of the sea-bird flings off the leaden-coloured rain and the colourless sands of the shore. Shelley had not only genius: he had courage; the most rare, most noble, and most costly of all forms of courage, that which rejects the measurements and the laws imposed upon the common majority of men by conventional opinion. And this praise, no slight praise, may be given to him, which cannot be given to many, that he had the courage to act up to his opinions. The world had never dominion enough over him to make him fear it, or sacrifice his higher affections to it. In this, as in his adoration of Nature and his instinctive pantheism, he was the truest poet the modern world has known.

To the multitude of men he must be forever unintelligible and alien; because their laws are not his laws, their sight is not his sight, their heaven of small things makes his hell, and his heaven of beautiful visions and of pure passions is a paradise whereof they cannot even dimly see the portals.

But to all poets his memory and his verse must ever be inexpressibly dear and sacred. His 'Adonais' may be repeated for himself. There is a beauty in the manner of his death which we must not grudge to him if we truly love him. It fitly rounded a poet's life. That life was short, as measured by years! but, ended so, it was more complete than it would have been had it stretched on to age. Who knows?—he might have become a magnate in Hampshire, a country squire, a member of Parliament, a sheriff for the county, any and all things such as the muses would have wept for; Shelley in England, Shelley old, would have been Shelley no more. Better and sweeter the waves of the Tyrrhene Sea and the violet-sown grave of Rome. Sadder and more painful than earliest death is it to witness the slow decay of the soul under the carking fret and burdensome conventionalities of the world; more cruel than the sudden storm is the tedious monotony of the world's bondage. The sea was merciful when it took the Adonais who sang of Adonais from earth when he was yet young. He and his friends, he and those who wrote the 'Endymion' and the 'Manfred,' were happy in their deaths; their spirits, eternally young, live with us and have escaped all contamination of the commonplace. Byron might have lived to wrangle in the Lords over the Corn Laws; Keats might have lived to become a London physician and pouch fees; Shelley might have lived to be *Custos Rotulorum* and to take his daughters to a court ball. Their best friend was the angel of death who came at Rome, at Missolonghi, at Lerici. 'Whom the gods love die young.'

The monotony, the thraldom and the pettiness of conventional life lie forever in wait for the man of genius, to sink him under their muddy waters and wash him into likeness with the multitude: Shelley, Byron and Keats escaped this fell embrace.

What may be termed the material side of the intellect receives assistance in England, that is to say, in the aristocratic and political world of England; wit and perception and knowledge of character are quickened and multiplied by it. But the brilliancy, liberty and spirituality of the imagination are in it dulled and lowered. If a poet can find fine and fair thoughts in the atmosphere of a London Square, he would be visited by far finer and fairer thoughts were he standing by the edge of the Adrian or Tyrrhene Sea, or looking down, eagle-like, from some high spur of wind-vexed Apennine. The poet should not perhaps live forever away from the world, but he should oftentimes do so.

The atmosphere of Italy has been the greatest fertiliser of English poetical genius. There is something fatal to genius in modern English life; its conditions are oppressive; its air is heavy; its habits are altogether opposed to the life of the imagination. Out-of-door life in England is only associated with what is called 'the pleasure of killing things,' and is only possible to those who are very robust of frame and hard of feeling. The intellectual life in England is only developed in gaslight and lamplight, over dinner-tables and in club-rooms, and although the country houses in some instances might be made centres of intellectual life, they never are so by any chance, and remain only the sanctuaries of fashion, of <u>gastronomy</u> and of sport. The innumerable demands on time, the routine of social engagements, the pressure of conventional opinion, are all too strong in England to allow the man of genius to be happy there, or to reach there his highest and best development. The many artificial restraints of life in England are, of all things, the most injurious to the poetic temperament, which at all times is quickly irritated and easily depressed by its surroundings. There is not enough leisure or space for meditation, or freedom to live as the affections or the fancy or the mind desires; and the absence of beauty—of beauty, artistic, architectural, natural and physical—oppresses and dulls the poetic imagination without its being sensible of what it is from the lack of which it suffers.

It has been said of a living statesman that he is only great in opposition. So may it be said of the poet who touches mundane things. He is only great in opposition. Milton could not have written a Jubilee Ode without falling from his high estate; and none can care for Shakespeare without desiring to expunge the panegyric on a Virgin Queen written for the Masque of Kenilworth. The poet is lord of a spiritual power; he is far above the holders of powers temporal. He holds the sensitive plant in his hand, and feels every innermost thrill of Nature; he is false to himself when he denies Nature and does a forced and unreal homage to the decrees and the dominion of ordinary society or of ordinary government.

'Both are alien to him, and are his foes.'

This line might fittingly have been graven on Shelley's tombstone, for it was essentially the law of his soul. The violence of his political imprecations is begotten by love, though love of another kind: love of justice, of truth, of tolerance, of liberty, all of which he beheld violated by the ruling powers of the state and of the law. With the unerring vision which is the birthright of genius, he saw through the hypocrisies and shams of kings, and priests, and churches, and council-chambers, and conventional morality, and political creeds. The thunder of the superb sonnet to England which begins with the famous line,

'An old, mad, blind, despised and dying king,'

came from his heart's depths in scorn of lies, in hatred of pretence, in righteous indignation as a patriot at the corruption, venality and hypocrisy of

'Rulers who neither see, nor feel, nor know,

But leech-like to their fainting country cling.'

It is perhaps to be lamented that the true poetic temperament should ever turn aside to share the fret and fever of political strife. It is waste of the spirit of Alastor to rage against Swellfoot. But the poet cannot wholly escape the influences of baser humanity, and, watching the struggles of 'the blind and battling multitude' from afar, he cannot avoid being moved either to a passion of pity or to a passion of disdain, or to both at once, in view of this combat, which seems to him so poor and small, so low and vile. Men of genius know the mere transitory character of those religions and those social laws which awe, as by a phantasm of terror, weaker minds, and they refuse to allow their lives to be dictated to or bound down; and in exact propor/tion to their power of revolt is their attainment of greatness.

The soul of Shelley was, besides, deeply imbued by that wide pantheism which makes all the received religions of men look so trite, so poor, so narrow and so mean.

'Canst those imagine where those spirits live
Which make such delicate music in the woods?

'Tis hard to tell:
I have heard those more skilled in spirits say,
The bubbles, which enchantment of the sun
Sucks from the pale, faint water-flowers that pave
The oozy bottom of clear lakes and pools,
Are the pavilions where such dwell and float
Under the green and golden atmosphere
Which noon-tide kindles through the woven leaves;
And when these burst, and the thin, fiery air,
The which they breathed within those lucent domes,
Ascends to flow like meteors through the night,
They ride on them, and rein their headlong speed,
And bow their burning crests, and glide in fire
Under the waters of the earth again.
If such live thus, have others other lives,
Under pink blossoms or within the bells
Of meadow flowers, or folded violets deep,
Or on their dying odours when they die,

Or on the sunlight of the sphered dell?'

The loveliness of Nature filled him with awe and deep delight.

'How glorious art thou, Earth! and if thou be

The shadow of some spirit lovelier still,

Though evil stain its work, and it should be

Like its creation, weak yet beautiful,

I could fall down and worship that and thee.'

'My soul is an enchanted boat,

Which, like a sleeping swan, doth float

Upon the silver waves of thy sweet singing;

And thine doth like an angel sit

Beside the helm conducting it,

Whilst all the winds with melody are ringing

It seems to float ever, forever.

Upon that many-winding river,

Between mountains, woods, abysses,

A paradise of wildernesses!

Till, like one in slumber bound,

Borne to the ocean, I float down, around

Into a sea profound, of ever-spreading sound.'

This intimate sympathy with Nature, this perception of beauty in things seen and unseen, this deep joy in the sense of existence, make the very life of Shelley's life; he is the ideal poet, feeding

'on the aerial kisses

Of shapes that haunt thought's wildernesses.'

Taine has said, with truth, of modern life,—

'Nous ne savons plus prendre la vie en grand, sortir de nous mêmes; nous nous contennons dans un petit bien-être personnel, dans une petite œuvre viagère.' [He is writing in the mountains beyond Naples.] 'Ici on reduit le vieux et le couvert au simple necessaire. Ainsi dégagée l'âme, comme les yeux, pouvait contempler les vastes horizons tout ce qui s'etend et dure au déla de l'homme.'

Modern life gives you six electric bells beside your bed, but not one court or chamber that a great artist would care to copy. The poet yawning among the electric bells becomes a common-place person, with a mind obscured by a gourmet's love of the table and the cellar; he is the chameleon who has lost his luminous and magical powers of transfiguration, and become a mere gorged lizard stuffed with sugar.

Byron, Shelley, Wordsworth, were in their different lives so great because they had all the power to reject the drowsy and dulling influences of the common world of men, and withdraw from it to Ravenna, to Lirici, to Rydal. The commonplace of life, whether in occupations, relationships, or so-called duties, eats away the poetry of temperament with the slow, sure gnawing of the hidden insect which eats away the tiger-skin until where the golden bronze and deep sable of the shining fur once glistened, there is only a bald, bare spot, with neither colour nor beauty left in it. There are millions on millions of ordinary human lives to follow the common tracks and fulfil the common functions of human life. When the poet is dragged down to any of these he is lost. The moth who descried the star lies dead in the kitchen fire, degraded and injured beyond recall.

'There is a path on the sea's azure floor;

No keel has ever ploughed that path before.'

Such should be the poet's passage through life. Not his is it to sail by chart and compass with common mariners along the sea roads marked out for safety and for commerce.

Above all else, the poet should be true to himself—to his own vision, his own powers, his own soul,

'like Heaven's pure breath

Which he who grasps can hold not; like death,

Who rides upon a thought, and makes his way

Through temple, tower and palace, and the array

Of arms.'

The supreme glory of Shelley is that he, beyond all others, did go where 'no keel ever ploughed before,' did dwell more completely than any other has ever dwelt

'on an imagined shore

Where the gods spoke with him.'

The poet is wisest, and his creations are most beautiful when his thoughts roam alone in

'fields of Heaven-reflecting sea,

Beneath the uplifting winds, like plains of corn

Swayed by the summer air;'
and when he, like Proteus, marks

'The shadow of fair ships, as mortals see
The floating bark of the light-laden moon
With that white star, it's sightless pilot's crest,
Borne down the rapid sunset's ebbing sea;
Tracking their path no more by blood and groans,
And desolation, and the mingled voice
Of slavery and command; but by the light
Of wave-reflected flowers, and floating odours,
And music soft and mild, free, gentle voices,
That sweetest music, such as spirits love.'

And he is wisest when he says, with Apollo,

'I shall gaze not on the deeds which make
My mind obscure with sorrow, as eclipse
Darkens the sphere I guide; but list, I hear
The small, clear, silver lute of the young Spirit
That sits i' the morning star.'

If ever poet held that lute on earth, Shelley held it all through his brief life; and if ever there be immortality for any soul, his surely is living now beside that Spirit in the light of a ceaseless day.

'Death is the veil which those who live call life;
They sleep, and it is lifted.'

SOME FALLACIES OF SCIENCE[K]

'Le génie fait les philosophes et les poetes: le temps ne fait
que les savants.' —Fontenelle.

Sir Lyon, *now* Lord, Playfair, read to the assembled members of the
British Association, when they met at Aberdeen, a discourse both eloquent
and well suited to excite the enthusiasm of his audience, already disposed
by taste and bias to salute its propositions as gospel. That there were truths
in it, no one would dispute; that it was exclusively composed of truth is
not so evident to minds unswayed by scientific prejudice. It, at all events,
was a curious and complete example of the scientific mind, of its views,
conclusions and expectations, and is therefore interesting in itself, if not as
overwhelming in its persuasions to the dispassionate reader as it was to
the sympathetic and selected audience to which it was addressed. Scientific
persons usually never address themselves to any other audience than one
thus pannelled and prepared. They like to see a crowd of their own disciples
in their halls ere they let fall their pearls of wisdom. The novelist does not
demand that he shall be only read by novelists. The painter does not think
that none but painters can be permitted to judge a painting. The sculptor
does not ask that every critic of his work shall be a Phidias. The historian
does not insist that none but a Tacitus shall pass judgment on him. But the
scientist does exact that no opinion shall be formed of him and of his works
except by his own brethren, and sweeps aside all independent criticism on a
principle which, if carried out into other matters, would forbid John Ruskin
ever to give an opinion on painting, and would prohibit Francisque Sareey
from making any critical observations on actors. This address satisfied its
audience, because that audience was composed of persons already willing
to be satisfied; but if we can imagine some listener altogether without such
bias, if we can suppose some one amongst the auditors with mind altogether
unprejudiced, such an one might without effort have found many weak
places in this fine discourse, and would have been sorely tempted to cry
'Question! Question!' at more than one point in it.

Taken as a whole, the address was an admirable piece of special
pleading in favour of science, and of her superior claims upon the resources
of all states and the minds of all men. But special pleading has always this
disadvantage: that it seeks to prove too much; and the special pleading

of the President of the Aberdeen meeting is not free from this defect. We know, of course, that, in his position, he could hardly say less; that with his antecedents and reputation, he would not have wished to say less; but those who are removed from the spell of his eloquence, and peruse his arguments in the serene air of their studies, may be pardoned if they be more critical than an audience of fellow-workers, and mutual admirers, if they lay down the pages of his admirably-worded praises of science, and ask themselves dispassionately: How much of this is true?

The main object of the discourse was to prove that science is the great benefactress of the world. But is it proved? To the mind of the scientist the doubt will seem as impious as the doubt of the sceptic always does seem to the true believer. Yet it is a doubt which must be entertained by those who are not led away by that bigotry of science, which has so much and so grievously in common with the bigotry of religions.

Let us see what are the statements which the President of the British Association brings forward in support of the position which he gives to Science as the goddess and the benefactress of mankind. First, to do this he casts down the Humanities beneath his feet, as the professors of science always do; and, as an illustration of the uselessness which he assigns to them, he asserts that were a Chrysoloras to teach Greek in the Italian universities he would not hasten perceptibly the onward march of Italy!

What does this mean? It is a statement, but the statement of an opinion, not of a fact.

What is comprised under the vague term 'the onward march of Italy?' Does it mean the return of Italy to her pristine excellence in all arts, her love of learning, her grace of living? or does it mean the effort of Italy to aggrandise herself at all cost, and to engage in foreign and colonial wars whilst her cities groan under taxation and her peasantry perish of pellagra? In the one case the teaching of Chrysoloras would be of infinite value; in the other it would, no doubt, not harmonise with the vulgar greeds and dangerous ambitions of the hour. If the 'onward march of Italy' means that she is to kneel to a Crispi, submit to a standing army, wait slavishly on Germany, and scramble for the sands of Africa, the teachings of Chrysoloras would be wasted; but if it mean that she is to husband her strength, cultivate her fertile fields, merit her gift of beauty, and hold a high place in the true civilisation of the world, then I beg leave to submit that Chrysoloras, or what his name is here taken to symbolise, would do more for her than any other teacher she could have, certainly more than any teacher she now possesses. Could the classic knowledge and all which is begotten by it of serenity, grace, trained eloquence and dispassionate meditation, be diffused once more through the mind of Italian youth, it would, I think, produce a generation which would not applaud Eritrea and Kassala, nor accept the political tyrannies of state-appointed prefects.

The scientists take for granted that the education of the schools creates intelligence; very often it does no such thing. It creates a superficial appearance of knowledge, indeed; but knowledge is like food, unless it be thoroughly assimilated when absorbed, and thoroughly digested, it can give no nourishment; it lies useless, a heavy and unleavened mass. It is the fashion in these times to despise husbandmen and husbandry, but it is much to be questioned if the city cad, with his smattering of education, his dabbling in politics, his crude, conceited opinions upon matters on which he is absolutely ignorant, be not a far more ignorant, as he is undoubtedly a far more useless, person than the peasant, who may never have opened a book or heard of arithmetic, but thoroughly understands the soil he works on, the signs of the weather, the rearing of plants and of animals, and the fruits of the earth which he cultivates. The man of genius may be many-sided; nature has given him the power to be so; but the mass of men do not and cannot obtain this Protean power; to do one thing well is the utmost that the vast majority can well hope to do; many never do so much, nor a quarter so much. To this vast majority science would say: you may be as indifferent weavers, ploughmen, carpenters, shopmen, what you will, but you must know where the spermatic nerves are situated in the ichneumon, and you must describe the difference between microzoaires and miraphytes, and you must understand the solidification of nitric acid. Nor is the temper which science and its teachers seem likely thus to give the human race, one of fair promise. How much have not the men of science added to the popular dread of cholera, which in its manifestation of cowardice and selfishness has so grossly disgraced the Continent of Europe of late years? Their real or imaginary creation, the microbe, has invested cholera with a fanciful horror so new and hideous in the popular mind, that popular terror of it grows ungovernable, and will, in great likelihood, revolt beyond all restraint, municipal or imperial, whenever the disease shall again revisit Europe with violence. Again, how many nervous illnesses, how many imaginary diseases, have sprung into existence since science, popularised, attracted the attention of mankind to the mechanism of its own construction? It is a familiar truth that a little knowledge is a dangerous thing, and of no knowledge is it truer than of physiological knowledge. It has been said, that every one at forty should be a fool or a physician, and so far as knowing what to eat, drink and avoid, every one should be so; but, unhappily, those who become the latter, *i.e.*, those who become capable of controlling their own constitutional ailments and weaknesses, are apt to contract in their study of themselves an overweening tendency to think about themselves. The generalisation of physiology amongst the masses means the generalisation of this form of egotism. A child who was told and shown something of anatomy, said, naively: 'Oh, dear me! now that I know how I am made, I shall be always thinking that I am coming to pieces.' In a less innocent way the effect of the popularisation of physiology is the same on the multitude as on this child: it increases valetudinarianism, nervousness and the diseases which spring from morbid fears and morbid desires. Those nervous illnesses which are the peculiar privilege of modern times, are largely due to the exaggerated attention to themselves which science has taught to humankind. The Greek and the Latin said: 'Let us eat and drink and enjoy, for to-morrow we die.' Modern science says: 'Let us concentrate our whole mind on ourselves and our body, although our mind like our body is only a conglomeration of gases which will go out in the dark.' The classic injunction and conclusion are the more healthy and the more logical, and produced a race of men more manly, more vigorous and more consistent with themselves.

To return to the assertions contained in this address which we now consider: in the address it is stated as a fact which all must rejoice over, that in Boston one shoe factory, by its machines, does the work of 30,000 shoemakers in Paris, who have still to go through the weary drudgery of hand-labour. Now, why is the 'drudgery' of sewing a shoe in any way more 'weary' than the drudgery of oiling, feeding and attending to a machine? Machine-work is, on the contrary, of all work the most mechanical, the most absolute drudgery. There is no kind of proof that, because the work of 30,000 shoemakers is done by a machine, mankind at large is any the happier for this. We know that all machine-made work is inferior to hand-work; inferior in durability, in excellence of quality, and in its inevitable lack of that kind of individuality and originality which handwork takes from the fingers which form it. In the *Seven Lamps of Architecture*, there is an admirable exposition of this immeasurable difference in quality which characterises hand-labour and machine-made work; of the stone cut by steam and the stone cut by hand. Let us only consider what ruin to the arts of India has been brought about by the introduction of machinery. The exquisite beauty of Oriental work is due to the individuality which is put into it; the worker, sitting beneath his grove of date-trees, puts original feeling, individual character, into each line graven on the metal, each thread woven in the woof, each turn given to the ivory. Machines destroy all this. They make machines of the men who tend them, and give a soulless and hateful monotony to everything which they produce.

Despite the vaunt of Playfair, the cobbler who sits on the village green, doing sound, if simple work, honestly, giving a personality to the shoe he labours on, and knowing on what foot it will be worn and whither it will go, is a man, and maybe in his own humble way a good artist; but the attendant who feeds the shoe-machine with oil, or takes from it its thousands of machine-cut leathers, is no better than a machine himself; so far from being 'set free,' he is in servitude. The cobbler on the village green knows far more of freedom than he.

This curious statement that hand-work, with its scope for originality and individual interest is slavery, whilst the work of factories, mechanical, monotonous and done in ugly chambers and unwholesome air, is liberty, is surely the oddest delusion with which the fanatical and biased mind of science ever delighted itself. Who can compare the freedom of the native child in a village of Benares, shaping an ebony or cocoanut toy under the palm-fronds of his home, with the green paroquets swinging, and the monkeys chattering in the sun-lit bamboos above his head, with the servitude of the poor little sickly and weary Hindoos, thronging in patient flocks the noisome factory-chambers of Bombay?

The President of the British Association seems to expect that all men whom machines 'set free' from the drudgery of their daily calling, will, all at once, do something infinitely better than they did before they were free. But this seems to me a very rash conclusion. If the 30,000 shoemakers are all 'set free' in Paris, by the introduction of the Boston machine, is it so certain that their freedom will produce anything better than a good pair of shoes? What greater freedom is there in attending to the machine if they select to do that, or in entering into another trade?—one thing or the other no doubt they must do, if they want to earn their bread? What have they gained by being 'set free, and passed from one kind of occupation to another?' I fail to see what they have gained. Have the public gained? It is open to doubt. Where will be the gain to their contemporaries, or to themselves, if these 30,000 shoemakers 'set free' become telegraph clerks or book-keepers? Something they must become, unless they are to live as paupers or mendicants. Where is their freedom? 'Set free' is a seductive and resonant expression, but analysed it simply means nothing in this instance. And, before quitting this subject, let me also remark that if Playfair knew as much about shoes as he does about science, he would know that a machine to make shoes is a most unwholesome invention, because every shoe or boot which is not made *expressly* for the foot which is to wear it, is an ill-made shoe, and will cause suffering and deformity to the unwise wearer. The vast mass of the population of every 'civilised' nation has deformed feet, because they buy and wear ready-made shoes, thrusting their extremities into houses of leather never designed for them. Machines which make shoes by the thousand can only increase this evil. As it is, we never see by any chance any one walk well, unless it be some one whose shoes are made with great care and skill, adjusted to his feet alone, or peasants who have never shod their feet at all and step out, with the bare sole set firmly and lightly on their mother earth. Science can, no doubt, turn out millions of cheap shoes, all exactly alike, but Nature will not consent to adopt such monotony of contour in the feet which will wear them.

The President of the British Association speaks of science always as of a Demeter, with blessings in her hands, creating the fulness of the fields and the joys of mankind. He forgets that the curse of Demeter brought barrenness: and if we resist the charm of his eloquence and look more closely at the tissue of it, we shall not be so content to accept his declarations. What does the expression mean, 'to benefit mankind?' I conclude that it must mean to increase its happiness and its health; all the wisdom of the ages will avail it nothing if it pule in discontent and fret in nervous sickness. Now, does science increase the sum of human happiness? It is very doubtful.

Let us take the electric telegraph as an instance of the benevolence of science. Can it be said to make men happier? I think not. Politicians and diplomatists agree that the hasty judgments and conflicting orders which it favours and renders possible, double the chances of internecine quarrels, and stimulate to irritation and haste, which banish statesmanship. In business the same defects are due to it, and many a rash speculation or unconsidered reply, an acceptance or refusal, forced on men without there being time for any mature consideration, have led to disastrous engagements and as disastrous failures. Even in private life its conveniences may have a certain value, but the many troubles and excitements brought by it are incalculable. Niobe hearing of the death of her children by a printed line on a yellow sheet of paper, has her grief robbed of all dignity and privacy, and intensified by a shock which deals her its fatal blow without any preparation of the mind to receive it. The telegraph, bridging space, may be, and is, no doubt, a wonderful invention, but that it has contributed to the happiness or wisdom of humanity is not so certain. Men cannot do without it now, no doubt; neither can they do without alcohol. The telegraph, like nearly all the inventions of the modern age, tends to shorten time but to harass it, to make it possible to do much more in an hour, a day, a year, than was done of old, but to make it impossible to do any of this without agitation, brain-pressure and hurry. It has impaired language and manners, it has vulgarised death, and it has increased the great evils of immature choice and hasty action; these drawbacks weighed against its uses must at the time prevent us from regarding its invention as an unmixed blessing. Of the telephone may be said as much, and more.[L]

Playfair, proceeding in his enumeration of the benefits which science confers on man, turns to that most familiar matter, air, and that equally familiar element, water. He speaks with pride of all which science has discovered concerning their component parts, and their uses and effects upon the world. His pride, no doubt, may be justified in much, but he passes over one great fact in connection with air and water, *i.e.*, that both have been polluted through the inventions of science in a degree which may well be held to outweigh the value of the discoveries of science.

Were we to awake an Athenian of the time of Phidias from his mausoleum, and take him with eyes to see and ears to hear and nostrils to smell, into Blackpool or Belfast, even into Zurich or Munich, he would ask us, in stupefaction, under what curse of the gods had the earth fallen that mankind should dwell in such hideous clamour, such sooty darkness, such foul stenches, such defiled and imprisoned air. He would survey the begrimed toilers of the mills and looms, the pallid women, the stunted offspring, the long lines of hideous houses, the soil ankle-deep with cinder-dust, the skies a pall of lurid smoke, the country scorched and blackened and accursed; he would survey all this, I say, asking by what malediction of heaven and what madness of mankind the sweetest and chief joys of Nature had been ruined and forgotten thus? He would behold the dwarfed trees dying under the fume of poisonous gases, the clear river changed to a slimy, crawling, stinking, putrid flood of filth; the buoyant air, once sweet as the scent of cowslips or clover-grass, made by the greed of man into a sickly, noxious, loathsome thing, loaded with the stench of chemicals and the vapours of engine-belched steam. He would stand amidst this hell of discordant sounds, between these walls of blackened brick, under this sky of heavy-hanging soot; and he would remember the world as it was; and if at his ears any prated of science, he would smile in their faces, and say,—'If these be the fruits of science let me rather dwell with the forest beast and the untaught barbarian.'

Yes; no doubt science can study air in her spectrum, and analyse water in her retorts; she can tell why the green tree dies in the evil gas, and the rose will not bloom where the blast-furnace roars: she can tell you the why and the wherefore, and can give you a learned treatise on the calcined dust which chokes up your lungs; but she cannot make the green tree and the wild rose live in the hell she has created for men, and she cannot make the skies she has blackened lighter, nor the rivers she has poisoned run clean. Even we who dwell where the air is pure, and the southern sun lights the smiling waves and the vine-clad hills, even we cannot tell how beautiful was the earth in the days of the Greek anthologists; when the silvery blue of wood-smoke alone rose from the hearth fires; when the flame of the vegetable oils alone illumined the fragrant night; when the white sails alone skimmed the violet seas; when the hand alone threw the shuttle and wove the web; and when the vast virgin forests filled the unpolluted air with their odorous breath. Even we cannot tell what the radiance of the atmosphere, of the horizons, of the sunrise and sunset, were when the world was young. Our loss is terrible and hopeless, like the loss of all youth. It may be useless to lament it, but in God's name let us not be such purblind fools that we call our loss our gain.

Repose, leisure, silence, peace and sleep are all menaced and scattered by the inventions of the last and present century. They are the greatest though the simplest blessings that mankind has ever had; their banishment may be welcomed by men greedy only of gold; but, meantime, the mad-houses are crowded, spinal and cerebral diseases are in alarming increase, heart-disease in divers shapes is general, where it once was rare, and all the various forms of bodily and mental paralysis multiply and crown the triumphs of the age.

Let us turn for a moment to the consideration of politics and of war as these are affected by the influence of science. Playfair speaks much of the superior wisdom, the superior education, the superior devotion to science, of Germany, as contrasted with those of any other nation; he lauds to the skies her enormous grants to laboratories and professors of physiology and chemistry and 'original research' (called by the vulgar, vivisection); but the only result of all this expenditure and instruction is a military despotism so colossal that, whilst it overawes and paralyses both German liberty and European peace, it yet may fall over from its own weight any day, like the giant of clay which it resembles. Are we not then justified in objecting to accept, whilst the chief issue of German culture is Militarism and anti-Semitism, such praises of Germany, and refusing to render such homage to her? 'By your fruits ye shall be judged,' is a just saying: and the fruits of Germany, in the concert of Europe and the sum of political life, are dissension, apprehension, absolutism, and the sacrifice of all other nations to the pressure of the military Juggernaut which rolls before her; whilst in her own national life the outcome of the sanguinary lessons given by the government is little better than the barbarism of the middle ages without its redeeming law of chivalry. The incessant and senseless duels which maim and disfigure German youth remain a disgrace to civilisation, and a duellist may fire three times at an adversary who *never returns the fire* and, killing him at the last, will only be punished by a slight imprisonment, whilst he will be admired and deified by his comrades.[M] Such barbarous brutality, such insensibility to generous feeling, such universal resort to the arbitration of every trifling dispute by the pistol or the sabre, is the chief characteristic of the nation in which science rules supreme! Conscription, that curse of nations, is forced on all weaklier powers by the enormous armed forces of Germany; art suffers, trades suffer, families suffer; and we are called on by a 'scientific' mind to admire as a model the nation which is the cause of this suffering, as we are bidden to admire as models also her mutilated and bandaged students, and her blue-spectacled and blear-eyed school children!

Again Playfair traces the defeat of France in 1870 to the inferiority of her university teaching, and gives the opinion of the Institut de France as his authority. It seems a singularly illogical and unphilosophical decision for such an august body to have given forth publicly. The causes of the defeat of France stretch farther back and have deeper roots than can be accounted for by the omission of the state to create more professors and laboratories. The whole teachings of history show that all states, after reaching their perihelion, gradually decline and sink into an inferior place amongst the nations. The day of France, as of England, is already past its noon. Neither will ever be what they have been. Neither will ever again give law to Europe as they gave it once. But so many causes, some near, some remote, have all contributed to bring about a decline which is as inevitable to nations as to individuals, that it is surely most unphilosophic to contend that such decay could have been averted by the creation of some hundred or thousand more professors of natural or other science. It may be excusable for such a professor to consider such professorships the one universal panacea for all ills; but it is not an opinion in which those who know France best and most intimately would be inclined to coincide. They would conclude that, on the contrary, she has too many professors already; that the grace, and wit, and courtesy, and wisdom and chivalry have gone out of her since she was ruled from the desks of the school-master, the physiologist and the notary, and that the whole system of French colleges is calculated to emasculate and injure the character of the schoolboy before he goes up for his baccalaureate.

The German invasion of France was supported by all which science could do, yet most military judges are agreed that unless the carelessness of her foe had afforded her a fortnight's preparation, Germany would have been hopelessly beaten on her own territory; whilst, look at the campaign how we may, it cannot stand a moment's comparison with the Eastern marches of Alexander, or the conquests of Roman generals. With none of the resources of modern warfare, these great conquerors carried fire and sword through the whole of the regions known to them, from the sands of Africa to the ice-plains of the Baltic. What is there in modern war, which can compare with the campaigns of Hannibal, the amazing victories of Julius Cæsar, the deeds of the young Pompeiins, the story of every Legion? In the English endeavour to rescue Gordon, with every aid which modern science can invent, and assisted by every facility which modern modes of transit lend to the transport of multitudes, an army was despatched from Great Britain with orders to reach a city on the Nile. The errand was too difficult to be accomplished; the generals returned with their mission unfulfilled; the country received them with honour. This is the height to which the assistance of modern science has brought the would-be Cæsars of the age.

What child's play would this expedition to Khartoum have seemed to Scipio Africanus or to Lucius Sylla! Yet all the 'resources of science' did not save the modern expedition from failure, and, in the face of Europe and Asia, it retreated in ignominy before the barbaric and untrained followers of a half-mad prophet, after an enormous expenditure of stores and treasure, and a perfectly useless waste of human life!

War has been almost incessant since the empire of science, but it has been characterised neither by magnanimity nor true triumph. Europe, armed to the teeth, is like a muzzled pack of blood-hounds; every nation lives in terror of the others; to such a pass has scientific warfare brought the world. The multiplication of engines of destruction is one of the chief occupations and boasts of a scientific age, and it can claim a melancholy pre-eminence in the discovery of the means to inflict the most agonising of all wounds through the medium of conical bullets and shells of nitro-glycerine. To have added unspeakable horror to death, and to have placed the power of secret and wholesale assassination in the hands of ignorant and envious men, is one of the chief benefits which this Egeria has brought to her eager pupil. And when her worshippers laud her to the skies, as does the president of the Aberdeen meeting, their silence on this side of her teaching is at once significant and ominous.

Playfair is obviously afraid that the Humanities will always obtain, in England at least, a larger place in public teaching and in public subsidies than pure science will be able to do. I wish his fear may be justified. My own fears are on the other side. Science offers prizes to the prurient curiosities and the nascent cruelties of youth with which literature can never compete. To study all the mysteries of sex in anatomy, and to indulge the power of a Nero in little when watching the agonies of a scientifically-tortured or poisoned dog, are enjoyments appealing to instincts in the frame of the school-boy, with which not even the most indecent passage in his Greek or Latin authors can ever pretend to measure attraction. The professors of science need have no fear as to the potency of the charm which their curriculum will exercise over the juvenile mind. Teaching which offers at once the penetration into corporeal secrets and the power of torture over animals, possesses a fascination for the minds of youth which it will never lose, because its appeals are addressed to those coarsest and crudest impulses which are strongest of all in the child and in the adolescent.

What science is preparing for the future of man, in thus putting the scalpel and the injecting-needle into the hands of children, is a darker and wider question. One thing is certain, that in the future, as in the streets and temples of Ancient Rome, there will be no altar to Pity.

The acknowledged doctrine of the professors of 'research,' that all knowledge is valuable because it is, or appears to be, knowledge, and that all ways and methods of obtaining it are justified and sanctified, bears so curious a likeness to the self-worship of the Papal dominion and of the Spanish Inquisition, that we see, with a sense of despair, how bigotry and despotism in some form or another are fated to reappear so long as human life shall last.

It is significant of the political immorality and readiness to tyrannise over others in the pursuit of their aims, which characterise the scientific classes, that they are willing to admire and support any government, however despotic, which is willing in return to endow their scholarships and erect their laboratories. They are inclined to surrender all political liberty, if by so doing they can obtain a ruler who will build them a number of new colleges, with every new instrument ready to their hands for animal torture and physiological or chemical experiment.

A Lorenzo di Medici, devoted exclusively to the sciences instead of to the arts, would be their ideal sovereign. Public liberties might perish under him as they should; he would give science her free scope, her desired endowments, her million living victims; he would be even too enlightened to refuse her human subjects for the physiological laboratory.

This curious willingness of the pursuers of science to join hands with tyranny, so long as tyranny helps themselves, is the darkest menace of the world's future. In time to come it may assume dimensions and aspects which are undreamed of now. The demand of biologists and chemists to be provided for out of the funds of the state, is a demand which has never been made by literature or art, and would not be tolerated from them. The exorbitant sums insisted on for the establishment of laboratories and professorships, rob science of that character of disinterested devotion which alone would make it worthy of esteem. 'Give me a thousand or fifteen hundred a year,' says the physiologist to the state; 'give me money-grants also for experiments which I may spend at my good option and for which I need return no account, and leave me to cut up dogs and cats and horses at leisure. In return I will give you some new facts about internal hydrocephalus or the length of time a new poison takes to kill a guinea-pig.' The agreement may, or may not, be worth the state's entering into with the physiologist, but in any case the physiologist cannot deny that he makes a good income out of his science, and cannot pretend to any disinterested or philanthropic selection of it. The moment that any man accepts a salary for intellectual work, he must submit to resign all claim to purely intellectual devotion to it. The claims of scientists to be paid and provided for out of national funds has many equivocal aspects, and will have many unwholesome results; whilst the rapacity and insistence with which they are put forward are as unbecoming as they are undisguised. The high priests of modern science are not likely to shed tears like the Greek philosopher Isocrates because they are compelled to take money. On the contrary, they clamour loudly for their maintenance by their nation, with a cupidity which has happily never disgraced either literature or art.

As modern socialism aspires to make the world into one vast allotment-ground, with every man's half-acre meted out to him on which to build his hut and hive his store, so science would change the world into one vast class-room and laboratory, wherein all humanity (paying very large fees) should sit at the feet of its professors, whom it would clothe with purple and fine linen, and whom it would never presume to oppose or to contradict.

The world will gain nothing by delivering itself, as it is gradually doing, from the bondage of the various churches and their priesthoods, if in their stead it puts its neck under the yoke of a despotism, more intellectual perhaps, but as bigoted, as arrogant, and as cruel. That this danger lies before it from its submission to the demands of science, no dispassionate student of humanity can doubt.

FEMALE SUFFRAGE

It is a singular fact that England, which has been always esteemed the safest and slowest of all factors in European politics, should be now seriously meditating on such a revolutionary course of action as the political emancipation of women. It is a sign, and a very ominous sign, of the restlessness and feverishness which have come upon this century in its last twenty years of life, and from which England is suffering no less than other nations, is perhaps even suffering more than they, since when aged people take the diseases natural to youth it fares ill with them, more ill than with the young. There are many evidences that before very long, whichever political party may be in office, female suffrage will be awarded at <u>Westminster</u>, and if it be so, it is scarcely to be doubted that the French Chambers and the Representative Houses at Washington will be loth to lag behind and resist such a precedent. The influence on the world will scarcely be other than most injurious to its prosperity and most degrading to its wisdom.

It is true that the wholesale exercise of electoral rights by millions of uneducated and unwashed men is a spectacle so absurd that a little more or a little less absurdity may be held not to matter very greatly. The intellectual world in political matters has voluntarily abdicated already and given its sceptre to the mob. 'Think you,' said Publius Scipio to the raging populace, 'then, I shall fear those free whom I sent in chains to the slave market?' But the modern politician, of whatever nation he be (with the solitary exception of Bismarck), does fear the slaves whose chains he has struck off before they know how to use their liberty, and has in him neither the candour nor the courage of Scipio.

Rationally, logically, political power ought to be alloted in proportion to the stake which each voter possesses in the country. But this sound principle has been totally disregarded in the present political systems of both Europe and America. Vapourings anent the inherent 'rights of man' have been allowed to oust out common-sense and logical action, and he whose contributions to the financial and intellectual power of his nation are of the largest and noblest order has no more electoral voice in the direction of the nation than the drunken navvy or the howling unit of the street-mob. This is esteemed liberty, and commends itself to the populace, because it levels, or seems to level, intellect and wealth with poverty and ignorance. It is probable that America will, in years to come, be the first to change this, the doctrine of democracy, as there are signs that the United States will probably grow less and less democratic with every century, and its large land-owners will create an aristocracy which will not be tolerant of the dominion of the mob. But meantime Europe is swaying between absolutism and anarchy, with that tendency of the pendulum to swing wildly from one extreme to the other which has been always seen in the whole history of the world; and one of the most curious facts of the epoch is that both democracy and conservatism are inclined to support and promote female suffrage, alleging each of them totally different motives for their conduct, and totally different reasons for the opinions which they advance in its favour.

The motives of the Tory leaders are as unlike those of Mrs Fawcett, Mrs Garratt, and the rest of the female agitators as stone is unlike water, as water is unlike fire. The conservative gentlemen wish to admit women into political life because they consider that women are always religious, stationary, and wedded to ancient and stable ways; the female agitators, on the contrary, clamour to have themselves and their sex admitted within the political arena because they believe that women will be foremost in all emancipation, innovation, and social democratic works. It is an odd contradiction, and displays perhaps more than anything else the utter confusion and the entire recklessness and abandonment of principle characteristic of all political parties in the latter half of the nineteenth century. It is very possible that as the English labourer obtained his vote through the confusion and jealousies of party against the sane, the serene, and the unbiased judgment of patriots, so woman in England, and if in England, ultimately in America, will obtain hers. Opportunist policies have always their sure issue in sensational and hurried legislation; and in Europe at the present hour, in England and France most especially, an opportunist policy is the only policy pursued.

What is there to be said in favour of female suffrage? It may be treated as an open subject, since both Reactionists and Socialists can advance for it claims and arguments of the most totally opposite nature. Perhaps it may be said that there is some truth in both sides of these arguments and entire truth in neither. It is probable that female politicians would be many of them more reactionary than the Reactionists, and many of them would be more socialistic than the Socialists. The golden mean is not in favour with women or with mobs.

In England, both the Conservative and Radical intentions are at present limited to giving the suffrage to such women alone as are possessed of real property. But it is certain that this limitation could not be preserved; for the women without property would clamour to be admitted, and would succeed by their clamour as the men without property have done. No doubt, to see a woman of superior mind and character, capable of possessing and administering a great estate, left without electoral voice, whilst her carter, her porter, or the most illiterate labourer on her estate possesses and can exercise it, is on the face of it absurd. But it is not more absurd than that her brother should have his single vote outnumbered and neutralised by the votes of the men-servants, scullions and serving-boys who take his wage and fill his servants' hall and kitchen. It would be more honest to say that the whole existing system of electoral power all over the world is absurd; and will remain so, because in no nation is there the courage, perhaps in no nation is there the intellectual power, capable of putting forward and sustaining the logical doctrine of the *just supremacy of the fittest*: a doctrine which it is surely more vitally necessary to insist on in a republic than in a monarchy. It is because the fittest have not had the courage to resist the pressure of those who are intellectually their inferiors, and whose only strength lies in numbers, that democracy has been enabled to become the power that it has. Theoretically, a republic is founded on the doctrine of the supremacy of the fittest; but who can say that since the days of Perikles any republic has carried out this doctrine practically? The lawyer or the chemist who neglects his business to push himself to the front in political life in France is certainly not the most admirable product of the French intellect; nor can it be said by any impartial student that every President of the United States has been the highest type of humanity that the United States can produce.

Alexander Dumas *fils*, the most accomplished, but the most rabid of the advocates of female suffrage, resumes what seems to him the absurdity of the whole system in a sentence. 'Mme. de Sévigné ne peut pas voter; M. Paul son jardinier peut voter.' He does not seem to see that there is as great an absurdity in the fact that were Mme. de Sévigné, Monsieur de Sévigné, and were she living now, all her wit and wisdom would fail to confer on her more voting power than would be possessed by 'Paul son jardinier.'

With all deference to him, I do not think that Mme. de Sévigné would have cared a straw to rival Paul, the gardener, in going to the electoral urn. Mme. de Sévigné, like every woman of wit and mind, had means of exercising her influence so incomparably superior to the paltry one of recording a vote in a herd that she would, I am sure, have had the most profound contempt for the latter. Indeed, her contempt would have probably extended to the whole electoral system and 'government by representation.' Women of wit and genius must always be indifferent to the opportunity of going up to the ballot booth in company with their own footman and coachman. To those who have a sense of humour the position is not one of dignity. Hypatia, when she feels herself the equal of Julian, will not readily admit that Dadus, however affranchised, is her equal.

Absurdities are not cured by adding greater absurdities to them; discrepancies are not remedied by greater discrepancies being united to them. Whether women voted or not would not change by a hair's breadth the existing, and to many thinkers the deplorable fact, that under the present electoral system throughout the world, the sage has no more electoral power than the dunce, that Plato's voice counts for no more than a fool's. The admission of women could do nothing to remedy this evil. It would only bring into the science of politics what it has too much of already—inferior intelligence and hysterical action. No: reply both the French essayist and the conservative advocates of female suffrage. Not so; because we should only admit women qualified to use it by the possession of property. But it would be impossible to sustain this limitation in the teeth of all the levelling tendencies of modern legislation; it would speedily be declared unjust, intolerable, aristocratic, iniquitous, and it would soon become impossible to deny to Demos's wife or mistress, mother or sister, what you award to Demos himself. If women be admitted at all to the exercise of the franchise they must be admitted wholesale down to the lowest dregs of humanity as men are now admitted. The apple-woman will naturally argue that she has as much right to it as the heiress; how can you say she has not when you have given the apple-man as much electoral voice as the scholar? It is idle to talk of awarding the female suffrage on any basis of property when property has been deliberately rejected as a basis for male suffrage.

The project often insisted on by the advocates of the system, to give votes only to unmarried women, may be dismissed without discussion, as it would be found to be wholly untenable. It would give votes to the old maids of Cranford village, and the enriched *cocottes* of great cities, and would deny them to a Mme. Roland or a Mme. de Staël, to Lady Burdett Coutts or to Mme. Adam. The impossibility of any such limitation being sustained if female suffrage be ever granted, renders it unnecessary to dwell longer on its self-evident defects.

Again, are women prepared to purchase electoral rights by their willingness to fulfil military obligations? If not, how can they expect political privileges unless they are prepared to renounce for them the peculiar privileges which have been awarded to them in view of the physical weakness of their sex? Dumas does, indeed, distinctly refuse to let them be soldiers, on the plea that they are better occupied in child-bearing, but in the same moment he asserts that they ought to be judges and civil servants. It is difficult to see why to postpone an assault to a beleaguered city because *Mme. la Générale est accouchée* would be more absurd than to adjourn the hearing of a pressing lawsuit because *Mme. la Jugesse* would be *sur la paille*. The much graver and truer objection lies less in the physical than in the mental and moral inferiority of women. I use moral in its broadest sense. Women on an average have little sense of justice, and hardly any sense whatever of awarding to others a freedom for which they do not care themselves. The course of all modern legislation is its tendency to make by-laws, fretting and vexatious laws trenching unjustifiably on the personal liberty of the individual. If women were admitted to political power these laws would be multiplied indefinitely and incessantly. The *infiniment petit* would be the dominate factor in politics. Such meddling legislation as the Sunday Closing Act in England, and the Maine Liquor Laws and Carolina Permissive Bill in the United States would be the joy and aim of the mass of female voters. Women cannot understand that you can make no nation virtuous by act of parliament; they would construct their acts of parliament on purpose to make people virtuous whether they chose or not, and would not see that this would be a form of tyranny as bad as any other. A few years ago a State in America (I think it was Maine or Massachusetts) decreed that because a few Pomeranian dogs were given to biting people, all Pomeranian dogs within the State, ill and well, young and old, should on a certain date be killed; and they were killed, two thousand odd in number. Now, this is precisely the kind of legislation which women would establish in their moments of panic; the disregard of individual rights, the injustice to innocent animals and their owners, the invasion of private property under the doctrinaire's plea of the general good, would all commend themselves to women in their hysterical hours, for women are more tyrannical and more self-absorbed than men.

Renan in his 'Marc-Aurèle' observes that the decline of the Roman Empire was hastened, and even, in much, primarily brought about by the elements of feebleness, introduced into it by the Christian sects' admission of women into the active and religious life of men. The woman-worship springing from the adoration of the virgin-mother was at the root of the emasculation and indifference to political and martial duties, which it brought into the lives of men who ceased to be either bold soldiers or devoted citizens.

I do not think the moral and mental qualities of the average woman so inferior to those of the average man as is conventionally supposed. The average man is not an intellectual nor a noble being; neither is the average woman. But there are certain solid qualities in the male creature which are lacking from the female; such qualities as patience and calmness in judgment, which are of infinite value, and in which the female character is almost invariably deficient; a lack in her which makes the prophecy of Dumas, that she will one day fill judicial and forensic duties, a most alarming prospect, as alarming as the prediction of Goldwin Smith that the negro population will eventually outnumber and extinguish the Aryan race in the United States.

There are men with women's minds, women with men's minds; masculine genius may exist in a female farm; feminine inconsistency in a male farm; but these are exceptions to the rule, and such exceptions are exceedingly rare.

The Conservative or patrician party in England advocates the admission of women into politics for much the same motives as influenced the early Christians; they believe that her influence will be universally exercised to preserve the moral excellences of the body politic, the sanctity of the home, the supremacy of religion, the cautiousness of timid and wary legislators. The class of which the Conservatives are always thinking as the recipients of female suffrage would possibly in the main part do so. They would be persons of property and education, and as such might be trusted to do nothing rash. But they would be closely wedded to their prejudices. They would be narrow in all their views. Their church would hold a large place in their affections, and their legislation would be of the character which they now give to their county society. Moreover, as I have said, the suffrage once given to women, it could not be restricted to persons of property. The female factory hand in her garret would assert that she has as much right to and need of a voice as the female landowner, and in face of the fact that the male factory hand and the male landowner have been placed on the same footing in political equality, the country would be unable to refute the argument.

The most intelligent and most eloquent of all the advocates of female suffrage is, as I have said, undoubtedly Dumas *fils*. No man can argue a case more persuasively; nor is any man more completely wedded to one side of an argument than he. Yet even he, her special pleader, in his famous *Appel aux Femmes*, admits that she would bring to science the scorn of reason, and the indifference to suffering which she has shown in so many centuries in the hallucinations and martyrdoms of religion; that she would throw herself into it with *audace et frénésie*; that she would hold all torture of no account if it solved an enigma, and would give herself to the beasts of the field, 'not to prove that Jesus lived, but to know if Darwin was right;' and he passes on to the triumphant prediction that in sixty years' time the world will see the offspring of men and female monkeys, of women and apes; though wherein this prospect for the future is glorious it were hard to say.

Stripped of that exaggeration which characterises all the arguments of a writer famous for anomaly, antithesis and audacity, his prediction that his favourite client Woman will bring into her pursuit of the mysteries of science, the same sort of *folie furieuse*, which Blandina and Agatha, and all the feminine devotees of the early years of Christianity brought into religion, is a prophecy undoubtedly correct. She will bring the same into politics, into legislation, if she ever obtain a preponderant power in them.

The most dangerous tendency in English political life is at this moment the tendency to legislate *per saltum*: female legislation would invariably be conducted *per saltum*. The grasshopper-bounds of Mr Gladstone would be outdone by the kangaroo-leaps of the female legislator when she moved at all. A 'masterly inactivity' would not be understood by her; nor the profound good sense contained in the advice which is variously attributed to Talleyrand, Melbourne and Palmerston, 'When in doubt do nothing.' There is the most mischievous desire in modern politicians to pull everything about, merely to look as if they were great reformers; to strew the ashes of the old order around them long ere they have even settled the foundations of the new; they do not consider the inevitable imperfection which must characterise all human institutions; they do not remember that if the system, whether political or social, works reasonably well, it should be supported, even if it be not symmetrically perfect in theory. These faults are characteristic of modern politicians, because modern politicians are for the most part no longer men trained from their youth in the philosophy of government, but opportunists who view politics as a field of self-advancement. Women will bring into politics these same faults greatly exaggerated and not balanced by that rough and ready common sense which characterises most men who are not specialists or visionaries. Whether the female legislator would imprison all people who do not go to church, or would imprison all people who do not attend scientific lectures, the despotism would be equal; and it is certain that she would desire to imprison either one class or the other.

Some writer has said, 'I can as little understand why any one should fast in Lent, as I can understand why others should object to their fasting if it please them.' But this would never be the attitude of the female politician in regard to either the fasting or the feasting of others. Sir Henry Thomson, in his admirable treatise on gastronomy, remarks on the unwisdom of those who, because a certain food is palatable and nutritious to themselves, recommend it to every one they know, making no account of the difference in constitution and digestion of different persons. There exists a similar difference in mind and character, for which women would never make any allowance when forcing on the world in general their political or social nostrums. As we again and again see the woman expecting from her son the purity of manners of a maiden, and making no account, because she ignores them entirely, of the imperious necessities of sex, so we should see her in matters of national or universal import similarly disregarding or ignoring all facts of which she chose to take no note. She would increase and intensify the present despotisms and weaknesses of political life, and she would put nothing in their place, for she would have lost her own originality and charm. Science, indeed, presumes that in educating her it would strengthen her reasoning powers and widen her mind into the acceptance of true liberty. But what proof is there that science would do anything of that sort? It has never yet showed any true liberality itself. Nothing can exceed the arrogance and the despotism of its own demands and pretensions, the immensity of its self-admiration, the tyrannical character of its exactions.

Dumas observes that happy women will not care for the suffrage because they are happy; he might have added, that brilliant women will not, because they have means of influencing men to any side and to any extent they choose without it. Who, then, will care to exercise it? All the unhappy women, all the fretful *déclassées*, all the thousands or tens of thousands of spinsters who know as much or as little of human nature as they do of political economy. What will such as these bring into political life? They can bring nothing except their own crotches, their own weakness, their own hysterical agitations. Happy women are fond of men, but unhappy women hate them. The legislation voted for by unhappy women would be as much against men, and all true liberty, as Dumas himself is against them and it. Men at present legislate for women with remarkable fairness; but women would never legislate for men with anything approaching fairness, and as the numerical preponderance of votes would soon be on the female side, if female electors were once accepted, the prospect is alarming to all lovers of true freedom.

The woman is the enemy of freedom. Give her power and she is at once despotic, whether she be called Elizabeth Tudor or Theroigne de Mirecourt, whether she be a beneficent or a malevolent ruler, whether she be a sovereign or a revolutionist. The enormous pretensions to the monopoly of a man's life which women put forward in marriage, are born of the desire to tyrannise. The rage and amazement displayed by the woman when a man, whether her lover or her husband, is inconstant to her, comes from that tenacity over the man as a property which wholly blinds her to her own faults or lack of charm and power to keep him. A very clever woman never blames a man for inconstancy to her: she may perhaps blame herself. Women as a rule attach far too great a value to themselves; the woman imagines herself necessary to the man because the man is necessary to her. Hence that eternal antagonism of the woman against the man which is one of the saddest things in human nature. Every writer like Dumas, who does his best to increase this antagonism, commits a great crime. The happiness of the human race lies in the good-will existing between men and women. This good-will cannot exist so long as women have the inflated idea of their own value which they now possess largely in Europe and still more largely in America. A virtuous woman may be above rubies, has said Solomon, but this depends very much on the quality of the virtue; and the idea prevailing among women that they are valuable, admirable and almost divine, merely because they are women, is one of the most mischievous fallacies born of human vanity, and accepted without analysis.

It has been passed, like many another fallacy, from generation to generation, and the enormous power of evil which lies in the female sex has been underestimated or conventionally disregarded for the sake of a poetic effect. The seducer is continually held up for condemnation, but the temptress is seldom remembered. It is common to write of women as the victims of men, and it is forgotten how many men are the victims in their earliest youth of women. Even in marriage the woman, by her infidelity, can inflict the most poignant, the most torturing dishonour on the man; the man's infidelity does not in the least touch the honour of the woman. She can never be in doubt as to the fact of her children being her own; but he may be perpetually tortured by such a doubt, nay, may be compelled through lack of proof to give his name and shelter to his offspring when he is morally convinced that they are not his. The woman can bring shame into a great race as the man can never do, and ofttimes brings it with impunity. In marriage, moreover, the influence of the woman, whatever popular prejudices plead to the contrary, is constantly belittling and injurious to the intelligence of the man. How many great artists since the days of Andrea del Sarto have cursed the woman who has made them barter their heritage of genius for the 'pottage' of worldly affluence? How much, how often, and how pitilessly have the petty affairs, the personal greeds, the unsympathetic and low-toned character of the woman he has unfortunately wedded, put lead on the winged feet of the man of genius, and made him leave the Muses for the god of barter beloved of the common people in the market-place? Not infrequently what is called with pious praise a good woman, blameless in her own conduct and devoted to what she conceives to be her duties, has been more fatal to the originality, the integrity, and the intellectual brilliancy of a man than the worst courtesan could have been. The injury which women have done the minds of men may fairly be set off against those social and physical injuries which men are said by M. Dumas to inflict so ruthlessly on women.

If outside monogamous marriage the woman suffers from the man, within it man suffers from the woman. It is doubtful if but for the obligation to accept it, which is entailed by property, and the desire for legitimate heirs, one man in a hundred of the richer classes would consent to marry. Whenever Socialism succeeds in abolishing property, monogamy will be destroyed with it perforce.

In the lower strata of society the conjugal association is made on more equal terms: both work hard and both frequently come to blows. The poor man loses less by marriage than the rich man, for he has his comforts, his food and his clothes looked after gratis, but the poor woman gains very little indeed by it; and if she got a hearing in the political world, she would probably brawl against it, or, which is still more likely, she would do worse and insist on marriage laws which should restrict the personal freedom of the man as severely and as tyrannically as the Sabbath observance laws do in Scotland, and as the Puritan exactions did in the early years of American colonisation.

The net result of the entrance of the woman into the political arena can never be for the happiness of humanity.

'Prevant leur revanche de l'immobilité à laquelle on les a condamnées elles vont courrir par n'importe quels chemins à côté de l'homme, devant lui si elles peuvent, contre lui s'il le faut à la conquête d'un nouveau monde. En matière de sensation la femme est l'extrême, l'excès, de l'homme.' Dumas recognises the inevitable hostility which will be begotten between the sexes if they war in the same public arena; but he passes over it.

If female suffrage become law anywhere, it must be given to all women who have not rendered themselves ineligible for it by criminality. The result will scarcely be other than the emasculation and the confusion of the whole world of politics. The ideal woman is, we know, the type of heroism, fortitude, wisdom, sweetness and light; but even the ideal woman is not always distinguished by breadth of thought, and it is here a question not of the ideal woman at all, but of the millions of ordinary women who have as little of the sage in them as of the angel. Very few women are capable of being the sympathetic mistress of a great man, or the ennobling mother of a child of genius. Most women are the drag on the wheel of the higher aspirations, to the nobler impulses, to the more original and unconventional opinions, of the men whom they influence. The prospect of their increased ascendency over national movements is very ominous. Is the mass of male humanity ready to accept it?

Women will not find happiness in hostility to men even if they obtain a victory in it, which is very doubtful. Women of genius have never hated men: they have perhaps liked them too well. To the woman of genius love may not be the sole thing on earth, as it is to Gretchen; it is only one amongst the many emotions, charms and delights of life; but she never denies its attractions, its consolation, its supreme ecstasy, its exquisite sympathies. Heloise and Aspasia can love better than Penelope.

Who, then, will become those enemies of men to whom Dumas looks for the emancipation of the weaker sex? All the *délaissées*, all the *déclassées*, all the discontented, jaded, unloved, embittered women in the world, all those, and their number is legion, who have not genius or loveliness, fortune or power, the wisdom to be mute or the sorcery to charm; women restless, feverish, envious, irritable, embittered, whose time hangs heavy on their hands and whose brains seethe under the froth of ill-assorted and ill-assimilated knowledge.

'Quarry the granite rock with razors,' wrote John Newman, 'or moor the vessel with a thread of silk; then may you hope, with such keen and delicate instruments as human knowledge and human understanding, to contend against these giants, the passions and the pride of man;'—or against the difference and the influence of sex.

I know not why women should wish or clamour at once to resemble and to quarrel with man. The attitude is an unnatural one; it is sterile, not only physically but mentally. It is true that the prejudices and conventionalities of society, and the fictions of monogamy have stranded a vast number of women, undistinguished and unhappy, with no career and no interests, who would imagine themselves disgraced if they enjoyed the natural affections of life outside that pale of propriety which the conventions of society have created. These are the women who would care for political power and would be allowed to exercise it. What could the world gain from such as these? What would it not lose of the small modicum of freedom, of contentment, and of wisdom which it already possesses?

To most women success is measured by the balance at the bank, by the applause of the hour, and nothing is esteemed which has not received the hall-mark of the world's approval. There are exceptions, no doubt; but they have been and are, I think, fewer than the advocates of female suffrage would have us believe. Men too often are mere *moutons de Panurge*, but women are so almost invariably. The Arab who weeps when a female child is born to him is perhaps more correct in his measurement of the sex than the American who is prepared to make her the spoiled and wayward sovereign of his household.

I have previously used the words 'mental and moral inferiority'; it is perhaps necessary to explain them. By mental inferiority I do not mean that the average women might not, if educated to it, learn as much mathematics or as much metaphysics as the ordinary man. I do not deny that Girton may produce senior wranglers or physiologists in time to come; it may do so. But the female mind has a radical weakness which is often also its peculiar charm; it is intensely subjective, it is only reluctantly forced to be impersonal, and it has the strongest possible tendency to tyranny, as I have said before. In public morality, also, the female mind is unconsciously unscrupulous; it is seldom very frank or honest, and it would burn down a temple to warm its own pannikin. Women of perfect honesty of intentions and antecedents will adopt a dishonest course, if they think it will serve an aim or a person they care for, with a headlong and cynical completeness which leaves men far behind it. In intrigue a man will often have scruples which the woman brushes aside as carelessly as if they were cobwebs, if once her passions or her jealousies are ardently involved. There is not much veracity anywhere in human nature, but it may always be roughly calculated that the man will be more truthful than the woman, in ninety-nine cases out of a hundred; his judgments will be less coloured by personal wishes and emotions, and his instincts towards justice will be straighter and less mobile than hers. Were women admitted into public life, bribery would become a still greater factor in that life than it now is, which is needless. All the world over, what is wanted for the health of the nations is the moral purification of politics, the elimination of venal and personal views, the disinterested advocacy and adoption of broad, just and magnanimous principles of action. Can it be said that the entry of women into politics would have this effect? He must be a sanguine man who can think that it would, and he must have but little knowledge of women.

On a les défauts de ses qualités. This is one of the most profound axioms ever evolved out of a study of human nature. And all which constitutes the charm of women, mutability, caprice, impressionability, power of headlong self-abandonment, mingled with intense subjectiveness and self-engrossment, would all make of women an inferior but of a most dangerous political force. Where Mr Gladstone has sent out troops and recalled them a dozen times, she, with similar but still greater oscillations of purpose, would send them out and recall them five hundred times. The *Souvent femme varie* of Francois the First is true to all time. But in all her variations it is the Sejanus, the Orloff, the Biron, the Bothwell of the moment, whom she would wade through seas of blood to please. This makes at once her dangerousness and her charm.

As scientists look forward to the time when every man will be bald from boyhood, thus having outgrown the last likeness to the beasts that perish, so enthusiasts for female suffrage look forward to a time when woman will have shed all her fair follies and rectified all her amusing inconsistencies. What will she be like then? Very unlovely it may safely be predicted, as unlovely as the men without hair; very mischievous for evil, it may also be deemed certain.

A French physiologist, who lectured in Russia not very long ago, was amazed at the howls of impatience and disdain which was aroused in the female students amongst his audience in Moscow by his simple statement that the claims of the arts must not be wholly lost sight of in the demands and inquiries of science. They would not tolerate even the mention of the arts; in their fanaticism they would only worship one God. The youths were willing to award a place to art; the maidens would hear of nothing but science. '*Une grande sécheresse de cœur domine la femme qui se donne à la Science;*' and with this dryness of the soul comes an unmerciful and intolerant disposition to tyranny over the minds of others.

It cannot be denied that the quality which in women bestows most happiness on those around them, is that which is called in French and has no exact descriptive word in English, *gaîte de cœur*. Not frivolous unusefulness, or passion for diversion and excitement, but a sweet and happy spirit, finding pleasure in small things and great, and shedding a light like that of Moore's wild freshness of morning on the beaten tracks of life. Where will this pleasant gaiety and smiling radiance go when, harassed, heated, and blown by the bitter winds of strife, the woman seeks to outshriek the man on political platforms, or when with blood-stained hands she bends over the torture-trough of the physiological laboratory?

The humanities do not harden a woman: erudition may leave her loveliness and grace of form and mind; though as proficient a Greek and Latin scholar as any of the learned Italian women of the Renaissance, yet she may be the joy of her home and the angel of the poor. A love of learning, of art, of nature, keeps long young the heart in which it has a place. But the noisy conflicts of the polling-booths and the pitiless cruelties of the laboratories will not do so. There is in every woman, even in the best woman, a sleeping potentiality for crime, a curious possibility of fiendish evil. Even her maternal love is dangerously near an insane ferocity, which at times breaks out in infanticide or child-murder. Everything which tends to efface in her gentler and softer instincts tends to make of her a worse curse to the world than any man has ever been. If, indeed, in the centuries to come she should develop into the foe of man, which Dumas *fils* wishes her to become, it is by no means improbable that men, in sheer self-defence, will be compelled to turn on her and chain her down into the impotency of servitude once more.

If she once leave the power which nature has given her over her lovers, her friends, her sons, to become the opponent, the jealous rival and the acrid enemy of men, then men, it may be with surety predicted, will not long keep the gloves on as they fight with her, but with the brutality which is natural to the male animal and which is only curbed, not effaced, by the graceful hypocrisies of society and of courtship, will with his closed fists send her down into that lower place of *la femelle de l'homme*, from which it has been the effort and the boast of Christianity and of civilisation to raise her. Woman can never truly conquer man, except by those irresistible weapons which the Queen of the Amazons leaned on in her strife with Alexander.

Man has, I repeat, been very fair in his dealings with women, as far as legislation goes; he could easily have kept her from all time to the harem, and it has been a proof of his fairness, if not of his wisdom, that he has not done so. I have but little doubt but that, before long, he will cede to her clamour, and let her seat herself beside him, or opposite to him, on the benches of his representative houses. When he does, he will, I think, regret the loss of the harem.

There is a lax and perilous inclination in the mass of mankind, in these latter days of the century, to give anything which is much asked for.

'To yield to clamour and to pallid fears,

What wisdom, temperance and truth deny;'

to let the reins go, and the steeds, which draw the chariot of national fate, gallop headlong, whither they will, downhill if they choose. The pessimism prevalent in the classes which think, lies at the root of their indifference to change, and their apathy and indolence before fresh demands. Men who do think at all, see how unsatisfactory all things are, how unreal all religions, how fictitious the bond of marriage, how mutable the laws of property, how appalling the future of the world, when there will not be even standing-room upon it for all the billions of peoples begotten. And they are, therefore, in that mood which makes them willing to try any new thing, even as men at death's door languidly affirm their despairing readiness to try any nostrum or panacea tendered to them.

Woman may, will, very possibly, snatch from the nerveless hand of the sick man those legal and legislative rights which she covets. The political movements of modern times have been always in the direction of giving unlimited power to blind and unmeasured masses, whose use of that which is thus rashly given them the boldest prophet dare not predict. Such movement will probably give political power to women.

I confess that I, for one, dread the day which shall see this further development of that crude and restless character of the nineteenth century, which, with sublime self-contentment and self-conceit, it has presumed to call Progress.

VULGARITY

If the present age were less of a hypocrite than it is, probably its conscience would compel it to acknowledge that vulgarity is excessively common in it; more common than in any preceding time, despite its very bountiful assumptions of good taste and generalised education.

Vulgarity is almost a modern vice; it is doubtful whether classic ages knew it at all, except in that sense in which it must be said that even Socrates was vulgar, *i.e.,* inquisitiveness, and in that other sense of love of display to which the tailless dog of Alkibiades was a mournful victim. We are aware that Alkibiades said he cut off his dog's tail and ears to give the Athenians something to talk of, that they might not gossip about what else he was doing. But though gossip was no doubt rife in Athens, still, vulgarity in its worst sense, that is, in the struggle to seem what the struggler is not, could have had no existence in times when every man's place was marked out for him, and the lines of demarcation could not be overstepped. Vulgarity began when the freedman began to give himself airs, and strut and talk as though he had been a porphyrogenitus; and this pretension was only possible in a decadence.

There may be a vast vulgarity of soul with an admirable polish of manners, and there may be a vast vulgarity of manner with a generous delicacy of soul. But, in this life, we are usually compelled to go by appearances, and we can seldom see beyond them, except in the cases of those few dear to, and intimate with us. We must be pardoned if we judge by the externals which are palpable to us and do not divine the virtues hidden beneath them.

An essayist has recently defined good manners as courtesy and truthfulness. Now this is simply nonsense. A person may be full of kindly courtesies, and never utter the shadow of an untruth, and yet he may have red-hot hands, a strident voice, an insupportable manner, dropped aspirates, and a horribly gross joviality, which make him the vulgarest of the vulgar. It is often said that a perfect Christian is a perfect gentleman, but this also is a very doubtful postulate. The good Christian may 'love his neighbour as himself,' and yet he may offend his ear with a cockney accent and sit down to his table with unwashed hands. 'Manners make the man,' is an old copy-book adage, and is not quiet true either: but it is certain that, without good manners, the virtues of a saint may be more offensive, by far, to society than the vices of a sinner. It is a mistake to confuse moral qualities with the social qualities which come from culture and from breeding.

I have said that Socrates must have been in a certain degree vulgar, because he was so abominably inquisitive. For surely all interrogation is vulgar? When strangers visit us, we can at once tell whether they are ill-bred or high-bred persons by the mere fact of whether they do, or do not, ask us questions. Even in intimacy, much interrogation is a vulgarity; it may be taken for granted that your friend will tell you what he wishes you to know. Here and there when a question seems necessary, if silence would imply coldness and indifference, then must it be put with the utmost delicacy and without any kind of semblance of its being considered a demand which must be answered. All interrogation for purposes of curiosity is vulgar, curiosity itself being so vulgar; and even the plea of friendship or of love cannot be pleaded in extenuation of it. But if love and friendship be pardoned their inquisitiveness, the anxiety of the general public to have their curiosity satisfied as to the habits, ways and scandals of those who are conspicuous in any way, is mere vulgar intrusiveness, which the 'society newspapers,' as they are called, do, in all countries, feed to a most pernicious degree. Private life has no longer any door that it can shut and bolt against the intrusion of the crowd. Whether a royal prince has quarrelled with his wife, or a country mayoress has quarelled with a house-maid, the press, large or small, metropolitan or provincial, serves up the story to the rapacious curiosity of the world-wide, or the merely local public. This intrusion on personal and wholly private matters is an evil which increases every day; it is a twofold evil, for it is alike a curse to those whose privacy it poisons, and a curse to those whose debased appetites it feeds. It would be wholly impossible, in an age which was not vulgar, for those journals which live on personalities to find a public. They are created by the greed of the multitude which calls for them. It is useless to blame the proprietors and editors who live on them; the true culprits are the readers—the legions of readers—who relish and patronise them, and without whose support such carrion flies could not live out a summer.

'It is so easy to talk about people' is the excuse constantly made by those who are reproved for gossiping about others who are not even, perhaps, their personal acquaintances. Yes, it is very easy; the most mindless creature can do it; the asp, be he ever so small, can sting the hero, and perchance can slay him; but gossip of a malicious kind is intensely vulgar, and to none but the vulgar should it be welcome, even if their vulgarity be such as is hidden under a cloak of good manners. It is true that there is a sort of spurious wit which springs out of calumny, and which is *malgré nous* too often diverting to the best of us, and this sort of personality has a kind of contagious attraction which is apt to grow even on those who loathe it, much as absinthe does. But it is none the less vulgar, and vulgarises the mind which admits its charm, as absinthe slowly eats up the vitality and the digestive powers of those who yield to its attraction. Were there no vulgarity, it may be said that there would be no scandal; for scandal is born of that marked desire to think ill of others, and that restless inquisitiveness into affairs that do not concern us, which is pre-eminently vulgar. When we talk of the follies of our friends, or the backslidings of our acquaintances, in a duchess's boudoir, we are every whit as vulgar as the fishwives or the village dames jabbering of the sins of Jack and Jill in any ale-house. The roots of the vulgarity are the same—inquisitiveness and idleness. All personalities are vulgar; and whether personalities are used as the base weapons to turn an argument, or as the equally base bait wherewith to make the fortunes of a newspaper, they are alike offensive and unpardonable. The best characteristic of the best society would be that they should be absolutely forbidden in it.

Another reason why the present age is more vulgar than any preceding it, may also be found in the fact that, in it pretension is infinitely more abundant, because infinitely more successful than it ever was before. An autocratic aristocracy, or a perfect equality, would equally make pretension impossible. But, at the present time, aristocracy is without power, and equality has no existence outside the dreams of Utopians. The result is, that the whole vast mass of humanity, uncontrolled, can struggle, and push, and strive, and sweat, and exhaust itself, to appear something that it is not, and all repose and calm and dignity, which are the foes of vulgarity, are destroyed.

Essayists have often attempted to define high breeding; but it remains indefinable. Its incomparable charm, its perfect ease, its dignity which is never asserted, yet which the most obtuse can always feel is in reserve, its very manner of performing all the trifling acts of social usage and obligation, are beyond definition. They are too delicate and too subtle for the harshness of classification. The courtier of the old story who, when told by Louis Quatorze to go first, went first without protest, was a high-bred gentleman. Charles the First, when he kept his patience and his peace under the insults of his trial at Westminster, was one also. Mme. du Barry screams and sobs at the foot of the guillotine; Marie Antoinette is calm.

True, I once knew a perfectly well-bred person who yet could neither read nor write. I can see her now in her little cottage in the Derbyshire woods, on the brown, flashing water of the Derwent River (Darron, as the people of Derbyshire call it), a fair, neat, stout, old woman with a round face and a clean mob cap. She had been a factory girl in her youth (indeed, all her womanhood had worked at the cotton mill on the river), and now was too old to do anything except to keep her one-roomed cottage, with its tall lancet windows, its peaked red roof, and its sweet-smelling garden, with its high elder hedge, as neat and fresh and clean as human hands could make them. Dear old Mary! with her racy, Chaucerian English, and her happy, cheerful temper, and her silver spectacles, which some of the 'gentry' had given her, and her big Bible on the little round table, and the black kettle boiling in the wide fireplace, and her casements wide open to the nodding moss-roses and the sweet-brier boughs! Dear old Mary! she was a bit of Shakespeare's England, of Milton's England, of Spenser's England, and the memory of her, and of her cottage by the brown, bright river often comes back to me across the width of years. She was a perfectly well-bred person; she made one welcome to her little home with simple, perfect courtesy, without flutter, or fuss, or any effort of any sort; she had neither envy nor servility; grateful for all kindness, she never either abused the 'gentry' or flattered them; and her admirable manner never varied to the peddler at her door or to the squire of her village; would never have varied, I am sure, if the queen of her country had crossed her door-step. For she had the repose of contentment, of simplicity, and of that self-respect which can never exist where envy and effort are. She could neither read nor write; she scrubbed and washed and worked for herself; she had never left that one little green nook of Derbyshire, or seen other roads than the steep shady highway which went up to the pine woods behind her house; but she was a perfectly well-bred woman, born of a time calmer, broader, wiser, more generous than ours.

A few miles off in the valley, where she never by any chance went, the excursion trains used to vomit forth, at Easter and in Whitsun week, throngs of the mill hands of the period, cads and their flames, tawdry, blowzy, noisy, drunken; the women with dress that aped 'the fashion,' and pyramids of artificial flowers on their heads; the men as grotesque and hideous in their own way; tearing through woods and fields like swarms of devastating locusts, and dragging the fern and hawthorn boughs they had torn down in the dust, ending the lovely spring day in pot-houses, drinking gin and bitters, or heavy ales by the quart, and tumbling pell-mell into the night train, roaring music-hall choruses; sodden, tipsy, yelling, loathsome creatures, such as make the monkey look a king, and the newt seem an angel beside humanity—exact semblance and emblem of the vulgarity of the age.

Far away from those green hills and vales of Derbyshire I pass to-day in Tuscany a little wine-house built this year; it has been run up in a few months by a speculative builder; it has its name and purpose gaudily sprawling in letters two feet long across its front; it has bright pistachio shutters and a slate roof with no eaves; it has a dusty gravelled space in front of it; it looks tawdry, stingy, pretentious, meagre, squalid, fine, all in one. A little way off it is another wine-house, built somewhere about the sixteenth century; it is made of solid grey stone; it has a roof of brown tiles, with overhanging eaves like a broad-leafed hat drawn down to shade a modest countenance; it has deep arched windows, with some carved stone around and above them; it has an outside stairway in stone and some ivy creeping about it; it has grass before it and some cherry and peach trees; the only sign of its calling is the bough hung above the doorway. The two wine-houses are, methinks, most apt examples of the sobriety and beauty which our forefathers put into the humblest things of life and the flimsy tawdriness and unendurable hideousness which the present age displays in all it produces. I have not a doubt that the one under the cherry tree, with its bough for a sign, and its deep casements, and its clean, aged look, will be soon deserted by the majority of the carters and fruit growers and river fishermen who pass this way, in favour of its vulgar rival, where I am quite sure the wines will be watered tenfold and the artichokes fried in rancid oil; its patrons will eat and drink ill, but they will go to the new one, I doubt not, all of them, except a few old men, who will cling to the habit of their youth. Very possibly those who own the old one will feel compelled to adapt themselves to the progress of the age; will cut the eaves off their roof, hew down their fruit trees, whitewash their grey stone, and turn their fine old windows into glass doors with pistachio blinds—and still it will not equal its rival in the eyes of the carters and fishers and gardeners, since it was not made yesterday! Neither its owners nor its customers can scarcely be expected to be wiser than are all the municipal counsellors of Europe.

Perfect simplicity is the antithesis of vulgarity, and simplicity is the quality which modern life is most calculated to destroy. The whole tendency of modern education is to create an intense self-consciousness; and whoever is self-conscious has lost the charm of simplicity, and has already become vulgar in a manner. The most high-bred persons are those in whom we find a perfect naturalness, an entire absence of self-consciousness. The whole influence of modern education is to concentrate the mind of the child on itself; as it grows up this egoism becomes confirmed; you have at once an individual both self-absorbed and affected, both hard towards others and vain of itself.

When pretension was less possible, vulgarity was less visible, because its chief root did not exist. When the French nobility, in the time of Louis Quatorze, began to *engraisser leurs terres* with the ill-acquired fortunes of farmer-generals' daughters, their manners began to deteriorate and their courtesy began to be no more than an empty shell filled with rottenness. They were not yet vulgar in their manners, but vulgarity had begun to taint their minds and their race, and their *mésalliances* did not have the power to save them from the scaffold. Cowardice is always vulgar, and the present age is pre-eminently cowardly; full of egotistic nervousness and unconcealed fear of all those physical dangers to which science has told all men they are liable. Pasteur is its god, and the microbe its Mephistopheles. A French writer defined it, the other day, as the age of the 'infinitely little.' It might be also defined as the age of absorbing self-consciousness. It is eternally placing itself in innumerable attitudes to pose before the camera of a photographer; the old, the ugly, the obscure, the deformed, delight in multiplying their likenesses on cardboard, even more than do the young, the beautiful, the famous, and the well-made. All the resources of invention are taxed to reproduce effigies of persons who have not a good feature in their faces or a correct line in their limbs, and all the resources of science are solicited to keep breath in the bodies of people who had better never have lived at all. Cymon grins before a camera as self-satisfied as though he were Adonis, and Demos is told that he is the one sacred offspring of the gods to which all creation is freely sacrificed. Out of this self-worship springs a hideous, a blatant vulgarity, which is more likely to increase than to diminish. Exaggeration of our own value is one of the most offensive of all the forms of vulgarity, and science has much to answer for in its present pompous and sycophantic attitude before the importance and the excellence of humanity. Humanity gets drunk on such intoxicating flattery of itself.

Remark how even what is called the 'best' society sins as these do who forsake the grey stone house for the slate-roofed and stuccoed one. There has been an endless outcry about good taste in the last score of years. But where is it to be really found? Not in the crowds who rush all over the world by steam, nor in those who dwell in modern cities. Good taste cannot be gregarious. Good taste cannot endure a square box to live in, however the square box may be coloured. That the modern poet can reside in Westbourne Grove, and the modern painter in Cromwell Road, is enough to set the hair of all the Muses on end. If Carlyle had lived at Concord, like Emerson, how much calmer and wiser thought, how much less jaundiced raving, would the world have had from him! That is to say, if he would have had the soul to feel the green and fragrant tranquillity of Concord, which is doubtful. Cities may do good to the minds of men by the friction of opinions found in them, but life spent only in cities under their present conditions is debasing and pernicious, for those conditions are essentially and hopelessly vulgar.

If the soul of Shelley in the body of Sardanapalus, with the riches of Crœsus, could now dwell in Paris, London, or New York, it is doubtful whether he would be able to resist the pressure of the social forces round him and strike out any new forms of pleasure or festivity. All that he would be able to do would, perhaps, be to give better dinners than other people. The forms of entertainment in them are monotonous, and trivial where they are not coarse. When a man colossally rich, and therefore boundlessly powerful, appears, what new thing does he originate? What fresh grace does he add to society; what imagination does he bring into his efforts to amuse the world? None; absolutely none. He may have more gold plate than other people; he may have more powdered footmen about his hall; he may have rosewood mangers for his stables; but he has no invention, no brilliancy, no independence of tradition; he will follow all the old worn ways of what is called pleasure, and he will ask crowds to push and perspire on his staircases, and will conceive that he has amused the world.

When one reflects on the immense possibilities of an enormously rich man, or a very great prince, and sees all the *banalité*, the repetition, and the utter lack of any imagination, in all that these rich men and these great princes do, one is forced to conclude that the vulgarity of the world at large has been too much for them, and that they can no more struggle against it than a rhinoceros against a quagmire; his very weight serves to make the poor giant sink deeper and quicker into the slime.

From his birth to his death it is hard indeed for any man, even the greatest, to escape the vulgarity of the world around him. Scarcely is he born than the world seizes him, to make him absurd with the fussy conventionalities of the baptismal ceremony, and, after clogging his steps, and clinging to him throughout his whole existence, vulgarity will seize on his dead body and make even that grotesque with the low comedy of its funeral rites. Had Victor Hugo not possessed very real qualities of greatness in him he would have been made ridiculous forever by the farce of the burial which Paris intended as an honour to him.

All ceremonies of life which ought to be characterised by simplicity and dignity, vulgarity has marked and seized for its own. What can be more vulgar than the marriage ceremony in what are called civilised countries? What can more completely take away all delicacy, sanctity, privacy and poetry from love than these crowds, this parade, these coarse exhibitions, this public advertisement of what should be hidden away in silence and in sacred solitude? To see a marriage at the Madeleine or St Philippe du Roule, or St George's, Hanover Square, or any other great church in any great city of the world, is to see the vulgarity of modern life at its height. The rape of the Sabines, or the rough bridal still in favour with the Turcomans and Tartars, is modesty and beauty beside the fashionable wedding of the nineteenth century, or the grotesque commonplace of civil marriage. Catullus would not have written 'O Hymen Hymenæ!' if he had been taken to contemplate the thousand and one rare petticoats of a modern trousseau, or the tricolored scarf of a continental mayor, or the chairs and tables of a registry office in England or America.

Modern habit has contrived to dwarf and to vulgarise everything, from the highest passions to the simplest actions; and its chains are so strong that the king in his palace and the philosopher in his study cannot keep altogether free of them.

Why has it done so? Presumably because this vulgarity is acceptable and agreeable to the majority. In modern life the majority, however blatant, ignorant or incapable, gives the law, and the *âmes d'elite* have, being few in number, no power to oppose to the flood of coarse commonplace, with which they are surrounded and overwhelmed. Plutocracy is everywhere replacing aristocracy, and has its arrogance without its elegance. The tendency of the age is not towards the equalising of fortunes, despite the boasts of modern liberalism; it is rather towards the creation of enormous individual fortunes, rapidly acquired and lying in an indigested mass on the stomach of Humanity. It is not the possessors of these riches who will purify the world from vulgarity. Vulgarity is, on the contrary, likely to live, and multiply, and increase in power and in extent. Haste is one of its parents, and pretension the other. Hurry can never be either gracious or graceful, and the effort to appear what we are not is the deadliest foe to peace and to personal dignity.

'Dans les anciennes sociétés l'aristocracie de l'argent était contrepesée par l'aristocracie de la naissance, l'aristocracie de l'esprit, et l'aristocracie du cœur. Mais nous, en abandonnant jusqu'au souvenir même de ces distinctions, nous n'avons laissé subsister que celles que la fortune peut mettre entre les hommes.... Dans les anciennes sociétés la fortune comme la noblesse représentait quelque chose d'autre, si je puis ainsi dire, et de plus qu'elle-même. Elle était vraiment une force sociale parcequ'elle était une force morale. On s'enrichssiait honêtement: de telle sorte que la richesse représentait non-seulement, comme je crois que disent les économistes, le travail accumulé de trois ou quatre générations, mais encore toutes les vertus modestes qui perpétuent l'amour du travail dans une même famille, et querque chose enfin de plus haut, de plus noble, de plus rare que lout cela: le sacrifice de l'égoïsme à l'intérèt, la considération, la dignité du nom. Il n'y a plus d'effort, il n'y a même pas de travail, à l'origine d'un grand nombre de ces nouvelles fortunes, et l'on peut se demander s'il y a, seulement de l'intelligence. Mais, en revanche, il y a de l'audace, et surtout cette conviction que la richesse n'a pas de juges mais seulement des envieux et des adorateurs. C'est ce qui fait aujourd'hui l'immoralité toute particulière et toute nouvelle de cette adoration que nous professons publiquement pour lui. Le temps approche où il ne sera pas fâcheux, mais honteux, d'être pauvre.'

These words of the celebrated French critic, Brunetière, written *apropos* of *La France Juive*, are essentially true, even if truth is in them somewhat exaggerated, for in the middle ages riches were often acquired by violence, or pandering to vice in high places. The modern worship of riches *per se* is a vulgarity, and as he has said, it even amounts to a crime.

Such opinions as his are opposed to the temper of the age; are called <u>reactionary</u>, old-fashioned and exclusive; but there is a great truth in them. If the edge were not rubbed off of personal dignity, if the bloom were not brushed off of good taste, and the appreciation of privacy and *recueillement* greatly weakened, all the personalities of the press and of society would never have been endured or permitted to attain the growth which they have attained. The faults of an age are begotten and borne out of itself; it suffers from what it creates. One looks in vain, in this age, for any indication of any new revolt against the bond of vulgarity, or return to more delicate, more dignified, more reserved manners of life. If socialism should have its way with the world (which is probable), it will not only be vulgar, it will be sordid; all loveliness will perish; and, with all ambition forbidden, heroism and greatness will be things unknown, and genius a crime against the divinity of the Eternal Mediocre. The socialism of Bakounine, of Marx, of Krapotkine, of Tolstoï, is the dreariest and dullest of all earthly things—an Utopia without an idea, a level as blank and hopeless as the dust plains of a Russian summer. It may be a vision, dreary as it is, which will one day be realised. There is hourly growing in the world a dull and sullen antagonism against all superiority, all pre-eminent excellence, whether of intellect, birth or manner; and this jealousy has the germs in it of that universal war on superiority which will be necessary to bring about the triumph of socialism. At present, society is stronger than the socialists; is stronger in Germany, in America, in Italy, in Russia, even in France; but how much longer it will have this superior strength who can say? Socialism being founded, not on love, as it pretends, but on hatred—hatred of superiority—appeals to a malignant instinct in human nature, in the mediocrity of human nature, which is likely to increase as the vast and terrible increase of population makes the struggle of existence more close and more desperate. Socialism will very possibly ravage and lay waste the earth like a hydra-headed Attila; but there will be nothing to be hoped for from it in aid of the graces, the charms, or the dignity of life. Were riches more careful of these, they would hold their own better in the contest with socialism. Were society more elegant, more self-respecting, more intelligent, more distinguished, it would give its defenders much more reason and strength to plead in favour of its preservation.

But society is on the whole both stupid and vulgar. It scarcely knows the good from the bad in anything. If a fashion is set, it follows the fashion sheepishly, without knowing why it does so. It has neither genuine conscience, nor genuine taste. It will stone A. for what it admires in B., and will crucify Y. for what it smilingly condones in Z. It has no true standard for anything. It is at once hypercritical and over-indulgent. What it calls its taste is but a purblind servility. It will take the deformed basset-hound as a pet, and neglect all the beautiful canine races; it will broil in throngs on a bare strip of sand, and avoid all the lovely places by wood and sea; it will worship a black rose, and never glance at all the roses which nature has made. If only Fashion decree, the basset-hound, the bare sand, and the black rose are to it the idols of the hour. It has no consistency; it will change the Japanese for the Rococo, the Renaissance for the Queen Anne, the Watteau for the Oriental, or mix them all together, at the mere weathercock dictate of fashion or caprice. It has no more consistency in its code of morals; it will ask Messalina anywhere as long as a prince speaks to her and she is the fashion; if the prince ceases to speak and she ceases to be the fashion, it puts up its fan at her vices, and scores her name out of its visiting list. There is no reality in either its pretensions to morality or good taste.

When we think of the immense potentialities and capabilities of society, of all that it might become, of all that it might accomplish, and behold the monotony of insipid folly, of ape-like imitation, of consummate hypocrisy, in which it is content to roll on through the course of the years, one cannot but feel that, if its ultimate doom be to be swallowed up and vomited forth again, lifeless and shapeless, by the dragon of socialism, it will have no more than its due; that it will fall through its own sloth and vileness as the empire of Rome fell under the hordes of the barbarians.

That charming writer Gustave Droz has said that railways are at once the symbol and the outcome of the vulgarity of the age; and that whoever lets himself be shot through space like a parcel through a tube, and condescends to eat in a crowd at a station buffet, cannot by any possibility retain dignity of appearance or elegance of manners. The inelegant scrambling and pushing, and elbowing and vociferating of a modern railway station form an exact and painful image of this restless, rude and gregarious century.

Compare the stately progress of a Queen Elizabeth, or a Louis Quatorze through the provinces, calm, leisurely, dignified, magnificent, with the modern monarch or prince always in movement as if he were a *commis-voyageur*, interviewed ridiculously on a square of red carpet on a station platform, and breathlessly listening to a breathless mayor's silly and verbose address of welcome; then rushing off, as if he were paid so much an hour, to be jostled at a dog show, hustled at an agricultural exhibition, and forced to shake hands with the very politicians who have just brought before the House the abolition of the royal prerogative. It is not the question here of whether royalty is, or is not, better upheld or abolished; but so long as royalty exists, and so long as its existence is dear to many millions, and esteemed of benefit by them, it is infinitely to be regretted that it should have lost, as it has lost, all the divinity which should hedge a king.

Recent publications of royal feelings and royal doings may be of use to the enemies of royalty by showing what twaddling nothings fill up its day; but to royalty itself they can only be belittleing and injurious in a great degree, whilst the want of delicacy which could give to the public eye such intimate revelations of personal emotions and struggles with poverty, as the publication of the *Letters of the Princess Alice of England* made public property, is so staring and so strange that it seems like the public desecration of a grave.

Books, in which the most trivial and personal details are published in print by those who should veil their faces like the Latin in sorrow and veil them in their purples, could only be possible in an age in which vulgarity has even reached up and sapped the very foundations of all thrones. One cannot but feel pity for the poor dead princess, who would surely have writhed under such indignity, when one sees in the crudeness and cruelty of print her homely descriptions of suckling her children and struggling with a narrow purse, descriptions so plainly intended for no eyes but those of the person to whom they were addressed. Better—how much better!— have buried with her those humble letters in which the soul is seen naked as in its prayer-closet, and which are no more fit to be dragged out into the garish day of publicity than the bodily nakedness of a chaste woman is fit to be pilloried in a market-place. I repeat, only an age intensely and despairingly vulgar could have rendered the publication of such letters as those royal letters to royal persons possible. Letters of intimacy are the most sacred things of life; they are the proofs of the most intimate trust and confidence which can be placed in us; and to make them public is to violate all the sweetest sanctities of life and of death.

La pudeur de l'âme is forever destroyed where such exposure of feelings, the most intimate and the most personal, becomes possible. In the preface to those letters it is said that the public will in these days know everything about us, and therefore it is better that they should know the truth from us. Not so; this attitude is indeed submission to the mob: it is unveiling the bosom in the market-place. Any amount of calumny cannot destroy dignity; but dignity is forever destroyed when it condescends to call in the multitude to count its tears and see its kisses.

The great man and the great woman should say to the world: 'Think of me what you choose. It is indifferent to me. You are not my master; and I shall never accept you as a judge.' This should be the attitude of all royalty, whether that of the king, the hero, or the genius.

THE STATE AS AN IMMORAL FACTOR

The tendency of the last years of the nineteenth century is toward increase in the powers of the state and decrease in the powers of the individual citizen. Whether the government of a country be at this moment nominally free, or whether it be avowedly despotic, whether it be an empire, a republic, a constitutional monarchy, or a self-governing and neutralised principality, the actual government is a substitution of state machinery for individual choice and individual liberty. In Servia, in Bulgaria, in France, in Germany, in England, in America, in Australia, anywhere you will, the outward forms of government differ widely, but beneath all there is the same interference of the state with personal volition, the same obligation for the individual to accept the dictum of the state in lieu of his own judgment. The only difference is that such a pretension is natural and excusable in an autocracy; in a constitutional or republican state it is an anomaly, even an absurdity. But whether it be considered admirable or accursed, the fact is conspicuous that every year adds to the pretensions and powers of the state, and every year diminishes the personal freedom of the man.

To whatever the fact be traceable, it is there, and it is probably due to the increase of a purely *doctrinaire* education, which with itself increases the number of persons who look upon humanity as a drill-sergeant looks upon battalions of conscripts; the battalions must learn to move mechanically in masses, and no single unit of them must be allowed to murmur or to fall out of the ranks. That this conscript, or that, may be in torture all the while matters nothing whatever to the drill-sergeant. That what would have been an excellent citizen makes a rebellious or inefficient conscript is not his business either; he only requires a battalion which moves with mechanical precision. The state is but a drill-sergeant on a large scale, with a whole nationality marched out on the parade-ground.

Whatever were in other respects the evils attendant on other ages than this, those ages were favourable to the development of individuality, and therefore of genius. The present age is opposed to such development; and the more the state manipulates the man, the more completely will individuality and originality be destroyed. The state requires a tax-paying machine in which there is no hitch, an exchequer in which there is never a deficit, and a public, monotonous, obedient, colourless, spiritless, moving unanimously and humbly like a flock of sheep along a straight, high road between two walls. That is the ideal of every bureaucracy; and what is the state except a crystallised bureaucracy? It is the habit of those who uphold the despotism of government to speak as though it were some impersonal entity, some unerring guide, some half-divine thing like the pillar of fire which the Israelites imagined conducted them in their exodus. In actual fact, the state is only the executive; representing the momentary decisions of a majority which is not even at all times a genuine majority, but is, in frequent cases, a fabricated and fictitious preponderance, artificially and arbitrarily produced. There can be nothing noble, sacred, or unerring in such a majority; it is fallible and fallacious; it may be in the right, it may be in the wrong; it may light by accident on wisdom, or it may plunge by panic into folly. There is nothing in its origin or its construction which can render it imposing in the sight of an intelligent and high-spirited man. But the mass of men are not intelligent and not high-spirited, and so the incubus which lies on them through it they support, as the camel his burden, sweating beneath it at every pore. The state is the empty cap of Gessler, to which all but Tell consent to bow.

It has been made a reproach to the centuries preceding this one that in them privilege occupied the place of law; but, though privilege was capricious and often unjust, it was always elastic, sometimes benignant; law—civil law, such as the state frames and enforces—is never elastic and is never benignant. It is an engine which rolls on its own iron lines, and crushes what it finds opposed to it, without any regard to the excellence of what it may destroy.

The nation, like the child, becomes either brutalised by over-drilling, or emasculated by having all its actions and opinions continually prescribed for it. It is to be doubted whether any precautions or any system could compass what the state in many countries is now endeavouring to do, by regulation and prohibition, to prevent the spread of infectious maladies. But it is certain that the nervous terrors inspired by state laws and by-laws beget a malady of the mind more injurious than the bodily ills which so absorb the state. Whether Pasteur's inoculation for rabies be a curse or a boon to mankind, there can be no question that the exaggerated ideas which it creates, the fictitious importance which it lends to what was previously a most rare malady, the nightmare horrors it invokes, and the lies which its propagandists, to justify its pretences, find themselves compelled to invent, produce a dementia and hysteria in the public mind which is a disease far more widespread and dangerous than mere canine rabies (unassisted by science and government) could ever have become.

The dissemination of cowardice is a greater evil than would be the increase of any physical ill whatever. To direct the minds of men in nervous terror to their own bodies is to make of them a trembling and shivering pack of prostrate poltroons. The microbe may be the cause of disease; but the nervous terrors generated in the microbe's name are worse evils than any bacillus. It is the physiologist's trade to increase these terrors; he lives by them, and by them alone has his being, but when the state takes his crotchets and quackeries in earnest and forces them upon the public as law, the effect is physically and mentally disastrous. The cholera as a disease is bad enough, but worse than itself by far are the brutal egotism, the palsied terror, the convulsive agonies, with which it is met, and which the state in all countries does so much to increase. Fear alone kills five-tenths of its victims, and during its latest visitation in the streets of Naples people would spring up from their seats, shriek that they had cholera, and fall dead in convulsions, caused by sheer panic; whilst in many country places the villagers fired on railway trains which they imagined might carry the dreaded malady amongst them. This kind of panic cannot be entirely controlled by any state, but it might be mitigated by judicious moderation, instead of being, as it is, intensified and hounded on by the press, the physiologists, and the governments all over the known world.

The state has already passed its cold, hard, iron-plated arms between the parent and the offspring, and is daily dragging and forcing them asunder. The old moral law may say 'Honour your father and mother,' etc., etc., but the state says, on the contrary: 'Leave your mother ill and untended whilst you attend to your own education; and summon your father to be fined and imprisoned if he dare lay a hand on you when you disgrace and deride him.' The other day a working man in London was sentenced to a fortnight's imprisonment with hard labour, because, being justly angry with his little girl for disobeying his orders and staying out night after night in the streets, he struck her twice with a leathern strap, and she was 'slightly bruised.' The man asked pertinently what was the world coming to if a parent might not correct his child as he thought fit. What can be the relations of this father and daughter when he leaves the prison to which she sent him? What authority can he have in her sight? What obedience will he be able to exact from her? The bruises from the strap would soon pass away, but the rupture, by the sentence of the tribunal, of parental and filial ties can never be healed. The moral injury done to the girl by this interference of the state is irreparable, ineffaceable. The state has practically told her that disobedience is no offence, and has allowed her to be the accuser and jailer of one who, by another canon of law, is said to be set in authority over her both by God and man.

The moral and the civil law alike decree and enforce the inviolability of property; anything which is the property of another, be it but of the value of a copper coin, cannot be taken by you without your becoming liable to punishment as a thief. This, by the general consent of mankind, has been esteemed correct, just and necessary. But the state breaks this law, derides it, rides rough-shod over it, when for its own purposes it requires the property of a private person; it calls the process by various names—condemnation, expropriation, annexation, etc.; but it is a seizure, a violent seizure, and a essentially seizure against the owner's will. If a man enter your kitchen-garden and take a few onions or a few potatoes, you can hold, prosecute and imprison him; the state takes the whole garden, and turns you out of it, and turns it into anything else which for the moment seems to the state excellent or advantageous, and against the impersonal robber you can do naught. The state considers it compensation enough to pay an arbitrary value; but not only are there many possessions, notably in land, for the loss of which no equivalent could reconcile us, but the state herein sets up a principle which is never accorded in law. If the man who steals the onions offers to pay their value, he is not allowed to do so, nor is the owner of the onions allowed to accept such compensation; it is called 'compounding a felony.' The state alone may commit this felony with impunity, and pay what it chooses after committing it.

The state continually tampers with and tramples on private property, taking for itself what and where and how it pleases; the example given to the public is profoundly immoral. The plea put forth in excuse for its action by the state is that of public benefit; the interests of the public cannot, it avers, be sacrificed to private interest or ownership or rights of any sort. But herein it sets up a dangerous precedent. The man who steals the potatoes might argue in his own justification that it is better in the interest of the public that one person should lose a few potatoes than that another person should starve for want of them, and so, either in prison or in poorhouse, become chargeable to the nation. If private rights and the sacredness of property can be set at naught by the state for its own purposes, they cannot be logically held to be sacred in its courts of law for any individual. The state claims immunity for theft on the score of convenience, so then may the individual.

If the civil law be in conflict with and contradiction of religious law, as has been shown elsewhere,[N] it is none the less in perpetual opposition to moral law and to all the finer and more generous instincts of the human soul. It preaches egotism as the first duty of man, and studiously inculcates cowardice as the highest wisdom. In its strenuous endeavour to cure physical ills it does not heed what infamies it may sow broadcast in the spiritual fields of the mind and heart. It treats altruism as criminal when altruism means indifference to the contagion of any infectious malady. The precautions enjoined in any such malady, stripped bare of their pretences, really mean the naked selfishness of the *sauve qui peut*. The pole-axe used on the herd which has been in contact with another herd infected by pleuro-pneumonia or anthrax would be used on the human herd suffering from typhoid, or small-pox, or yellow fever, or diphtheria, if the state had the courage to follow out its own teachings to their logical conclusions. Who shall say that it will not be so used some day in the future, when increase of population shall have made mere numbers of trifling account, and the terrors excited by physiologists of ungovernable force?

We have gained little by the emancipation of human society from the tyranny of the churches if in its stead we substitute the tyranny of the state. One may as well be burned at the stake as compelled to submit to the prophylactic of Pasteur or the serum of Roux. When once we admit that the law should compel vaccination from small-pox, there is no logical reason for refusing to admit that the law shall enforce any infusion or inoculation which its chemical and medical advisers may suggest to it, or even any surgical interference with Nature.

On the first of May, 1890, a French surgeon, M. Lannelongue, had a little imbecile child in his hospital; he fancied that he should like to try trepanning on the child as a cure for imbecility. In the words of the report, —

'Il taillait la suture sagittale et parallèlement avec elle une longue et étroite incision cranienne depuis la suture frontale à la suture occipitale; il en resulta pour la partie osseusse une perte de substance longue de 9 centimetres et large de 6 millimetres, et il en resulta pour le cerveau un véritable débridement.'

If this child live, and be no longer imbecile, the parents of all idiots will presumably be compelled by law to submit their children to this operation of trepanning and excision. Such a law would be the only logical issue of existing hygienic laws.

In the battlefield the state requires from its sons the most unflinching fortitude; but in civil life it allows them, even bids them, to be unblushing poltroons.

An officer, being sent out by the English War Office this year to fill a distinguished post in Hong Kong, was ordered to be vaccinated before going to it; and the vaccination was made a condition of the appointment. In this instance a man thirty years old was thought worthy of confidence and employment by the state, but such a fool or babe in his own affairs that he could not be trusted to look after his own health. You cannot make a human character fearful and nervous, and then call upon it for the highest qualities of resolve, of capacity, and of courage. You cannot coerce and torment a man, and then expect from him intrepidity, presence of mind and ready invention in perilous moments.

A few years ago nobody thought it a matter of the slightest consequence to be bitten by a healthy dog; as a veterinary surgeon has justly said, a scratch from a rusty nail or the jagged tin of a sardine-box is much more truly dangerous than a dog's tooth. Yet in the last five years the physiologists and the state, which in all countries protects them, have succeeded in so inoculating the public mind with senseless terrors that even the accidental touch of a puppy's lips or the kindly lick of his tongue throws thousands of people into an insanity of fear. Dr Bell has justly said: 'Pasteur does not cure rabies; he creates it.' In like manner the state does not cure either folly or fear: it creates both.

The state is the enemy of all volition in the individual: hence it is the enemy of all manliness, of all force, of all independence, and of all originality. The exigencies of the state, from its monstrous taxation to its irritating by-laws, are in continual antagonism with all those who have character uncowed and vision unobscured. Under the terrorising generic term of the law, the state cunningly, and for its own purposes, confounds its own petty regulations and fiscal exactions with the genuine solemnity of moral and criminal laws. The latter any man who is not a criminal will feel bound to respect; the former no man who has an opinion and courage of his own will care to observe. Trumpery police and municipal regulations are merged by the ingenuity of the state into a nominal identity with genuine law; and for all its purposes, whether of social tyranny or of fiscal extortion, the union is to the state as useful as it is fictitious. The state has everywhere discovered that it is lucrative and imposing to worry and fleece the honest citizen; and everywhere it shapes its civil code, therefore, mercilessly and cunningly towards this end.

Under the incessant meddling of government and its offspring, bureaucracy, the man becomes poor of spirit and helpless. He is like a child who, never being permitted to have its own way, has no knowledge of taking care of itself or of avoiding accidents. As, here and there, a child is of a rare and strong enough stuff to break his leading-strings, and grows, when recaptured, dogged and sullen, so are there men who resist the dogma and dictation of the state, and when coerced and chastised become rebels to its rules. The petty tyrannies of the state gall and fret them at every step; and the citizen who is law-abiding, so far as the greater moral code is concerned, is stung and whipped into continual contumacy by the impertinent interference of the civil code with his daily life.

Why should a man fill up a census-return, declare his income to a tax-gatherer, muzzle his dog, send his children to schools he disapproves, ask permission of the state to marry, or do perpetually what he dislikes or condemns, because the state wishes him to do these things? When a man is a criminal, the state has a right to lay hands on him; but whilst he is innocent of all crime his opinions and his objections should be respected. There may be many reasons—harmless or excellent reasons—why publicity about his life is offensive or injurious to him; what right has the state to pry into his privacy and force him to write its details in staring letters for all who run to read? The state only teaches him to lie.

'You ask me things that I have no right to tell you,' replied Jeanne d'Arc to her judges. So may the innocent man, tormented by the state, reply to the state, which has no business with his private life until he has made it forfeit by a crime.

The moment that the states leaves the broad lines of public affairs to meddle with the private interests and actions of its people, it is compelled to enlist in its service spies and informers. Without these it cannot make up its long lists of transgressions; it cannot know whom to summon and what to prosecute.

That duplicity which is in the Italian character so universally ingrained there that the noblest natures are tainted by it—a duplicity which makes entire confidence impossible, and secrecy an instinct strong as life—can be philosophically traced to the influences which the constant dread of the detectives and spies employed under their various governments for so many centuries has left upon their national temperament. Dissimulation, so long made necessary, has become part and parcel of the essence of their being. Such secretiveness is the inevitable product of domestic espionage and trivial interference from the state, as the imposition of a gate-tax makes the peasantry who pass the gate ingenious in concealment and in subterfuge.

The requisitions and regulations of the state dress themselves vainly in the pomp of law; they set themselves up side by side with moral law; but they are not moral law, and cannot possess its impressiveness. Even a thief will acknowledge that 'Thou shalt not steal' is a just and solemn commandment: but that to carry across a frontier, without declaring it, a roll of tobacco (which you honestly bought, and which is strictly your own) is also a heinous crime, both common-sense and conscience refuse to admit The Irish peasant could never be brought to see why the private illicit whisky-still was illicit, and as such was condemned and destroyed, and the convictions which followed its destruction were amongst the bitterest causes of Irish disaffection. A man caught in the act of taking his neighbour's goods knows that his punishment is deserved; but a man punished for using or enjoying his own is filled with chafing rage against the injustice of his lot. Between a moral law, and a fiscal or municipal or communal imposition or decree, there is as much difference as there is between a living body and a galvanised corpse. When in a great war a nation is urged by high appeal to sacrifice its last ounce of gold, its last shred of treasure, to save the country, the response is willingly made from patriotism; but when the revenue officer and the tax-gatherer demand, threaten, fine and seize, the contributor can only feel the irritating impoverishment of such a process, and yields his purse reluctantly. Electoral rights are considered to give him a compensating share in the control of public expenditure; but this is mere fiction: he may disapprove in every item the expenditure of the state; he cannot alter it.

Tolstoï has constantly affirmed that there is no necessity for any government anywhere: it is not *a* government, but *all* governments, on which he wages war. He considers that all are alike corrupt, tyrannical and opposed to a fine and free ideal of life. It is certain that they are not 'the control of the fittest' in any actual sense, for the whole aspect of public life tends every year more and more to alienate from it those whose capacity and character are higher than those of their fellows: it becomes more and more a routine, an *engrenage*, a trade.

From a military, as from a financial, point of view this result is of advantage to the government, whether it be imperial or republican; but it is hostile to the character of a nation, morally and æsthetically. In its best aspect, the state is like a parent who seeks to play Providence to his offspring, to foresee and ward off all accident and all evil, and to provide for all possible contingencies, bad and good. As the parent inevitably fails in doing this, so the state fails, and must fail, in such a task.

Strikes, with their concomitant evils, are only another form of tyranny; but they have this good in them—that they are opposed to the tyranny of the state, and tend to lessen it by the unpleasant shock which they give to its self-conceit and self-complacency. Trades-unions turn to their own purposes the lesson which the state has taught them—*i.e.*, a brutal sacrifice of individual will and welfare to a despotic majority.

There is more or less truth and justification in all revolutions because they are protests against bureaucracy. When they are successful, they abjure their own origin and become in their turn the bureaucratic tyranny, sometimes modified, sometimes exaggerated, but always tending towards reproduction of that which they destroyed. And the bureaucratic influence is always immoral and unwholesome, were it only in the impatience which it excites in all courageous men and the apathy to which it reduces all those who are without courage. Its manifold and emasculating commands are to all real strength as the cords in which Gulliver was bound by the pygmies.

The state only aims at instilling those qualities in its public by which its demands are obeyed and its exchequer is filled. Its highest attainment is the reduction of mankind to clockwork. In its atmosphere all those finer and more delicate liberties which require liberal treatment and spacious expansion inevitably dry up and perish. Take a homely instance. A poor, hard-working family found a little stray dog; they took it in, sheltered, fed it, and attached themselves to it; it was in one of the streets of London; the police after a time summoned them for keeping a dog without a licence; the woman, who was a widow, pleaded that she had taken it out of pity, that they had tried to lose it, but that it always came back to them; she was ordered to pay the amount of the dog-tax and two guineas' costs; *i.e.*, the state said to her: 'Charity is the costliest of indulgences; you are poor; you have no right to be humane.' The lesson given by the state was the vilest and meanest which could be given. This woman's children, growing up, will remember that she was ruined for being kind; they will harden their hearts, in accordance with the lesson; if they become brutal to animals and men, it is the state which will have made them so.

All the state's edicts in all countries inculcate similar egotism; generosity is in its sight a lawless and unlawful thing: it is so busied in urging the use of disinfectants and ordering the destruction of buildings and of beasts, the exile of families and the closing of drains, that it never sees the logical issue of its injunctions, which is to leave the sick man alone and flee from his infected vicinity: it is so intent on insisting on the value of state education that it never perceives that it is enjoining on the child to advance itself at any cost and leave its procreators to starve in their hovel. The virtues of self-sacrifice, of disinterested affection, of humanity, of self-effacement, are nothing to it; by its own form of organism it is debarred from even admiring them; they come in its way; they obstruct it; it destroys them.

Mr Ruskin, in one of the papers of his *Fors Clavigera*, speaks of an acacia tree, young and beautiful, green as acacias only are green in Venice, where no dust ever is; it grew beside the water steps of the Academy of the Arts and was a morning and evening joy to him. One day he found a man belonging to the municipality cutting it down root and branch. 'Why do you murder that tree?' he asked. The man replied, *'Per far pulizia'* (to clean the place). The acacia and the municipality of Venice are an allegory of the human soul and its controller, the state. The acacia was a thing of grace and verdure, a sunrise and sunset pleasure to a great soul; it had fragrance in its white blossoms and shade in its fair branches; it fitly accompanied the steps which lead to the feasts of Carpaccio and the pageants of Gian Bellini. But in the sight of the Venetian municipality it was irregular and unclean. So are all the graces and greenness of the human soul to the state, which merely requires a community tax-paying, decree-obeying, uniform, passionless, enduring as the ass, meek as the lamb, with neither will nor wishes; a featureless humanity practising the goose-step in eternal routine and obedience.

When the man has become a passive creature, with no will of his own, taking the military yoke unquestioningly, assigning his property, educating his family, holding his tenures, ordering his daily life, in strict accord with the regulations of the state, he will have his spirit and his individuality annihilated, and he will, in compensation to himself, be brutal to all those over whom he has power. The cowed conscript of Prussia becomes the hectoring bully of Alsace.[O]

'Libera chiesà in libero stato' is the favourite stock phrase of Italian politicians; but it is an untruth—nay, an impossibility—not only in Italy, but in the whole world. The church cannot be liberal because liberality stultifies itself; the state cannot be liberal because its whole existence is bound up with dominion. In all the political schemes which exist now, working themselves out in actuality, or proposed as a panacea to the world, there is no true liberality; there is only a choice between despotism and anarchy. In religious institutions it is the same; they are all egotisms in disguise. Socialism wants what it calls equality; but its idea of equality is to cut down all tall trees that the brushwood may not feel itself overtopped. Plutocracy, like its almost extinct predecessor, aristocracy, wishes, on the other hand, to keep all the brushwood low, so that it may grow above it at its own pace and liking. Which is the better of the two?

Civil liberty is the first quality of a truly free life; and in the present age the tendency of the state is everywhere to admit this in theory, but to deny it in practice. To be able to go through the comedy of the voting-urn is considered privilege enough to atone for the loss of civil and moral freedom in all other things. If it be true that a nation has the government which it deserves to have, then the merits of all the nations are small indeed. With some the state assumes the guise of a police officer, and in others of a cuirassier, and in others of an attorney; but in all it is a despot issuing its petty laws with the pomp of Jove; thrusting its truncheon, or its sword, or its quill into the heart of domestic life, and breaking the backbone of the man who has spirit enough to resist it. The views of the state are like those of the Venetian municipality concerning the acacia. Its one aim is a methodical, monotonous, mathematically-measured regularity: it admits of no expansion; it tolerates no exceptions; of beauty it has no consciousness;

of any range beyond that covered by its own vision it is ignorant. It may work on a large scale—even on an enormous scale—but it cannot work on a great one. Greatness can be the offspring alone of volition and of genius: it is everywhere the continual effort of the state to coerce the one and to suffocate the other.

The fatal general conception of the state as an abstract entity, free from all mortal blemish, and incapable of error, is the most disastrous misconception into which the mind of man could possibly have fallen. If the human race would only understand, and take the trouble to realise, that government by the state can be nothing better than government by a multitude of clerks, it would cease to be enamoured of this misconception. Government, absolute and unelastic, by a million of Bumbles, the elevation to supreme and most meddlesome power of a Bureaucracy employing an army of spies and informers in its service; this is all that the rule of the state can ever be, or can ever mean, for mankind. It is impossible that it should ever be otherwise.

Were there some neighbouring planet, populated by demi-gods or some angels, from whom the earth could obtain a superior race to undertake its rule, the domination of this superior race might be beneficial, though it is questionable whether it would, even then, be agreeable. Socialism calls itself liberty, but it is the negation of liberty, since it would permit the state, *i.e.*, the bureaucracy, to enter into and ordain every item of private or of public life. The only sect which has any conception of liberty is that which is called Individualism, and it is singular and lamentable how few followers Individualism obtains. It is due, perhaps, to the fact that so few human beings possess any individuality.

The mass of men are willing to be dominated, have no initiative, no ambition, no moral courage; it is easier to them to join a herd and be driven on with it; it saves them thought and responsibility. Were Individualism general, there would be no standing armies, there would be no affiliation to secret societies, there would be no formation of the public mind by the pressure of a public press, there would be no acceptance of the dicta of priests and physicians, there would be no political councils, there would be no ministers of education. But Individualism is extremely rare, whether as a quality or a doctrine. Where it does exist, as in Tolstoï or Auberon Herbert, it is regarded by the mass of men as abnormal, as something approaching a disease. Yet it will be the resistance of Individualism which will alone save the world (if it be saved indeed) from the approaching slavery of that tyranny of mediocrity which is called the authority of the state. For government by the state merely means government by multitudes of hired, blatant, pompous official servants, such as we are now blessed with; but with the powers of those official servants indefinitely extended until the tentacles of the state should stretch out like that of the octopus and draw into its maw all human life.

No one who studies the signs of the times can fail to be struck by the growing tendency to invoke the aid of what is called the state in all matters; and those who would be alarmed and disgusted at the despotism of a single ruler, are disposed meekly to accept the despotism of the impalpable, impersonal and most dangerous legislator. No one who has observed the action of a bureaucracy can, without dread, see its omnipotence desired; for the fact cannot be too often repeated, that the omnipotence of the state is the omnipotence of its minions in a multitude of greater or smaller offices throughout the country cursed by them. Through whom can the espionage which is necessary to secure the working of permissive bills, of total abstinence laws, of muzzling regulations, of medical and hygienic interference, be exercised, and the vast machinery of fines and dues which accompany these be manipulated, except by hordes of officials gaining their livelihood by torturing the public?

The state is always spoken of as if it were an impersonal force, magnified into semi-divinity of more than mortal power and prescience, wholly aloof from all human error, and meteing out the most infallible justice from the purest balance. Instead of that the state is nothing, can be nothing, more than a host of parasites fastened on the body politic, more or less fattening thereon, and trained to regard the public as a mere taxable entity, always in the wrong and always to be preyed upon at pleasure. It may be unintelligible why mankind ever laid its head under the heel of a single human tyrant, but it is surely more perplexing still why it lies down under the feet of a million of government spies and scriveners. That there is a singular increase in public pusillanimity everywhere is unquestionable; its outcome is the tendency, daily increasing, to look to the government in every detail and every difficulty.

THE PENALTIES OF A WELL-KNOWN NAME

When in childhood, if we be made of the stuff which dreams ambitious dreams, we see the allegorical figure of Fame blowing her long trumpet down the billowy clouds, we think how delightful and glorious it must be to have a name which echoes from that golden clarion. Nothing seems to us worth the having, except a share in that echoing windy blast. To be famous: it is the vision of all poetic youth, of all ambitious energies, of all struggling and unrecognised talent. To be picked out by the capricious goddess and lifted up from the crowd to sit beside her on her throne of cloud, seems to the fancy of youth the loftiest and loveliest of destinies.

In early youth we know not what we do, we cannot measure all we part with in seeking the publicity which accompanies success; we do not realise that the long trumpet of our goddess Fame will mercilessly blow away our dearest secrets to the ears of all, and so strain and magnify them that they will be no more recognised by us, though become the toy of all. We do not appreciate, until we have lost it, the delightful unregarded peace with which the obscure of this world can love, hate, caress, curse, move, sit still, be sick, be sorry, be gay or glad, bear their children, bury their dead, unnoted, untormented unobserved.

It is true that celebrity has its pleasant side. To possess a name which is an open sesame wherever it is pronounced is not only agreeable, but is often useful. It opens doors easily, whether they be of palaces or of railway stations; it saves you from arrest if you be sketching fortifications; it obtains attention for you from every one, from ministers to innkeepers; in a word, it marks you as something out of the common, not lightly to be meddled with, or neglected with impunity. It has its practical uses and its daily advantages, if it have also this prosaic drawback, that, like other conspicuous personages, you pay fifty per cent. dearer than ordinary people for everything which you consume.

Fame, like position, has its ugly side; whatever phase of it be taken, whatever celebrity, notoriety, distinction, or fashion, it brings its own penalties with it, and it may be that these penalties underweigh its pleasures.

The most cruel of its penalties is the loss of privacy which it entails; the difficulty which it raises to the enjoyment of free and unobserved movement. Whether the owner of a well-known name desire privacy for the rest of solitude, for the indulgence of some affection of which it is desired that the world shall know nothing, for the sake of repose, and ease, or for the pursuit of some especial study, the *incognito* sighed for is almost always impossible to obtain.

Find the most retired and obscure of places, amidst hills where no foot but the herdsman's treads, and pastures which feel no step but those of the cattle, a mountain or forest nook which you fondly believe none but yourself and one other know of as existing on the face of the globe; yet brief will be your and your companion's enjoyment of it if your lives, or one of your lives, be famous; the press will track you like a sleuth-hound, and all your precautions will be made as naught, and, indifferent to the harm they do or the misery they create, the Paul Prys of broadsheets will let in the glare of day upon your dusky, mossy dell.

The artist has, no doubt, in this much for which to blame himself: why does the dramatist deign to bow from his box? why does the composer salute his audience? why does the painter have shows at his studio? why does the great writer tell his confidences to the newspaper hack?

Because they are afraid of creating the enmity and the unpopularity which would be engendered by their refusal. Behind this vulgar, intrusive espionage and examination there lies the whole force of the malignity of petty natures and inferior minds, *i.e.*, two thirds of the world. The greater is afraid of the lesser; the giant fears the sling or the stone of the pigmy; he is alone, and the pigmies are multitudinous as the drops in the sea.

We give away the magic belt which makes us invisible, without knowing in the least all that we give away with it: all that delightful independence and repose which are the portion of the *humbles de la terre*, who, all the same, do not value it, do not appreciate it; do not, indeed, ever cease from dissatisfaction at it In their ignorance they think how glorious it must be to stand in the white blaze of the electric light of celebrity; how enviable and delightful it surely is to move forever in a buzz of wondering voices and a dust of rolling chariots, never to stir unchronicled and never to act uncommented. Hardly can one persuade them of the treasure which they possess in their own obscurity? If we tell them of it, they think we laugh at them or lie.

Privacy is the necessity of good and great art, as it is the corollary of dignity and decorum of life. But it is bought with a price; it is bought by incurring the dislike and vindictiveness of all who are checked in their petty malice and prying curiosity and are sent away from closed doors.

The ideal literary life is that of Michelet; the ideal artistic life is that of Corot. Imagine the one leaving the song of the birds and the sound of the seas to squabble at a Copyright Congress, or the other leaving his green trees and his shining waters to pour out the secrets with which nature had intrusted him in the ear of a newspaper reporter! If a correspondent of the press had hidden behind an elder-bush on a grassy path at Shottery, methinks Shakespeare would have chucked him into the nearest ditch; and if a stenographer had inquired of Dante what meats had tasted so bitter to him at Can Grande's table, beyond a doubt the meddler would have learned the coldness and the length of a Florentine rapier. But then no one of these men was occupied with his own personality, none of them had the restless uneasiness, the morbid fear, which besets the modern hero, lest, if his contemporaries do not prate of him, generations to come will know naught of him.

In modern life also, the fox, with his pen and ink hidden under his fur, creeps in, wearing the harmless skin of a familiar house-dog, and the unhappy hare or pullet, who has received, caressed, and fed him without suspicion, sees too late an account of the good nature and of his habitation travestied and sent flying on a news sheet to the four quarters of the globe. Against treachery of this kind there is no protection possible. All that can be done is to be very slow in giving or allowing introductions; very wary in making new acquaintances, and wholly indifferent to the odium incurred by being called exclusive.

Interrogation is always ill-bred; and an intrusion that takes the form of a prolonged interrogation is an intrusion so intolerable that any rudeness whatever is justifiable in its repression.

The man of genius gives his work, his creation, his *alter ego*, to the world, whether it be in political policy, in literary composition, in music, sculpture, painting, or statuary. This the world has full right to judge, to examine, to applaud, or to condemn; but beyond this, into the pale of his private life it has no possible title to entry. It is said in the common jargon of criticism that without knowing the habits, temperament, physique and position of the artist, it is impossible to correctly judge his creation. It is, on the contrary, a hindrance to the unbiassed judgment of any works to be already prejudiced *per* or *contra* by knowledge of the accidents and attributes of those who have produced them. It is a morbid appetite, as well as a vulgar taste, that makes the public invade the privacy of those who lead, instruct, or adorn their century, and these last have themselves to thank, in a great measure, for the pests which they have let loose.

Every day any one who bears a name in any way celebrated receives requests or questions from persons who are unknown to him, demanding his views on everything from Buddhism to blacking, and inquiring into every detail of his existence, from his personal affections to his favourite dish at dinner. If he deign to answer them, he is as silly as the senders.

Sometimes you will hear that a town has been named after you in America, or Australia, or Africa; it is usually a few planks laid down in a barren plain, and you are expected to be grateful that your patronymic will be shouted on a siding as the railway train rushes by it. Sometimes an enthusiastic and unknown letter writer will implore you to tell him or her 'everything' about yourself, from your birth onwards; and if, as you will certainly do if you are in your senses, you consign the impudent appeal to the waste-paper basket, your undesired correspondent will probably fill up the *lacuna* from his or her own imagination. Were all this the offspring of genuine admiration, it might be in a measure excused, though it would always be ill-bred, noxious and odious. But it is either an impertinent curiosity or a desire to make money.

The moment that your name is well known, the demands made upon you will be as numerous as they will be imperative. Though you may never have given any permission or any data for a biography, the fact will not prevent hundreds of biographies appearing about you: that they are fictitious and unauthorised matters nothing either to those who publish or to those who read. Descriptions, often wholly inaccurate, of your habits, your tastes, your appearance, your manner of life, will be put in circulation, no matter how offensive or how injurious to you they may be. Your opinions will be demanded by strangers whose only object is to obtain for themselves some information which they can turn to profit. From the frequency or rarity of your dreams to the length of your menu at dinner, nothing will escape the insatiable appetite of an unwholesome and injurious inquisitiveness. Obscure nonentities from Missouri or Nevada will imagine that they honour you by writing that they have baptised their brats in your name, and requesting some present or acknowledgment in return for their unwelcome effrontery in taking you as an eponymus.

It is probable, nay, I think, certain, that in no epoch of the world's history was prominence in any art or any career ever rendered so extremely uncomfortable as in ours, never so heavily handicapped with the observation and penalty-weight of inquisitive misrepresentation. All the inventions of the age tend to increase a thousandfold all that minute examination of and impudent interference with others which were alive in the race in the days of Miltiades and Socrates, but which has now, in its so-called scientific toys, the means of gratifying this mischievous propensity in an infinitely greater and more dangerous degree.

The instant that any man or woman accomplishes anything which is in any way remarkable, the curiosity of the public is roused and fastens on his or her private life to the neglect and detriment of his or her creations. The composer of the 'Cavalleria Rusticana,' an opera which, whatever may or may not be its artistic merit, has had charm and melody enough to run like a flame of fire across Italy, awakening the applause of the whole nation, had dwelt in obscurity and poverty up to the moment when his work aroused a fury of delight in his country people. Lo! the press immediately seizes on every detail of his hard and laborious life, and makes a jest of his long hair. What has his life or his hair to do with the score of the 'Cavalleria Rusticana?' What has the fact that he has written music which, if not original, or spiritual, has the secret of rousing the enthusiasm of the populace, to do with the private circumstances, habits, or preferences of his daily existence? It is an intolerable impudence which can presume to pry into the latter because the former has revealed in him that magic gift of inspiration which makes him momentarily master of the souls of others.

The human mind is too quickly coloured, too easily disturbed, for it to be possible to shake off all alien bias and reflected hues; and it is more just to the dead than to the living, because it is not by the dead moved either to that envy or detraction, that favour or adulation, which it unconsciously imbibes from all it hears and knows of the living.

Whoever else may deem that the phonograph, the telephone, and the photographic apparatus are beneficial to the world, every man and woman who has a name of celebrity in that world must curse them with deadliest hatred. Life is either a miserable and weak submission to their demands, or a perpetual and exhausting struggle against and conflict with their pretensions, in the course of which warfare enemies are made inevitably and continually by the tens of thousands. He who bends beneath the decrees of the sovereign spy is popular at the price of dignity and peace. Those who refuse to so stoop are marked out for abuse and calumny from all those who live by or are diverted by the results of the espionage. There is no middle way between the two; you must be the obedient slave or the irreconcilable opponent of all the numerous and varied forms of public inquiry and personal interference. The walls of Varzin have never been high enough to keep out the interviewer, and the trees of Faringford have never been so thickly planted that they availed to screen the study of the poet. The little, through these means and methods, have found out that they can annoy, harass, torment, and turn to profit, the great. Who that knows humanity could hope that the former would abstain from the exercise of such power?

The worst result of the literary clamour for these arrays of facts, or presumed facts, is that the ordinary multitude, who have not the talent of the original seekers, imitate the latter, and deem it of more importance to know what any famous person eats, drinks, and wears, in what way he sins, and in what manner he sorrows, than it does to rightly measure and value his picture, his position, his romance, or his poem. Journalistic inquisitiveness has begotten an unwholesome appetite, an impudent curiosity, in the world, which leaves those conspicuous in it neither peace nor privacy.

The press throughout the whole world feeds this appetite, and the victims, either from timidity or vanity, do not do what they might do to condemn and resist it. The interviewer too often finds his impertinent intrusion unresented for him, or the public which employs him, to reach any consciousness of his intolerable effrontery. He has behind him those many-handed powders of anathema, misrepresentation, and depreciation which are called the fourth estate, and almost all celebrity is afraid of provoking the reprisals in print which would follow on a proper and peremptory ejection of the unsought visitor.

Because a man or woman more gifted than the common multitude bestows upon the world some poem or romance, some picture, statue, or musical composition, of excellence and beauty, by what possible right can the world pry into his or her privacy and discuss his or her fortunes and character? The work belongs to the public, the creator of the work does not. The invasion of private life and character never was so great or so general as it is in the last years of this century. It is born of two despicable parents, curiosity and malignity. Beneath all the flattery, which too frequently covers with flowers the snake of inquisitiveness, the snake's hiss of envy may be plainly heard by those who have ears to hear. It is the hope to find, sometime, some flaw, some moral or physical disease, some lesion of brain or decay of fortune, in the private life of those whom they profess to admire or adore, which brings the interviewer crawling to the threshold and peering through the keyhole. What rapture for those who cannot write anything more worthy than a newspaper paragraph to discover that the author of 'Salammbo' was an epileptic! What consolation for those who cannot string rhymes together at a child's party to stand beside the bedside of Heine and watch 'the pale Jew writhe and sweat!'

In Dalou's monument to Eugene Delacroix he represents the great painter with his chin sunk in the *cache-nez*, which his chilly and fragile organisation led to his wearing generally, no matter whether the weather were fine or foul. Dalou has outraged art, but he has delighted his contemporaries and crystallised their taste; the *cache-nez* about the throat of the man of genius enchants the common herd, which catches cold perpetually, but could not paint an inch of canvas or a foot of fresco, and feels jealously, restlessly, malignantly, grudgingly, that the creator of the 'Entreé des Croises' and the 'Barque de Dante,' who was so far above them in all else is brought nearer to them by that folded foulard. The monument in the gardens of the Luxembourg is an epitome of the sentiment of the age; time, glory and art bend before Delacroix and offer him the palms of immortality; Apollo throws his lyre away in sympathy and ecstasy; but what the mortal crowds see and applaud is the disfiguring neckerchief!

It is the habit of scholars to lament that so little is known of the private life of Shakespeare. It is, rather, most fortunate that we know so little, and that little but vaguely. What can we want to know more than the plays tell us? Why should we desire to have records which, drawing earthwards the man, might draw us also downwards from that high empyrean of thought where we can dwell through the magic of the poet's incantations?

It may be a natural instinct which leads the crowd to crave and seek personal details of the lives of those who are greater than their fellows, but it is an instinct to be discouraged and repressed by all who care for the dignity of art. The cry of the realists for *documents humains* is a phase of it, and results from the poverty of imagination in those who require such documents as the scaffolding of their creations. The supreme gift of the true artist is a rapidity of perception and comprehension which is totally unlike the slow piecemeal observations of others. As the musician reads the page of a score at a glance, as the author comprehends the essence of a book by a flash of intelligence, as the painter sees at a glance the points and lines and hues of a landscape, whilst the ordinary man plods through the musical composition note by note, the book page by page, the landscape detail by detail, so the true artist, whether poet, painter, or dramatist, sees human nature, penetrating its disguises and embracing all its force and weakness by that insight which is within him. The catalogues, the classifications, the microscopic examinations, which are required to make up these '*documents*,' are required by those who have not that instantaneous comprehension which is the supreme gift of all supreme talent. The man who takes his notebook and enumerates in it the vegetables, the fish, the game, of the markets, missing no bruise on a peach, no feather in a bird, no stain on the slab where the perch and trout lie dying, will make a painstaking inventory, but he will not see the whole scene as Teniers or Callot saw it.

When the true poet or artist takes up in his hand a single garden pear or russet apple, he will behold, through its suggestions, as in a sorcerer's mirror, a whole smiling land of orchard and of meadow; he will smell the sweet scent of ripe fruit and wet leaves; he will tread a thousand grassy ways and wade in a thousand rippling streams; he will hear the matin's bell and the even song, the lowing kine and the bleating flocks; he will think in a second of time of the trees which were in blossom when Drake and Raleigh sailed, and the fields which were green when the Tudor and Valois met, and the sunsets of long, long ago, when Picardy was in the flames of war, and all over the Norman lands the bowmen tramped and the fair knights rode.

The phrasing of modern metaphysics calls this faculty assimilation; in other days it has been called imagination: be its name what it will, it is the one essential and especial possession of the poetic mind, which makes it travel over space, and annihilate time, and behold the endless life of innumerable forests as suggested to it by a single green leaf. When the writer, therefore, asks clamorously for folios on folios of *documents humains,* he proves that he has not this faculty, and that he is making an inventory of human qualities and vices rather than a portrait of them.

THE LEGISLATION OF FEAR

To any one convinced of what seems to be a supreme truth, that the happiness of humanity can only be secured by the liberty of the individual, the tendency of opinion in Europe in this present year must be a matter of grave anxiety. The liberty of the public is everywhere suffering from the return to reaction of their governments. The excesses of a few are made the excuse for the annoyance and restriction of the many. Legislation by fear is everywhere replacing legislation by justice, and is likely to continue to do so. The only statesman who has spoken of anarchy in any kind of philosophic spirit is Lord Rosebery, who called it 'that strange sect of which we know so little.' All other political speakers have treated of it only with blind abuse. In truth we do know almost nothing of it; we do not know even who are its high priests and guiding spirits. We know that it is a secret society, and we know that secret societies have always had, in all climes and for all races, the most singular and irresistible fascination. To meet it, ordinary society has only its stupid and brutal police system; its armies of spies, who, as the journey of Caserio from Cette to Lyons proves, are hopelessly useless, even when they are truthful.

It is true that, in the long run, secret societies have always been conquered and dispersed by ordinary society, but they are constantly reappearing in new forms, and it is certain that they have an extreme attraction for certain minds and classes of men, that they exact and receive an universal obedience which is never given to ordinary laws. They constitute a phase, a phenomenon, of human nature which is in itself so strange that it ought to be examined with the most calm and open-minded philosophy, instead of being judged by the screams of frightened crowds and the coarse invective of such politicians as Crispi. The curious power which can induce young men to risk their lives, and give them willingly to the scaffold, cannot be worthily examined and met by a rough classification of these men amongst monsters and wretches. That they have been brought, in their youth, to entire insensibility to personal danger and absolute indifference to death, whether to suffer it or cause it, is an indisputable fact; but no one seems to care to investigate the means by which they are brought to this state of feeling, nor the social causes by which this doctrine of destruction has been begotten. They are classed amongst criminals and sent to the scaffold. But it is certain that they are different to ordinary criminals; they may be much worse than they, but they are certainly different, and are in a sense entirely free from egotism, which is the usual motive of common crimes, except so far as they are seduced by the egotism of vanity.

It is impossible not to recognise great qualities allied to great cruelties in anarchists and nihilists, and, in the former, to great follies. When we remember the ghastly punishment of even the slightest political offences in Russia, yet see continually that some one is found who dares place on the Tsar's dressing-table or writing-table a skull, a threatening letter, a dagger, or some other emblem and menace of death; that to do this, access is obtained into the most private and carefully-guarded apartments of imperial palaces; that who it is that does this can never be ascertained (*i.e.*, there is no traitor who betrays the secret), and that the most elaborate and constant vigilance which terror can devise and absolutism command is impotent to trace the manner in which entrance is effected, we must admit that no common organisation can be at work, and that no common qualities must exist in those affiliated to it. There is no doubt that anarchism is a much more vulgar and much more guilty creed than nihilism. The latter has the reason of its being in the most brutal government that the world holds; it lives in a hell and only strives to escape from that hell, and liberate from it its fellows. Anarchy, with no such excuse, strikes alike at the good and the bad; strikes indeed at the good by preference. Yet there are qualities in it which we have been accustomed to consider virtues; there are resolution, patience, *sang froid* and absolute indifference to peril; it is these which make it formidable. It also cannot be doubted that behind its Caserios and its Vaillants there must be some higher intelligence, some calm, trained, dominant minds. It has grown up in the dark, and by stealth; unsuspected, unseen, until it is strong enough to shake like an earthquake the existing institutions of the world. We see the bomb, the pistol, the knife; but we do not see the power which directs these, any more than we see that volcanic stratum which makes the solid earth divide and crumble.

The existing clumsy machinery of tribunals and police offices will not have more faculty to detect it than has the public in general. There are no seismographic instruments in the political world. There are only a scaffold and a house of detention. This age, which is squeamish about execution, has invented the infernal torture of solitary confinement. It need not surprise us if there be a return to rack and thumbscrew, these primitive agencies being refined and intensified by the superior resources of science. It is, I believe, proved that Stambuloff tortured his political prisoners with the old-fashioned forms of torture. These can scarcely be worse than the solitary confinement in humid underground cells in which Francesco Crispi causes those who displease him to be confined. Men in the freshness of youth, in the full promise of talent, are shut up in these infernal holes in solitude for a score of years, their health ruined and their minds distraught. Many of these men have no fault whatever except that the authorities are afraid of their political doctrines and of the sympathy the populace feel for them. Where is the regard for 'life' in these fell sentences? Death would be a thousand times more merciful.

A youth of twenty-one was in the second week of July condemned at Florence to fifteen months' imprisonment for having called the *pretore* of a petty court and his subordinate *vigliacchi* (scoundrels); an expression so appropriate to the officials of these vicious and corrupt little tribunals that it was unpardonable. If at the end of the fifteen months this lad comes out of prison at war with society, a second Caserio, a second Vaillant, whose will be the fault?

A young lady of good family saved a little dog from the guards in Paris, and when she had seen it safely up its staircase turned in righteous indignation on the men. 'Are you not ashamed to persecute innocent little animals?' she said to them. 'You would be better employed in catching thieves.' This just remark so infuriated them, as a similar observation did the Florentine *pretore*, that they seized her, cuffed her, dragged her along under repeated blows, tearing some of her clothes off her back, and, reaching the police-station, locked her up with the low riff-raff of the streets. This took place in a fashionable quarter of Paris. If the male relatives of the young gentlewoman had lynched the guards who thus outraged her they would only have done their duty; but we know that the Parisian tribunals would have condemned them had they done so, and absolved the rascally myrmidons of the law. There is no justice anywhere if police are compromised by it.

At Mantua, in the month of August of this year, a poor woman, who has five children to maintain by her daily labour, was arrested by a guard for bathing in a piece of water outside the town (she ought to have been rewarded for her unusual cleanliness); and being taken before the tribunal she was sentenced to a fine. She exclaimed as she heard the sentence, 'And the brigadier who brought this misery on me has his decoration!' She was condemned to further punishment for the rebellious utterance; her defender, a young lawyer, in vain protested, and, for thus protesting, was himself arrested and charged with the misdemeanour of endeavouring 'to withdraw a prisoner from just authority'! Can anything be more infamous?

In July at Ravenna eight young lads were flung into prison for singing the Hymn of Labour.

Yet more absurd still. In Florence a band of young men were arrested for singing the choruses from the *Prophète*, which sounded revolutionary to the ears of the police. At the same time, the indulgence shown to the crimes of the police is boundless.

A poor man named Pascia was, in the same city, last week condemned to thirty-five days' imprisonment for having said an impudent word to the guards. On hearing the sentence his wife, a young woman with a baby in her arms, expostulated, asking who would now earn her own and her child's bread. She was arrested, and locked up for the night on the charge of 'outraging authority.'

On the twenty-second of April of this year, Alfredo Ghazzi, Customs-house guard on the Italian border of the Tresa, fired into a fishing-boat on the Tresa, having received no provocation whatever, and maimed two men, named Zennari and Zannori, of whom the former died; the latter, after a long illness recovered. The military tribunal of Milan *entirely* absolved the guard Ghazzi.

For an offence of the kind (*reanto arbitrario in servizio*), even though ending in its victim's death, the legal maximum of punishment is only two years' imprisonment; but in this instance not even a fine was levied.

In Prussia the murder of men, women and children is frequent by the bayonets and the bullets of guards and sentinels. The other day a little boy was on the grass of a square in Berlin; the guard tried to arrest him; the child, frightened, ran away; the guard shot him dead. Such occurrences are frequent. If a newspaper condemns them the editor is imprisoned. It is wholly illogical to tell anarchists that human life is sacred when its sanctity can be disregarded at will by any soldier or police officer. The public was convulsed with horror before the assassination of Carnot; quite rightly; but why is it wholly unmoved at the assassination of the fishermen of Tresa, or of the child of Berlin?

The English nation has not perhaps been greatly interested in the fate of the conscript Evangelisto; has perhaps never heard of him. Briefly, he was, in the spring of this year, a young trooper, a peasant who had recently joined at Padua, could not learn to ride and had weak health; he was bullied to death by the officer immediately over him; he was made to ride with his feet tied beneath his horse, when he fell he was pulled up into the saddle and beaten, his hands being tied; once again he fell, and then never rose again; they swore at him and flung water over him in vain; he was dead. The officer who killed him is still at large and retains his position in the cavalry; being young, rich, and of rank, he drives four-in-hand about Udine, where he is now quartered, and when he is hissed and hooted by the country people they are arrested. Now, if the Italian press were to say what it has not said about this disgraceful affair under the new law, such lawful and proper censure would be called calumny of the army, and would be visited with fine and imprisonment.

The soldier is to be inviolable and revered as a god, when his bayonet or his sabre are the instruments of oppression of the government; but at other times he is considered as carrion with which his superiors may do whatever they choose.

It is constantly stated that the officer who tortured Evangelisto to death will be brought to trial, but months have elapsed since the tragedy and the young man is still enjoying himself[P] in full possession of his military rank. How could any public writer, who does his duty to the public, castigate too severely such atrocities as these?

Yet even to hint at the brutality which goes on in the barracks is considered almost treason in Italy even as in Germany.

The legislation of fear goes hand in hand with a military despotism. The one is the outcome of the other.

The commercial world, the financial world, and the world of pleasure are beside themselves with terror. In Italy this passion of fear is being used to secure the passing of laws which will completely paralyse the press and enable the government on any pretext to carry away its foes out of the Chambers, and to confine to *domicilio coatto* any person, male or female, in whom it may suspect any danger to itself, or who may be merely personally disliked by the men in office.

There is no exact equivalent in English for *domicilio coatto*; it means the right of Government to send anyone it pleases to reside in any district it selects, for as long a period as it may choose to ordain. A journalist was the other day arrested in Rome whilst talking with a friend, his offence being the expression of republican opinions. He was ordered to reside in an obscure village where he had been born, but which he had left when in swaddling clothes; his house, family and means of livelihood were all in Rome. He had been previously domiciled in Bologna, whence he had been expelled for the same offence of opinion. The confinement of a man of this profession to an obscure and remote village is, of course, the deprivation of all his means of livelihood. There is nothing he can do in such a place; meanwhile his family must starve in Rome or wherever they go.

Another journalist, merely accused of *desiring another form of government than the monarchial*, was put in the felon's dock, loaded with chains and surrounded by gendarmes, in the same place where Paolo Lega had been sentenced an hour before. A seller of alabaster statuettes and ornaments, though there was nothing against him except the suspicion of the police, was so harrassed by the latter in Civita Vecchia that he sold off all his stock at ruinous prices, and went towards Massa, his native place, hoping to dwell there in peace; he was, however, arrested at Corneto, on a vague charge of anarchism and flung into prison. These are only a few examples out of thousands. Can any better plan be devised for the conversion of industrious, harmless and prosperous persons into paupers and criminals?

It apparently seems a little thing to the violent old man who throughout 1894 has been unfortunately paramount in Italy, to uproot men from their homes and occupations and pitchfork them into some hamlet where they were born, or some barren sea-shore or desolate isle. But to a man who maintains himself by the work of either his hands or his brain, such deportation from the place where all his interests lie, is a sentence of ruin and starvation for him and his family; and if the Government gives him a meagre pittance to keep life in him (which it does not do unless he is actually a criminal or one condemned as such), all the women and children belonging to him must fall into complete misery, being deprived of his support. The English Press takes no notice of these seizures of citizens, and their condemnation to *domicilio coatto*, perhaps it does not comprehend what *domicilio coatto* means; or perhaps it thinks that it would not matter at all to a journalist, a solicitor, or a merchant, living and working in York, in Exeter, or in London, to be suddenly transported thence to some obscure hamlet in Hants, in Connaught, or in Merionethshire, and ordered never to leave that place.

There is a project for deporting all those thus uprooted and condemned in Italy to '*domicilio coatto*,' to an island on the Red Sea, there to rot out their wretched lives in fever and famine. On a barren shore, where not a blade of grass will grow, in face of a sun-scorched sea which no vessel ever visits save once a year, the skiffs of pearl-fishers, many of the most intelligent, the most disinterested, and the most patriotic men of Italy will be left to die by inches in the festering heat, deriving what consolation they may from the reflection that whilst honest men are thus dealt with for the sin of political opinion, the men who forged, robbed and disgraced their nation, at the Banca Romana, are set at liberty and caressed and acclaimed by the populace.

'I hope the country will draw a parallel between Tanlungo and ourselves,' said Dr Barbato, a man of high talent and character, who has been condemned to the agonies of solitary confinement in the prisons of Perugia for political offences; he is well known as a writer; and when the famous Liberal deputy, Cavallotti, was allowed to see him the other day, he merely said that he hoped he might be allowed more air, as the confinement to his cell made him suffer from almost continual vertigo, which prevented him from pursuing any intellectual thought.

The fortresses, prisons and penitentiaries are crowded all over Italy with prisoners, many of them as worthy of respect as Dr Barbato, as innocent as Molinari, as high-spirited and noble-hearted as De Felice. Under the additions which have been made to the Code in the last parliamentary sessions these captives will be increased by thousands.

Here is the text of some articles in the draft of the new laws recently passed at Montecitorio:—

'Whoso uses the press to excite to crime, does not merely commit an offence of the press but commits a common felony, with the aggravation of turning to a felonious purpose an instrument designed to uphold education and instruction. Whereas the destructive aim of those who would reduce existing society to the last gasp, is above all, to inoculate the army with the passion of discord and insubordination, the army which is our joy and pride by its example of patriotism, of self-denial, and of self-sacrifice, we propose, with the second article of this projected addition to the code, a punishment for this especial offence which, as the code stands at present, escapes penal chastisement. Thus we propose that any incitement to lawlessness, any propaganda leading to insubordination and rebellion, do not cease to be felonious offences because the offender employs the medium of the press instead of that of speech, and ... this form of offence should also be raised to the honour (*sic*) of a crime meet to be judged by the assizes whenever the offender shall use for such purpose the public press, and the greater gravity of the offence shall render it more ignoble, and shall not any longer allow it to escape under an aureole of political glory.'

It then proceeds to provide that such offence shall be punishable by a term of not less than five and of not more than ten years; and it is plain with what ease this clause may be stretched to comprehend and condemn every phase of liberal opinion in any way obnoxious to the Government in power.

Literature itself is threatened in the most perilous and insolent manner by the following lines in Article 2 of this Crispian programme:—

'Whosoever by means of the press, or in whatever other figurative sense (*qualsiasi altro senso figurativo*) instigates the military to disobey any law, or to be lacking in respect to their superiors, or to violate in any manner the duties of discipline, or the decorum of the army or of men under arms, or exposes it to the dislike or the ridicule of civil persons, shall be punished by imprisonment of a term varying from three to thirty months, and with the fine of from three hundred to three thousand francs.'

With such a comprehensive decree as this the delightful *Abbozzi Militare* of De Amicis might be condemned as wanting in respect, whilst Dante, were he living, would be sent much further than Ravenna.

Every one who attacks in print existing institutions is to be dragged into a criminal court, and from thence to prison; the philosophic republican, the meditative layman, who dares to bring his well-weighed thoughts to bear against existing institutions, will be set in the same dock with the thief, the forger, and the murderer, and from the dock will pass to the *ergastolo*, to the diet, the clothes, and the existence, of common felons.

This is a violation of intellectual and personal liberty which does not concern Italian writers alone; it is one which should rouse the alarm, the indignation and the sympathy of every thinker in every clime who from his study endeavours to enlighten and liberate the world.

Stripped of its pompous verbiage this addition to the Code will enable the government to silence and put away every public writer, orator, pressman, or deputy, who is displeasing or annoying to them. Observe the provision to treat as penal all judgments of the press passed on verdicts of the tribunals. The tribunals are at present merely held in some slight check by the expression of public opinion given in the daily press. This check is to be removed and the most conscientious, the most honourable of journalists, may be treated as a common malefactor and deprived of trial by jury. To be judged by jury has hitherto been the inalienable right of newspaper proprietors or of contributors to the press. It is impossible to exaggerate this menace to the liberties of the press. An insolent and unscrupulous minister, and a timid and servile parliament, have reduced the Italian press to the level of the Russian press.

There is scarcely any political article which the ingenuity of a public prosecutor could not twist into a criminal offence, and this project of law is so carefully worded that the meshes of its net are wide enough to entrap all expressions of opinion. Anything by its various sections may be construed into incitement to disorder or rebellion. John Bright and Stuart Mill would be condemned with Krapotkine and Tolstoï. A writer writing against conscription would be treated as equally guilty with one writing in favour of regicide.

The assassination of opinion is a greater crime than the assassination of a man. John Milton has said that, 'It is to hit the image of God in the eye.'

The whole provisions of these new laws are no less infamous; they will legalise arbitrary and unexplained arrest, and will condemn to '*domicilio coatto*' any deputy or citizen who may be suspected or obnoxious, and the law can be stretched to include and smite the simplest expression of individual views, the mere theory and deductions of philosophic studies.

This paper could under it be easily attacked as an *apologia pro anarchia*.

The printing press may not be an unmixed good, but it is certain that the absolute freedom of its usage is its right and its necessity.

The purpose of anarchism in its outrages is no doubt to make all government impossible through terror, but they will probably only succeed in making through terror every government a tyranny. The extent to which terror can carry already existing governments is nowhere seen so conspicuously as in Italy, where reaction is violent and entirely unscrupulous in its paroxysm of fear.

It is grotesque, it is impudent, of such governments as exist at the close of this century to expect that any writer, gifted with any originality of thought and having the courage of his opinions, should be content with them or offer them any adulation. The governments of the immediate moment are conspicuous for all the defects which must irritate persons of any intelligence and independence. All have overwhelmed their nations with fiscal burdens; all lay the weight of a constant preparation for war on their people; all harass and torment the lives of men by meddlesome dictation; all patronise and propagate the lowest forms of art; all muddle away millions of the public treasure; all are opportunists with neither consistency nor continuity. There is not a single government which can command the respect of any independent thinker. Yet we are told to revere government as a sacred custodian throned upon the purity of spotless snows!

'Two things are necessary to this country—liberty and government,' said Casimir-Perier in his opening address. He might have added that no one has ever yet succeeded in making the two dwell in unison. Liberty and government are dog and cat; there can be no amity or affinity between them. Governments are sustained because men make a sacrifice, sometimes compulsory, sometimes voluntary, of their liberties to sustain government. What is the idea of liberty which Casimir-Perier has in his mind? This kind of nobly sounding phrase is much beloved by <u>politicans;</u> they usually mean nothing by them. He will certainly leave the Prefectures and all their subordinates as he finds them; he will allow the Department of Seine et Oise to be poisoned, despite its inhabitants' piteous protests; he will sustain and probably give still more power to the police and the detective system; he will not prevent arbitrary arrests in the streets of innocent persons, nor domiciliary visits on suspicion to private houses; he certainly will not touch conscription; he in all likelihood will revive obsolete press laws, and he will without doubt harass and muzzle the socialists on every occasion; he will have his *Cabinet Noir* and secret services like the ministers of the Empire, and he will not alter by a hair's breadth the spoliation of the public for taxation, the worry of the citizen by bye-laws, the corruption of municipal and political elections, and the impossibility for any Royalist to obtain justice at any *mairie*, prefecture, or tribunal.

As the Republican can obtain no justice in Germany, as the Jew can obtain none in Russia, as the Ecclesiastic and the Socialist alike can obtain none in Italy, so the Royalist and the Socialist alike can obtain none in France. The same tendency to mete out justice by political weights and measures is to be observed in England, although not to so great an extent, because in England the character and position of judges and magistrates are far higher and less accessible to corruption and prejudice. Yet even there, since political bias is allowed to influence the issue of cards for State balls, and admittance to the opening of State Ceremonies, it will soon inevitably influence legal decisions in the country. Interference with the freedom of the press would not yet in a political sense be tolerated in England, but its tribunals have come grievously near to it in some recent verdicts, and the mere existence of Lord Campbell's Vigilance Society is an invasion of the liberty of literature; whilst the steps to be taken are not many which would carry the *Times* the *Post* the *Standard*, and many other journals from their servile adulation of the sham Sylla of Italy to the advocacy of a similar tyranny to his over Great Britain. Neither Conservatism nor Radicalism is any protection against tyranny, *i.e.*, incessant interference with the individual liberty of the citizen; and republics are as opposed to individualism as monarchies and empires.

Carnot lies dead in the Pantheon, and liberty lies dying in the world. His tender and unselfish heart would have ached with an impersonal sorrow, greater even than his grief for those he loved, could he have known that his death would have been made an excuse for intemperate authority and pusillanimous power to gag the lips and chain the strength of nations.

Footnotes

A. A Zoological Menagérie has been placed in the park of the Villa Borghese!

B. Since this was written it has been done, entirely obliterating republican Florence, and creating a new enormous debt for the town.

C. Deputy for Corteolona, and leader of the Extreme Left.

D. Since this was written, one-half of these gardens have been destroyed; the other half bought by the Marchese Ginori.

E. This altar has been since, at the entreaty of the people, replaced in San Giovanni.

F. 'I have in myself wondered strangely many a time how it is possible that in men who from their earliest youth have been used at the lowest price to bear bales of wool as porters and baskets of silk as carriers, and in a word to be little better than slaves all the day long, and to spend a great part of the night at carding and spinning, can in so many cases display, when there is opportunity and need, so much greatness of soul and such high and noble thoughts, and cannot only say but do such beautiful things as are said and done by them.'

Zanaiuoli means, literally, 'whoever carries a basket'; there is no exact English equivalent.

G. It was not cancelled, and Molinari is now in the *ergustolo* of Oneglia.

H. To such an extent is the espionage on the salt-tax carried that a poor man living on the seashore is not allowed to take up more than one pail of sea-water to his house in one day lest he should expose the water to the heat of the sun and use the few salt crystals which its evaporation would leave at the bottom of the pail.

I. The taxes of the Government amounted to four hundred millions odd in 1873; in 1893 they amount to over eight hundred millions.

J. A footman of Lord Darnley's was sentenced to pay £2 by the Rochester magistrates for having killed a dog by heaping burning coals on it! This in the end of the year 1894.

K. Suggested by an Address to the British Association at Aberdeen, 1885.

L. Science having shouted many hallelujahs over the telephone, now discovers that it is a terrible disseminator of disease!

M. See *Times* of September 19, 1885: account of duel in Munich.

N. See article 'The Failure of Christianity.'

O. Whoever may care to study the brutal treatment of conscripts and soldiers in Germany by their officers is referred to the revelations published this year by Kurt Abel and Captain Miller, both eye-witnesses of these tortures.

P. Since this was written, the officer, Blanc-Tassinari, has been tried by a *civil tribunal*, found guilty of 'culpable homicide and abuse of authority,' and condemned to five months' detention in a fortress, and a fine of £20 (500 fr.). This punishment will entail no privation, as he is rich, and will live as he pleases in the fortress, and when the five months have expired, will rejoin his regiment as if nothing had happened. De Felice, Molinari, Garibaldi-Bosco, Barbato, and hundreds of intelligent and disinterested patriots are brought before military courts, are sentenced to twenty, twenty-five, thirty years' imprisonment, are condemned to prison diet, to shaved heads, to forced labour, to solitary cells, whilst this young brute, who made the lives of his soldiers a martyrdom, and is found guilty of culpable homicide, receives practically no chastisement whatever. And the English Press upholds and justifies the Government under which such enormities are possible.